Y0-BST-274

WITHDRAWN
UTSA Libraries

The Idea Of Disability
in the Eighteenth Century

TRANSITS:
LITERATURE, THOUGHT & CULTURE 1650 — 1850

Series Editor
Greg Clingham
Bucknell University

Transits is the next horizon. This series of books, essays and monographs aims to extend recent achievements in eighteenth century studies, and to publish excellent work on any aspects of the literature, thought and culture of the years 1650-1850. Without ideological or methodological restrictions, Transits seeks to provide transformative readings of the literary, cultural, and historical interconnections between Britain, Europe, the Far East, Oceania, and the Americas in the long eighteenth century, and as they extend down to the present time. In addition to literature and history, such "global" perspectives might entail considerations of time, space, nature, economics, politics, environment, and material culture, and might necessitate the development of new modes of critical imagination, which we welcome. But the series does not thereby repudiate the local and the national, for original new work on particular writers and readers in particular places in time continues to be the bedrock of the discipline.

Titles in the Series

The Family, Marriage, and Radicalism in British Women's Novels of the 1790s: Public Affection and Private Affliction
Jennifer Golightly

Feminism and the Politics of Travel After the Enlightenment
Yaël Schlick

John Galt: Observations and Conjectures on Literature, History, and Society
Regina Hewitt

Performing Authorship in Eighteenth-Century English Periodicals
Manushag N. Powell

Excitable Imaginations: Eroticism and Reading in Britain, 1660–1760
Kathleen Lubey

The French Revolution Debate and the British Novel, 1790–1814: The Struggle for History's Authority
Morgan Rooney

For a complete list of titles in this series,
please visit http://www.bucknell.edu/universitypress

TRANSITS

The Idea Of Disability in the Eighteenth Century

EDITED BY

CHRIS MOUNSEY

LEWISBURG
BUCKNELL UNIVERSITY PRESS

Published by Bucknell University Press
Copublished with Rowman & Littlefield
4501 Forbes Boulevard, Suite 200, Lanham, Maryland 20706
www.rowman.com

10 Thornbury Road, Plymouth PL6 7PP, United Kingdom

Copyright © 2014 by Rowman & Littlefield

All rights reserved. No part of this book may be reproduced in any form or by
any electronic or mechanical means, including information storage and retrieval
systems, without written permission from the publisher, except by a reviewer who
may quote passages in a review.

British Library Cataloguing in Publication Information Available

Library of Congress Cataloging-in-Publication Data

The Idea of Disability in the Eighteenth Century / edited by Chris Mounsey.
    pages cm. — (Transits: Literature, Thought & Culture, 1650-1850)
  Includes bibliographical references and index.
  ISBN 978-1-61148-559-2 (cloth : alk. paper) — ISBN 978-1-61148-560-8
(electronic) 1. People with disabilities in literature. 2. People with disabilities—
History. 3. Disability studies. 4. Sociology of disability. 5. Literature—18th
century—History and criticism. I. Mounsey, Chris, 1959– editor of compilation.

  PN56.5.H35I34 2014
  808.83'93527—dc23

2013049457

♾️^{TM} The paper used in this publication meets the minimum requirements of
American National Standard for Information Sciences—Permanence of Paper for
Printed Library Materials, ANSI/NISO Z39.48-1992.

Printed in the United States of America

Library
University of Texas
at San Antonio

CONTENTS

T HE COLLECTION of essays in this book began its life in a discussion about disability with Paul Kelleher, instigated by George Haggerty, in 2010, in San Antonio, Texas. These conversations led to a pair of panels at the American Society for Eighteenth-Century Studies Annual Conference in Vancouver in 2011. The panels were perhaps the first to explore disability in the period at that gathering and led to the foundation of a Disability Studies Caucus, guaranteeing panels every year.

The debates about disability studies have become established as an important element in the study of any historical period, and the essays herein go far beyond the original papers to encompass the philosophy, theory, and experience of disability. In order to bring this about I must acknowledge the help of friends and institutions: Helen Deutsch, Rosemarie Garland-Thompson and Michael Davidson, who helped focus my ideas about where disability studies could go; and from the University of Winchester, which financed trips to conferences and a period of study leave to complete the volume. Last and by no means least, I would like to acknowledge the vital assistance of Stan Booth whose eyes have been replacing mine for the past two years, noticing things I cannot see and guiding me to places I would otherwise not be able to go. His help has been made possible by the British Government's Access to Work programme, and I remain eternally grateful to them for not writing me off. Disabled people have a lot to give, and it is assistance programmes like Access to Work that allow us to flourish.

Variability: Beyond Sameness and Difference

Chris Mounsey

A S EARLY AS 1982, Henri-Jacques Stiker argued in *A History of Disability* for a celebration of the exceptional disabled body and against the "rhetoric of sameness" of the body that he claimed pervaded twentieth-century Europe. His book was couched in the Foucauldian philosophy of its time[1] and warned that bringing the disabled body into the center of study should not "normalize" it: should not deny its "abnormality" against which a majority defined itself as "normal." For Stiker, disabled people should not be "assimilated" by a liberal culture that desired equality for all, but rather the disabled body could only be truly accepted by society in its incommensurateness. Acceptance of bodily difference, he argued, would produce a more flexible and tolerant society.

While I largely agree with this position, I believe that Stiker chose the methodology of analysis since, as he argued, "At the present time a historicist study of disability is not possible: there are too few in-depth studies. There are only soundings."[2] I believe that the time has now come for just such historicist readings of the body in all its variations, of which this collection of essays is intended to be a part. I hope to demonstrate in this introduction that we have reached a point in the progress of the study of the history of disability where detailed historicist readings are not only possible but also necessary. I shall also propose a new analysis of the body—Variability—that goes beyond the rhetoric of sameness and difference that concerned scholars in the twentieth century.

Disability is a narrow vein of study which, I believe, should not be separated off into its constituent parts (blindness, deafness, learning or physical disability, deformity, etc.) since each person's disability (under whichever banner it may subtend) is unlike any other person's, while the experience of being disabled is the same for each disabled person. I am partially sighted and am accorded the same protections under legislation as all other vision impaired people in Britain. But I am also the first with the group of symptoms that my physician has recorded. I am unique, different, exceptional even among people "like me." At the same time I share with my friend Robert, who is in a wheelchair, the desire to go for a walk by myself. Our experience of one of the limitations of our disability is the same, although our disabilities are very different. We are the "same only different." Likewise, Robert and I are the "same only different" from people who do not class themselves as disabled. We all have a body that has its different capacities, we all make decisions about what we believe are the capabilities of that body and we all encounter other bodies with their peculiar capacities and capabilities and learn from them.

The History of the Study of Disability

Since Stiker, disability has been grouped with race, class, gender, and sexuality as a means for examining culture. Each analysis follows the poststructuralist methodology of bringing the excluded into the center of the debate, to demonstrate that white races define themselves negatively against the nonwhite, the upper classes define themselves negatively against the lower, men define themselves negatively against women, heterosexuals define themselves negatively against homosexuals, and the able-bodied define themselves negatively against the disabled. In want of a shared characteristic, the poststructuralist methodology suggests that the dominant "we" of a culture defines itself negatively as "not you" and casts its gaze at these five (among other) out-groups to define exactly what it is by excluding what it is not. By reversing the process of exclusion, or in the Foucauldian archaeology, by exploring carefully the history of the dominant group, the importance of those who have been excluded is demonstrated. The archaeology expects to find the excluded groups to have been relatively acquiescent, or the victims of injustice, and explores the moment when political activism brought about change that made society more flexible and tolerant. This methodology is clearly dominant in the study of disability after Stiker.

Susan Burch gives an excellent account of the various approaches to the study of disability published before 2005, which there is no need to rehearse fully here.[3] Briefly, there are two types, both of which follow the Foucauldian analysis, one with a focus on disability as a topic, and the other which explores the intersections between disability and other theoretical concerns. Of the approaches to disability alone we find studies that are inclusive of a number of disabilities and others that treat exclusively with one. In *The New Disability History: American Perspectives*, Paul K. Longmore and Laurie Umansky state that "disability belongs with race, class, and gender as a 'standard analytical tool' of historical analysis" and present the history of the Americans with Disabilities Act of 1990 (ADA), an act they demonstrate was the result of disability activism and one that marked a change in cultural values.[4] However, a question is left unanswered by the study. Because of its goal, despite containing essays on a wide range of disabilities, the collection does not delve into history before the nineteenth century. We might ask why, in a country which is still governed by an amended eighteenth-century constitution, there was no mention or amendment made to it which would benefit disabled people. Was it because impairment, as David Turner points out,[5] was always understood as part of eighteenth-century life as a badge of frail humanity to which all would eventually succumb? Was it because, as the later history of Ellis Island exclusions of disabled immigrants demonstrates, because there was a tacit requirement of able-bodiedness in Lazarus's lines:

> Give me your tired, your poor,
> Your huddled masses yearning to breathe free,
> The wretched refuse of your teeming shore.
> Send these, the homeless, tempest-tost to me,
> I lift my lamp beside the golden door![6]

Or had something dramatic happened to the view of the body in the shift between the eighteenth century and the nineteenth when the poem was written? This is not to say that Longmore and Umansky's book is not a useful contribution to the history of disability, but that, since it concentrates on the events that led to the moment of change, the ADA, it calls out further work: a study of the prehistory of the history they give, which this book hopes to begin to address.

Writing exclusively about deafness, Lennard J. Davis's *Enforcing Normalcy* also declares that "disability [is] the missing term in the race, class and gender triad" and at the same time that "deaf history is at once part of and separate from disability history."[7] Explaining this paradox, he argues for his Foucauldian methodology that "the first task is to understand and theorize the discourse of disability, to see that the object of disability studies is not the person using the wheelchair or the Deaf person but the set of social, historical, economic, and cultural processes that regulate and control the way we think through the body."[8] The move is eminently poststructuralist and follows Derrida's famous dictum "Il n'ya pas d'hors text," there is no outside of the text.[9] In other words, everything we think and experience is textual. There is no real world out there that is unmediated by language. The power of the move is that if disability is treated as a discourse then one disability is a representative of all disabilities and Davis can explore all through the study of one. But to this I would question whether or not Davis is guilty of making all disabilities the same and ignoring difference: the very "rhetoric of sameness" that Stiker criticized in 1982. It might equally be argued that disability is not only a discourse but also a lived experience, a "thinking through the body" of a disabled person: the "person using the wheelchair or the Deaf person" each of whom "think through" bodies that are the same but impaired in different ways.

The third class of texts to which Burch also draws our attention are collections of essays that explore the intersections between disability and other theoretical concerns, such as *Deviant Bodies* edited by Jennifer Terry and Jacqueline Urla and *Gendering Disability* edited by Bonnie G. Smith and Beth Hutchinson.[10] Again, these are fascinating studies, which are made possible by the similarity of the Foucauldian analyses of sexuality, gender, and disability. Also, they mark the moment in the history of the academy when hiring took place each year at the Modern Language Association Annual Conference for an expert in the next new theory. I have published extensively in the history of sexuality, and it might seem logical that this book attempt to shed light on disability with the same sort of theoretical intersection. However, as I suggested in my latest (last?) collection on sexuality,[11] when Caroline Gonda and I set up the Queer People conferences at Christ's College in Cambridge in 2002, we were searching for our foremothers and forefathers, for the experiences of people who shared our same-sex sexualities but who lived in the eighteenth century or earlier. We were working in parallel with the theoretical using a historicist methodology to describe case studies of sexualities. Careful not to read ourselves into our subjects, the papers at the conferences explored examples of sexualities within their own peculiar context. The methodology was derived from the belief that rather than reducible to a discourse or a set of discourses, sexuality is better explained as the body acting upon its mind's desires. Sexuality was the link (or at least one link) between the mind and its body. And disability is perhaps another link, although it works in a different way.

I believe that my experience of my homosexuality is radically different from my experience of my vision impairment. I have always known I was a homosexual and never practiced any other form of sexuality, nor have I deliberately tried to pass as heterosexual. When I discuss my sexuality with friends, I explain that it was never possible for me to have tried heterosexuality since encounters with women never led to my having an erection, while those with men did. My sexuality was never fluid or changeable. Sexually, I could never be other than I always have been.

My sight problem is equally deep seated as I have, until recently, been able to "get by adequately" with the vision I was born with. However, although I always felt there was something wrong with my sight from an early age, because I had no experience of anyone else's sight against which to gauge the deficiencies of my own, I did not know how impaired my sight was until I was fifty when a new set of circumstances led to my first diagnosis. In consequence I have lived (or at least passed) as a sighted person most of my life. This is not to say that all experiences of sexuality and disability are the same as mine. On the contrary, I would argue that all experiences of sexuality and disability are different and they should be treated as different. But this is my point. My experiences of my sexuality and my disability are not commensurate with each other, and nor are they commensurate with those of other people. So I would question whether the intersections that are noticeable in the Foucauldian analyses of sexuality and disability may be products of the analytical tool rather than the history. My conclusion becomes clearer as vision impairment and homosexuality are remarkably the same for me politically since British laws protect me from discrimination both as a homosexual man and as a disabled man. My experience of each in my daily life may be very different but nevertheless I have learned the value of antidiscrimination legislation to gain me equality of access.

For this reason I neither criticize nor repudiate the Foucauldian analysis, nor the political activism it underpinned. I am a beneficiary of the work done to bring about the ADA and the British Equality Act of 2010. And while neither piece of legislation is perfect, and while I continue to struggle to get equal access for blind and partially sighted people to texts in the form they can use, which sighted people have, I believe that the Foucauldian part of disability history has reached its goal and we can move on to explore the histories of our disabled foremothers and forefathers in a different way. What I am suggesting is that disability studies should follow the typical academic trajectory of a subject area beginning with the general and all-encompassing theory and move toward the specific, local, and personal. When I discuss my vision impairment, my friends who have poor vision tell me they understand my problem because they too are blind when they do not wear their glasses. But their sympathy is predicated against the medical algorithm of dysfunction, diagnosis, treatment, cure, which starts from an unstable binary between able-bodiedness and disability. However, where my bespectacled friends can understand the binary because their sight is correctable (when they are clothed they can see properly and when not they are blind), mine is not correctable and never has been. I have no concept of what seeing properly is other than that which I have learned from talking to others. Therefore, I can have no proper understanding of the able-bodied and disabled binary.

It could therefore be argued further that the medical algorithm, which holds up cure as a possible future, might be the source of the idea that disability exists in a binary with able-bodiedness. My retinologist has discharged me because I am incurable. My future is not as a patient, patiently waiting to be cured. And it is for this reason I believe that we should begin our histories of disability from the disabled person who by the very fact of being disabled is not in a socially constructed binary with able-bodiedness. Disabled people are defined by their disability, not by their relationship with the able-bodied. We therefore need not be interested in the able-bodied: they have histories of their own. We need histories that are about us.

Recent Developments

Taking up the bibliography of disability history where Burch left off in 2005,[12] there have been many new studies of disability in history of the types she listed, but all have remained within the Foucauldian fold.[13] However, embedded within them at several places is the suggestion that lived experience of disabled people might be a way forward. Again I shall be brief rather than comprehensive and explore only three texts, the first being a special issue of *Radical History Review*, edited by Teresa Meade and David Serlin.[14] The collection of essays continues the history of the ADA and similar laws worldwide, exploring civil disobedience tactics by disabled people. Most exciting for me is a declaration in the introduction where Meade and Serlin declare war not only on the effects of oppression of and injustice suffered by disabled people but also on the results of poststructuralist nihilism, declaring that:

> Definitions and meanings attached to disability are always historically and culturally specific and never ideologically neutral. Yet this does not mean that disability is merely an artifact of poststructural dematerialization of the individual body of subjective experience.[15]

Furthermore, the collection is billed by its publishers in a way that suggests it parallels the local and specific of the queer project, "disclos[ing] how the ways in which we define 'disability' may expose biases and limitations of a given historical moment rather than a universal truth."[16] Together these two propositions, that disability is an embodied state rather than textual and that the analyses should be confined to the disabled body in particular historical moments, might suggest that the collection fulfills the criteria I suggested above. The cover photograph of CeCe Weeks, a disabled activist who chained himself to a wheelchair in Berkeley, California, seems to confirm this, as does the discussion of the historical moment of his protest about a cinema showing the extraordinary 1978 film about disability, *Coming Home*, which could not admit wheelchair-bound viewers.[17] However, the discussions of individuals tend to flash by while the greater (if not universal) conclusions are drawn. The underlying problem with this otherwise excellent collection becomes clear when the editors note the paucity of premodern histories of disability. They wonder whether this is

> because academic scholarship on disability rests largely on articulations of individualism and bodily sovereignty that have been shaped by constitutional democracies in North America and Europe since the late eighteenth century.[18]

This is the moment when the analytical tool, which is still at its heart Foucauldian, hijacks what is an otherwise wonderful project. Although the editors' intention is to present micro-histories, the concept of social construction is still dominant not only of disability but also of the sense of the individuality, which can see itself as disabled, the victim of injustice, and so be moved to activism. Meade and Serlin end on a note of hope that their collection will stimulate further research, and there has certainly been an increase in the production of historical work on disability. But the question of whether this new work marks a move forward methodologically is still not clear.

One way forward has been to widen the field of study to put an earlier date on the "articulations of individualism and bodily sovereignty" than the late eighteenth century, as does Kim E. Neilsen's *A Disability History of the United States*.[19] Another has been to deepen the level of detail of the history of the disabled subjects under study, to encompass more of their political, social, and cultural selves as does David M. Turner's *Disability in eighteenth-century England: Imagining Physical Impairment*.[20]

Neilsen's approach is to present the whole history of the United States from pre-Columbian times to the present day through the lens of disability, an unprecedented task, or as she puts it:

> No-one has attempted to create a wide-ranging chronological history narrative told through the lives of people with disabilities.[21]

With so wide a historical sweep, the "lives of people with disabilities" must necessarily be explained carefully, so Neilsen spends some time defining, "Who are people with disabilities? And conversely what does it mean to be nondisabled?" The process does not lead to a definition but rather to a statement of intent:

> Disability is not the story of someone else, it is the story of someone we love, the story of who we are and who we may become, and it is undoubtedly the story of our nation.

However, while declaring that

> this is not to argue that we should all hold hands and cheerfully insist that we are all disabled in some way or another

The underlying binary between disability and "ableism" remains the book's main analytical tool. In her attempt to give us a history that is not freighted with the negative view of disability, which she will go on to demonstrate was prevalent in much of the history of the United States, Neilsen cannot rid herself of a binary approach that turns the negative stereotype upon those whom she will term "ableist."

To attempt a greater depth of engagement than Nielsen, David M. Turner's *Disability in eighteenth-century England* explores a narrower field in terms of time and place (eighteenth-century England) and disability (only deformity).[22] It is a really useful survey of that century, which by closing in the focus on deformity, is able to elicit details that more general studies cannot (nor are intended to). But the balance between the particular and the general remains weighted toward the general because Turner is still using race, class, and gender alongside disability as tools of analysis, which at times occlude some of the more subtle questions that arise.

For example, in his sketch of the life of William Hay, who wrote *Deformity: An Essay* in 1754,[23] Turner notes that "he [Hay] 'never much valued' the mockheroic epithet 'My Lord' that was commonly applied to people of small stature yet it was 'grown into such a habit with the Rabble.'" Following his analytical principles, Turner glosses this with the comment that "those who were 'deformed' could expect little of the respect that normally accrued to rank."[24] But how can we be certain that this true to Hay's response to name calling? Did he necessarily see himself as superior to those who carried him through the streets of London in sedan chairs? Hay was not entitled to be called "My Lord" being only a member of the landed gentry. Was perhaps his label of "the Rabble" given only to those who called him "My Lord"? Hay was not just a small man with a curved spine, he was a poet, politician, husband, and father. Perhaps his response to chair-men[25] who called him "My Lord" was a defense mechanism against casual abuse he used in front of his wife and children? After all, Hay was a Whig member of parliament and his party stood for social equality rather than *noblesse oblige.*

Turner's book, of course, does not have room for such detailed speculations since it is trying to cover the whole eighteenth century. The section on Hay is only seven pages long and although it is longer than the 1,000 word entry for William Hay in the *Oxford Dictionary of National Biography* (*ODNB*),[26] Turner adds little factually to the story told there. What is interesting in a comparison between these two accounts is that while Turner describes Hay's life from the perspective of his deformity, Stephen Taylor's *ODNB* entry does not mention that Hay was "born a hunchback dwarf" until the second to last paragraph, although we are told chronologically that his sight was damaged after smallpox while he was studying law in London. What would seem to be going on in the two versions of Hay is that Turner is centering on Hay the disabled person, while Taylor is giving us Hay the politician and writer. But this produces anomalies in each account. When Taylor tells us of the depth of Hay's dedication to Whiggism and its leader (after Robert Walpole) the Duke of Newcastle, Thomas Pelham-Holles, he evidences:

> The link with the powerful Newcastle connection at which this dedica-
> tion hinted was confirmed on 3 May 1731 by Hay's marriage to Eliza-
> beth Pelham (1709–1793), the second daughter of Thomas Pelham of
> Catsfield Place, Sussex, and a cousin of the duke.

But this information is given before Taylor's readers would know (if they knew nothing about Hay) that he was deformed and a dwarf. The wedding is thus presented without a sense of how it was understood in the eighteenth century. Was it seen as strange for a deformed man to marry at all? Was the marriage considered dynastic (as Taylor's account suggests) or companionate? How were the four resulting children received? It might have been that Elizabeth loved and cherished William and their marriage bed was a happy one as well as fruitful. Nevertheless, we ought not avoid the question about how Hay saw himself as one partner in the alliance with Elizabeth, after all he published his *Essay on Deformity* a year before his death, which suggests that it was very important to him that it was published, and in it he records that he was never free from casual abuse about his shape. Was Hay's wife subject to the same vilification? Did Hay suffer when he thought about the things that were said to the woman he loved? Was his suffering from abuse and the consequent desire to be treated as equal to those who were not small and with curved spines the reason for his Whiggish principles? The example demonstrates that to treat disabled people as though their disability were marginal to their lives can miss something of great importance to them and theirs. Again, to be fair, it might be asked whether an *ODNB* entry is the right place for such speculations. But should a major and life defining disability be mentioned only in passing?

Turner's approach to Hay is also open to accusations of missing subtleties while putting a spin on his subject. And the fact of the *Essay* being an early example of a first-hand account of disability perhaps makes it more important than the rest of Hay's life to a book on deformity. Turner notes that Hay published *Remarks on the Laws relating to the Poor, with Proposals for their better Relief and Employment* (1731).[27] But this is the only one mention of the wide range of other texts of which Hay was author, including *An Essay on Civil Government* (1728); *Mount Caburn: A Poem* (1730); *Religio Philosophi: or, the principles of morality and Christianity illustrated from a view of the universe, and man's situation in it* (1753); *Martials Epigrammata Selecta* (1755).[28] Confronted with such riches, one wonders whether we ought to read Hay only for his contribution to the way we understand deformity. Hay was after all a politician who left one of the most complete parliamentary diaries of the early eighteenth century.[29]

If we do not give a full context to Hay's life and writing, can we begin to pick up the subtleties of how he understood himself as a deformed man living in the eighteenth century? To give an example, in his *Essay* Hay attacks Francis Bacon for making the stereotypical claim that people with irregular bodies have twisted minds.[30] Exonerating his subject, Turner notes that on the republication of Hay's complete writing,[31] the *Critical Review* glossed Hay's *Essay* with a comparison with Alexander Pope:

> Hay's good-humoured treatment of his subject was contrasted with the work of another writer with spinal curvature, Alexander Pope—described [in the *Critical Review*] as "the irritable poet of Twickenham"—whose barbed attacks in the *Dunciad* and other satirical works (together with other anti-social qualities of his character that [Samuel] Johnson had described) seemed to embody the "scorn" that Bacon had attributed to "deformed" people.[32]

For Turner, the *Critical Review* would thus seem to suggest that Hay was the "good deformed man" while Pope was the "bad." But what Turner fails to explore is the detail of Pope's and Hay's knowledge of one another and one another's work, especially while Hay was writing his translation and imitation of Martial's *Epigrams*, which are as barbed as Pope's, and use Pope's name over and over again as the modern literary model for his satire.[33] In the light of Hay's deference to Pope, it would seem difficult to argue as the *Critical Review* did, and the difference between the two men as poets may be suggested instead to be that Pope, the professional poet, had the temerity to publish his barbed attacks while he and his victims were still alive, while Hay, the poet politician, was careful of his public reputation and waited until he and his victims were dead before his barbed attacks were published by the best London publisher, Robert Dodsley. Hay himself would seem to make this case when he questions his decision to publish in his imitation of Martial's Epigram IV, which is used as a preface to his book:

> Why in Pall-Mall with *Dodsley* will you dwell,
> When in my desk you still might lodge so well?[34]

The reason Hay thought his translations ought to remain hidden in his drawer was that he like Martial (and Pope) might be attacked:

> You who castration dread, who hate my strokes,
> And grave correction of your idle jokes, . . .[35]

When we read the rest of the imitated epigrams, it becomes clear that Hay, like Martial, and like Pope, did not hide who he attacked. For example, Epigram XI names a phthisic Lady Mary Belair who is being wooed for her fortune as she dies of consumption:

> To Lady Mary Belair makes addresses;
> Presents he makes, sighs, presses, and professes.
> Is she so fair?—No lady so ill off.
> What is so captivating then?—Her cough.[36]

In want of careful research, Lady Mary Belair and her suitor remain unknown to us for the present, but the pair would have been easily identifiable to readers of the epigram in manuscript when it was fresh and the barbed comment would have stung its targets or given rise to laughter in its readers.

But if this would seem to give the lie to Hay's attack on Bacon and make him out to be like Pope, and both like Richard III, and all "determined to prove a villain," then we miss out on the fun and the intention of eighteenth-century satire and imitation. What Hay, Pope, and Samuel Johnson attempted in their satirical imitations of the classical poets, respectively Martial, Virgil, and Juvenal, was to give classical weight to their jokes at the expense of the vanity of human wishes that they saw around them. But satire had been the dominant form of poetry only in the early century and Pope is attacked in the *Critical Review* in 1796 because a form of writing more at ease with sensibility had taken its place after 1760 and Pope was out of favor. Hay comes away clean footed in comparison because his victims were never named and Lady Mary long dead before the epigram was published, and Hay himself died in the year of publication of his Martial. But the fact that the *Critical Review* could still make the attack on Pope's shape, and Samuel Johnson's ticks and physical oddities were the subject of mimicry by James Boswell and David Garrick, while Hay's attitude to his is applauded requires further study of these men as whole men, living and working in the eighteenth century, and negotiating their personal disability with dignity and humor.

Two thirds of this project has been carried out already by Helen Deutsch in *Resemblance and Disgrace*, and *Loving Dr. Johnson*,[37] two books which laid the ground work for much of what I have argued needs to be done to deepen and widen the scope of disability history in the eighteenth century. Each is a book length study of a disabled person that explores his life and work. *Resemblance and Disgrace* reads Alexander Pope "for deformity," that is to say it explores the intersections between Pope's work and his self-presentation as its author, his language and subject matter, his poetical intentions and his detractors' criticisms, from whom the title comes. Deutsch reads Pope's deformity as a metaphor of literature and how literature works to explore the experience of embodiment. While her book is specific to Pope it is also as wide ranging as Pope's influence on British poetry, but at the same time Deutsch is writing against the traditions of Pope criticism that are, she argues, "blind[. . .] to the way in which deformity for Pope is both a biographical fact and a literary method, a mode of conceiving."[38]

Extending her visual metaphor Deutsch explains the problem of a deformed man writing poetry that imitates a classical and therefore supposedly perfect preexisting form in the neo-classical period when representations of perfect physical forms were a common subject of painting and ceramics as well as poetry:

> What I hope will become visible in the process is the function of Pope's deformity as a sign of the monstrosity of imitative authorship, a phenomenon which caused Lady Mary Wortley Montagu to brand both the poet's body and his printed book "at once Resemblance and Disgrace" of originals both artificial and natural.[39]

What "becomes visible" in *Resemblance and Disgrace* is the balance between the personal and the society in which people find and define themselves, which is clearly negotiated in literature: which is perhaps the function of literature. Thus, in this case, Deutsch argues that "literary imitation is Pope's generic portrait,"[40] while at the same time the book explores Pope's poetry as the topos of the encounter between the global and the local:

> While *Windsor Forest* expands a garden to encompass an English empire, Pope's garden at Twickenham creates a counter-empire within the confines of individuality and with the seemingly stable material of land.[41]

Later in the book imitative poetry presents an encounter between the classical (defined by its having survived from time immemorial) and the ephemerality of an individual human life, in the figure of the medal, or coin.

> [It is the medal's] defense against entropy and chaos in the shape of a human body which Pope wants print to perform in Horace's likeness.[42]

In these examples (as well as others in the book) Pope's curved spine intervenes in the concept of "imitation" as his body's unlikeness to the classical athlete imposes itself upon his attempts to create the most beautiful classical imitations in poetry.

While Deutsch's work has set us a wonderful example of how to proceed, *Resemblance and Disgrace* has not exhausted the subject of imitation and disability in the eighteenth century. If I may enter into a debate with Deutsch about her interpretation of William Hay—and debate about interpretation is that on which literary scholarship thrives—she argues:

> Hay closes his text with two complimentary gestures. He prints a "Last Will" in which he leaves his body to science and asks that it be opened, made a biological specimen and preserved in a medical museum (part of what he wishes to display is the efficacy of a particular brand of soap for ingestion as a cure for various ills). The body which he recommends as both educational oddity and potential commodity.[43]

I would like to offer an alternate reading of Hay's intention for leaving his body to Sir Hans Sloane: which is to demonstrate that his deformed body is still a body that can act as an example for other bodies. Hay's deformed body is an adequate "imitation" (or perhaps iteration) of any other body since it works in the same way and can be helped by the use of a soap based medication to prevent bladder stones. Hay's body is the same only different as that of the classical athlete. Hay's attitude toward himself seems also to point out how much he thought he was "the same only different" from other people and that while Pope thought himself unfit for marriage, Hay did marry and had four children.

It is interpretations and comparisons between the experiences of disabled people that fuel the current collection, so I include this dialogue with Deutsch as an example of how important it is to continue to work with disabled subjects and to develop the methodologies with which we make such interpretations.

Variability: A New Analytical Tool

As early as 1999, Elizabeth Bredberg noticed that

> in disability history, . . . accounts of the lived experience of disabled people remain very much under-represented. Disability history, in ironic consequence, seems to sustain the depersonalized and institutionalized representation of disabled people that its authors undoubtedly deplore.[44]

At the same time the paper notes that there are several collections of biographies of deaf people, and she concludes with the suggestion that

> any real development in disability history will come from the work of investigators who have developed interpretive competence with [primary experiential accounts] as well.[45]

However, the question is left unanswered as to what "interpretive competence" might be, but I believe this is the nub of the matter, although probably in a different way from that which Bredberg intended. If we put together the undoubted fact that at this moment there is more work in deaf history than any other disability[46] with the question of interpretive competence we might find an answer. Deaf people write books because they can use them. There is a deaf university (Gallaudet) in Washington DC, which has an active academic publishing house. There are even two pictorial histories of the deaf, one of Britain and one of the United States.[47]

The reason I draw attention to this undoubted fact is that the deaf even call themselves "the people of the eye." Although much of their history has been a fight to use sign language as their main means of communication, the written word is the place where this fight has been recorded for posterity. Sign language is evanescent, like speech, and disappears as the signs are made, to become a personal mental image in the signer's and signee's minds. A conversation can be remembered, but memory of it becomes more and more indistinct as time passes. On the other hand, words on a page exist forever and can be studied again and again in a relationship between the eye and the colored characters. Words on a page may also be interpreted again and again, but they remain identical each time they are seen. An eye can skim in many different ways across the page to pick up different nuances of meaning by noticing connections between words that exist simultaneously and come in and out of focus as the eye moves over the page. Sign language and speech leave only a passing impression that can never be revisited.

For text-disabled people, access to words is always like sign language or speaking. We also have our own language for which we have fought, braille, but touching white dots on a page, is as temporal an experience as listening to a voice. There is no simultaneity equivalent to perusing words on a page when reading requires the temporal pass of the finger. A braille reader can never stop and ponder a single word and take in all its letters in one view.

I have no competence with braille as I could learn to read print as a child, so I cannot comment on the experience of reading that way. My main language of textual communication is aural: either text-to-voice (for work) or audio book (for pleasure). In either form text cannot come to me simultaneously and I have to study it in a linear temporality, although I fold time back and forth as I click the "back 30 seconds" button to pick up pieces of information I have missed in a moment of inattention as the voice moves smoothly on.

The process of re-educating myself to read this way took about two years, and now I can read and grade student essays at 120 words a minute: a speed that my students cannot even hear as language. I can even hear spelling mistakes. During the process of relearning to read, I was writing my book, *Being the Body of Christ*,[48] which was intended to have a wider range of authors, one to a chapter, and only about 10,000 words on E.F Benson's *David Blaize* trilogy. But I finally gave up on trying to read paper books after writing the chapters on Oscar Wilde, Alan Hollinghurst, Jeanette Winterson, and Edward Carpenter, and turned to text to voice. In the event, the detail I picked up from having to listen linearly word by word to Benson's lovely books, led me to writing 40,000 words on them. My whole method of working changed. Since I could never read properly, I would spy out useful phrases by skimming over text very quickly with one eye held tightly shut to find relevant passages by recognizing word shapes, which I would then write out or type in order to read properly. After reading by sight became impossible I had to listen to every word, word by word, going back and forth across the text so as to remember which incident came before which. Until five years ago I could retain the shape of paragraphs on a page and hold a mental image of the page, or the copied out text, to bring me the experience of seeing words simultaneously. Now linear time has replaced simultaneity for me and I would argue that this is another language experience equally valid as sign language or braille.

Now, text-to-voice has become so dominant a language of work for me that when I am at a conference and hear a paper which describes the work of "Foo-coh" I wonder for a moment whose work is being referenced, until I remember the sound pattern "Fow-oo-coh-ault" which my computer reads to me when speaking the letters "Foucault."[49]

When I am reading for pleasure, and turn to audio books, that is, books that are performed for the listener by a professional reader, I touch the limits of my new access to text. If I am unfamiliar with a sound pattern I can lose out on levels of meaning, as for example, recently when I was reading Robert Jordan's fantasy novel, *The Eye of the World,*[50] I heard the sound pattern "Eye-Siddeye," which the text tells me are some kind of magicians, but the sound has no obvious homopho-nic metaphors to the ear. I checked out the word and discovered that it was spelled "Aes Sedai" in the printed version of the text, which abounds with suggestions of Aois Dàna (Aes Dana) the Old Irish race of bards, whom they resemble.

Thus, I might argue, in work and leisure, I am more disabled than deaf readers. When I have finished this book you are now reading and it comes back to me for proofing, I will not be able easily to understand these last two paragraphs with text-to voice. A deaf person only has to look at them to understand them.

But here I am not trying to set up a hierarchy of disability where deaf/blind people might be "more disabled" than either blind or deaf people. And there is an excluded third party to the discussion, those who can both hear and see, what of them? Is their relationship to us the visually impaired, and you the deaf, the most important thing to know? I do not think so. The most important thing that identifies us is our differing capacities. We visually impaired access text the way we can, the deaf the way they can, each in our own peculiar way, and those who can both see and hear in theirs. Access for each group is different, valid, and has its strengths and weaknesses. It would be otiose to suggest that one type of access is better than another. But varying capacities might be a useful fact on which to base an analysis of people in history. Furthermore, since no one is totally "able" (in this example, to be totally able might be to see all words all at once on a page) and no one totally "disabled" (with no access to language at all), then we might dispense with the word "disabled" with its binary opposite, and call everyone "Variable." I would argue that this addresses the question that arose in reading Kim Neilsen's *Disabled History of the United States* since we no longer have to define who are the disabled and who the able. We are all simply Variable people.[51]

When we turn to look for more detail about the whole lives of historical people, Variability might also be of some help. Variability is no means transhistorical, as it would expect blind people in the eighteenth century to be different from blind people in the twenty-first century in the way they were treated or understood, in the same way that we would expect that every person in each century had different experiences of and with their peculiar abilities. But Variability would nevertheless expect that someone who was blind in the eighteenth century would have similar difficulties in, say, accessing text, as blind people in the twenty-first century, although they would understand themselves in a different way and expect different solutions. Above all, Variability would not suggest that difference was binary. Deaf people in the eighteenth-century were as different from blind people as they were different from those who thought themselves normal. There never was a reference point of "normal" that defined those who were not. Variability would expect that every "normal" person was as different (Variable) as every other "normal" person.

Variability is a concept that enshrines uniqueness, has the patience to discover the peculiarities of each individual and by so doing captures particular people rather than an "institutionalized representation of disabled people." As such it is a useless concept for those who are seeking "power relations" between groups who define themselves as the same against an other. But it is a good way to notice people in history.

If this sounds difficult, then try to untangle my experience of sight. I have always been visually impaired, but as I used to be able to see texts, I was educated in a mainstream school that did not know that I had a visual anomaly so did not treat me as disabled. Instead, as I coaxed my mind to use the vision I had to find some pattern to the words on the page, I was thought to be educationally subnormal. Now I am a full professor of English Literature although I cannot work with paper texts. When asked to describe my experience of vision, I say that "I can see everything but I can make out nothing." If I see letters and am asked to say what I've seen I say "letters." If I see a friend it is more than likely a stranger wearing my friend's face. If someone comes towards me with a smile (which I can obviously see) I greet them with the name I think goes with them and am often wrong. So I must have a visual memory of the friend that I cannot and could never see.

Have patience with me, don't simply call me blind, since I can see, or stupid as my school did, since I am really quite clever. Do not think of me as some "Other" who you are definitely not, since I share a lot of visual (and other) experiences with you. I like modern architecture (it is big and does not move and has little detail) and I love to walk around cities with you. Just don't let me try to cross a road because I cannot see the traffic since it moves. Protect me and cherish me, not as different from you but as a Variable of you. I am "the same only different" from you. My visual capacity is not the same as yours. But it has its recompenses. Learning to read with text-to-voice brought me a wholly new way of working that has enhanced my life immeasurably, and I recommend it to you even if you can read paper texts.

However, those recompenses are in my conscious decision to accept or deny. My oldest friend has macular degeneration, another genetic condition, that means she has like me had to face blindness at the height of her active life. We meet regularly and laugh and weep together about our past and present and futures. But if we share the experience of losing sight in middle age, we do not share a future. My friend does not understand the recompenses of being blind. She refuses to be registered blind or get a travel permit or read audio books. She will not go to art galleries anymore because she says "she cannot see the wall, let alone the painting." She would not go with me to the recent Edvard Munch exhibition in London[52] even though some of the paintings represented his experience of her condition. Instead she sits at home poring over visual text magnified to the highest level her kindle will manage, reading for half an hour a day before she is too exhausted and has to sleep.

My response to what I understand as a "same only different" future has been to accept my visual anomaly with its limitations and to relearn how to read. Furthermore, nothing will keep me out of art galleries where I stand and peer at artworks through my dark glasses. I used to despise conceptual art, but now prefer the gross visual stimulus to the intricate detail of a pre-Raphaelite painting.

What is different between me and my friend with macular degeneration is our capability to live with our altered capacity. Capability I understand as the mind's facility to accept difference and live with it or deny it. I can accept the physical constraints of my visual impairment, my friend cannot. Capability is experiential and nonjudgmental. It is not predictable and adds to the peculiarity of an individual. It is another element to be added to capacity as a way of noticing people in history. But if I seem to have set up yet another binary between capacity as body and capability as mind, then I must now point out that both capacity and capability only become apparent in encounters with others, and the three exist as a triplet.

What I want to maintain in the analysis of Variability, is the immediacy of individual lived experience. I believe that the three elements capacity, capability, and encounter, (which are not necessary to the central concept) can help to guide the analysis of experience, and highlight the relationship between body mind and other people as in the example I have just given.

The Essays

The essays illustrate different aspects of this volume: *The Idea of Disability in the Long Eighteenth Century*, and separate themselves neatly into three sections, the Methodological, the Conceptual, and the Experiential. The first group consider philosophies of the body before and after empiricism, and present an overall picture suggesting that empiricism, which might be argued to be the basis of the current scientific way people understand themselves as agents in the world, is filled with anxiety about failures in its method to explain different experiences of embodiment, and which, in the eighteenth century, was only one way to understand the body in all its forms—the others of which are more inclusive of aberration and empathetic toward difference. The second group of essays explores ways disability was conceptualized in the eighteenth century, in terms of literature and public consciousness, and we discover how literature disguises its representations of disability, while periodical and pamphlet literature was starkly direct in exposing the terrible tortures inflicted upon disabled people—especially the mentally disabled. The third group of essays, which explore the lives of disabled people throughout the century, demonstrates the dynamic tension between the personal desire for disabled people to be accepted and treated as autonomous individuals, while at the same time wanting to be part of groups either of other disabled people or of a wider community. In fact they demonstrate the way in which disabled people expressed concerns about their lives typical of the human social animal.

Theorizing Disability—Methodological Essays:

These consider philosophical writing dating between 1663 and 1788, a time in which the understanding of disability altered dramatically. We begin with Margaret Cavendish, whose natural philosophy was based upon an all but Hermetic view of "as above so below," that led her to reject ideas of superiority or inferiority between individuals based upon physical or mental difference. We then move to John Locke, the founder of empiricism in 1680, who believed that the basis of knowledge was observability, but who, faced with the lack of anything to observe, broke his own epistemological rules in his explanation of mental illness. Quite probably understanding the problems that empiricism set up, Anthony Ashley Cooper, Lord Shaftesbury, turned in 1711 to moral philosophy, but also founded his philosophy on a flaw. While he believed in the harmony of "the aesthetic trinity of beauty, truth, and virtue" he could not believe that a disabled friend whom he knew to have been moral before his physical alteration could change inside. Lastly, we turn to Thomas Reid who returned to the body as the ground of philosophical enquiry, but this time in terms of power. The body seen as a whole is, for Reid, complete in itself, and wanting nothing, be it missing a sense (Reid was deaf) or a physical or mental capacity.

Working on the late seventeenth-century natural philosopher, Margaret Cavendish, Holly Nelson and Sharon Alker's essay demonstrates that before empiricism there was no simple binary opposition between able bodies and disabled bodies, which might be used in Foucauldian negative definition. Rather they argue that Cavendish believed in a diversity of physical and mental states akin to my own idea of Variability. This means that from as early as the seventeenth century, the language of superiority and inferiority is undermined. Nelson and Alker also explain that Cavendish treated only with the body and left incorporeal spiritual truths to churchmen, which took the religious sting out of disability. For her pains, Cavendish was routinely thought to be mad herself, though she does not seem to have cared much about the appellation.

Jess Keiser's paper examines the problem with eighteenth-century empiricism's understanding of mental disability by examining a contradiction in John Locke's *Essay concerning Human Understanding*. Although Locke states plainly that his work will not "meddle with the Physical Consideration of the Mind," (that is neurophysiology, a term coined by Locke's teacher, Thomas Willis) his writings on madness point to the flux of animal spirits in the brain as a probable cause for mental derangement, thus: "the brain tricks the mad into perceiving otherwise irrational connections in the mind's ideas." In spite of this contradiction, Locke's writings on madness share with the rest of the *Essay* a concern that we cannot discover the mechanisms of the body because the real source of those mechanisms remains just out of sight, an insoluble problem, which led to the skepticism of David Hume and George Berkeley, and Shaftesbury's turn to describe morality. By surveying the similarities in these disparate moments in the *Essay*, Keiser's paper brings to light the anxiety around the hidden interactions of body and brain that pervades Locke's writings, to which we might conclude: empiricism is not a fit tool for explaining the complexities of how the disabled body works.

Paul Kelleher's essay begins where Locke's methodology failed—trying to comment upon a subject that could not be observed—in this case moral philosophy. However, Shaftesbury's "vision of moral harmony" as an "inward anatomy" in *Characteristics of Men, Manners, Opinions, Times* (1711) was also not free from criticism for its treatment of disabled subjects, this time that his work follows the Baconian model that the outwardly deformed must be morally deformed also. As

Kelleher writes: "moral philosophy addresses the fundamental question of what constitutes the good life: what is a life well lived, it asks, and how is such a life conducted in a world shared by others and sustained in a world comprised of materials and objects?" Any answers to these questions necessarily implicate those who, at different times, have been regarded as monstrous, deformed, freakish, deviant, or disabled. As even a cursory glance reveals, the pages of moral-philosophical treatises are replete with invocations—or more accurately, deprecations—of "deformity." Nevertheless, after a careful reading of the *Characteristics*, and a brief look at Shaftesbury's philosophical notes, the *Askêmata* (recently published in full for the first time), Kelleher demonstrates that if we "respect the ambiguities of any body of thought" we discover that Shaftesbury did not simply accept "the aesthetic trinity of beauty, truth, and virtue" and denigrate "the deformed, false and vicious." For example, if a friend whom we know to be morally virtuous travels in "the remotest parts of the East and the hottest countries of the South" and becomes physically deformed by disease, our friend has not changed morally because they are now ugly: "It is not we who change when our complexion or shape changes." Thus, Kelleher argues that Shaftesbury's aestheticization of morality—or what comes to the same, his *moralization of aesthetics*—does not overtly argue that what we today refer to as "disability" is synonymous with "moral deformity."

Emile Bojesen explores the way the Scottish philosopher Thomas Reid criticizes the binary of disabled able-bodied, finding it the product of empiricism and skepticism. As an alternative, Reid offers a common sense philosophy of power, where power is what differentiates beings with a "will" from those without, and makes them the author of their actions and their life. The idea is a complex one, the more so since empiricism and skepticism have become so engrained in our culture, but the outcome is liberating since, according to Reid, the agent has power over their dis/ability rather than their dis/ability having power over them. Power dictates the direction of the will and locates the will as being subject to the various bodily faculties: emphasizing the Variable experience of the body and mind before the direction of the will. No two bodies are the same, be they able or disabled, but they are all fully capable of doing what they can.

Thinking about Disability—Conceptual Essays

At the heart of the study of any historical artifact is the question of where to look for evidence, and when looking for evidence of disability, we have largely to rely upon texts. However, texts come in many forms, and the two essays here explore three types, the novel, the periodical and the pamphlet, which pour out their riches in different ways.

Anna K. Sagal's paper explores the intersections between language and disability in Laurence Sterne's character of Uncle Toby in *Tristram Shandy*. What becomes more complex here, is the fact that although Toby can be read as an equivalent of a modern traumatized war veteran, he was also an eighteenth-century man who used that century's language to express and come to terms with his disability, which makes for a fascinating comparison. The language games which so famously define Sterne's novel do not cease to be played when we try to pin down any of its characters, who are "in search for their own comprehensible narratives within a larger narrative," which might be a personal search for the meaning of one's disability. What becomes tragic, however, is that this meaning must be hidden within the language games themselves as a puzzle that needs to be solved in order to be expressed as disability is too awful to be expressed on the polite page of the novel.

Dana Gliserman Kopans's essay argues that the claim that literary portrayals of false imprisonment for insanity are overstated needs to be reconsidered in the light of contemporary periodical and pamphlet accounts which fed widespread fears that the "trade in lunacy" was so voracious that no one was safe. While the essay considers the problem of false imprisonment for insanity in a case documented by Daniel Defoe in *The Review*, and two others by the falsely imprisoned James Bruckshaw and James Belcher, the punishment handed out to the unnamed woman and the two men must have been typical of that meted out to those who were really mentally disabled. The essay gives a truly harrowing account of the dreadful treatment of mentally disabled people in the eighteenth century, set within the contemporary regimes of incarceration for insanity: William Battie's private confinement (in St Luke's) for vitiated senses and John Monro's public display (in Bedlam) for vitiated judgment, both of which led to mentally disabled people being tortured. What is most ironic about this is that it was Battie and Monro who testified to the 1763 House of Commons Report on the state of madhouses in England, a trade in which both had made vast fortunes, and which neither wanted to be questioned about their running private prisons for the incarceration of unwanted relatives.

Living with Disability—Experiential Essays

Not all people have left a large body of work on which to base biographical accounts, and with relatively few disabled people (there are, for example only fifteen blind writers noted on Eighteenth-Century Collections Online) the evidence is even more sparse and the lives even more evanescent. These four essays begin to bring to light little known disabled people, or people who are little known for their disability, giving various forms of biographical accounts of Susanna Harrison, Sarah Scott, Priscilla Poynton, and Thomas Gills, who are all but forgotten in the academic (Scott perhaps less so) as well as the public consciousness. When I was researching Thomas Gills in Bury St. Edmunds, I told the archivists about their blind poet but none had even heard of him, though he sold his pamphlets at the steps of St Mary's church every day until he died in 1716—a few yards from their door.

Jamie Kinsley's essay on the devout poetry of Susanna Harrison explores the way this pain-wracked poet followed successfully the economic example of another religious poet, Elizabeth Singer Rowe, while at the same time giving a voice to her own suffering and her methods of coping with daily unmitigated pain. The result gives us an extraordinarily personal experience of disability. What is interesting is how Harrison writes for a supportive coterie, and how her longing to be always a part of the public worship of her congregational community is necessary for her understanding of her sense of herself as part of a divine family. In this sense, Harrison's poetry gives us a glimpse of what Lennard J. Davis has suggested is the period in which the signifiers for disability begin shifting from perceived vice to perceived virtue. At the same time the fact that Harrison's poems were edited by her minister and presented as the work of a poor disabled poet, we might find a reason for the shift was connected with the economics of charity rather than the purported divine purpose of using the suffering of the disabled body as an example of the suffering of Jesus: a process that the essay argues marginalizes disabled people.

Jason Farr also develops Lennard J. Davis's idea about the change in consciousness about and of physical deformity during the eighteenth century from public spectacle to a test for virtue to overcome, using the eighteenth-century concept of sensibility. His essay argues against the idea of a docile minority of deformed people, suggesting rather William Hay's challenge to the ugly club is another example of how he subverts established modes of thinking that were promoted by both the literary establishment, represented by Steele, and scientific thought, epitomized by Bacon. Instead, Farr argues that the writings of William Hay and Sarah Scott go beyond merely procuring sympathy for the disabled: they attempt to reconfigure cultural perceptions about the body by extolling deformity as a most desirable physical condition. By rereading Sarah Scott's novel, *Agreeable Ugliness*, Farr's essay demonstrates that people afflicted by facial deformity were not subject to the wishes of a dominant public or familial pressure to conform, but used their wit and intelligence to get what they wanted.

Jess Domanico presents a study of Priscilla Poynton, a blind poet who discusses her own experience of life as a blind woman in her autobiographical poetry. Although noting that there are few other facts known about her life other than her two collections of poetry, the paper becomes a call for a full-length piece of work to be done on Poynton, who was part of the tradition of blind people making an economic life for themselves in whatever ways they could. The paper also notes the limits of the understanding of disability both in the eighteenth century and now, and asks that we listen to the individual explain their own disability. Domanico also suggests that Poynton's "blindness is actually enabling—i.e. it enables her to read her own life as she envisions it." This challenging essay therefore suggests that we can read the poet herself through her own writing about herself as an example of Variability—as the woman she was rather than as a blind prisoner of her disability. Poynton's poetry, Domanico argues, is where we encounter Poynton reading herself—and subsequently defining herself—as a woman writer.

My essay also gives a study of a blind poet, Thomas Gills of Bury St. Edmunds, who wrote poetry in order to help himself to economic independence. The essay discusses the place of literary studies in the history of disability, and argues that a carefully contextualized account of a disabled person can bring to light a great deal about the whole person working within the ebbs and flows of historical change and continuity, while remaining aware of the fact that presenting evidence from a variety of disparate sources, and using all the tricks and partial truths that the construction of a single narrative implies, the resultant "total vision" will be to a degree distorted. In the same vein, I argue that the language of address by the poor to their benefactors comprised various forms: as the example of Gills's various publications and his publication strategy imply.

Notes

1. Stiker's bibliography cites: "Foucault, Michel. *Histoire de la Folie à l'Age classique*. Plon, 1961. Reprint, Ed.Gallimard, 1972. Foucault, Michel. *Naissance de la Clinique*. PUF, 1963. Foucault, Michel. *Surveiller et punir*. Ed. Gallimard, 1975," as well as Gilles Deleuze's book on Foucault: "*Foucault*, Ed. De Minuit, 1968." Stiker's bibliography also cites four books by the structuralist anthropologist Claude Levi-Strauss: "*Anthropologie Structurale*. 1958. Reprint Plon, 1974. *La Pensée sauvage*. Plon, 1962. *Anthropologie structural deux*. Plon, 1973. *L'impossible prison. Recherches sur le système pénitentiare au XIXe siècle*, ed. Michelle Perrot. Le Seuil, 1980." The lack of a reference to the works of Jacques Derrida would suggest that Stiker had come down on the side of Foucault in the poststructuralist debate sparked off by Derrida's attack on Foucault in 1962, published as

"Cogito and the History of Madness," in *Writing and Difference*, trans. Alan Bass, 36-77 (London: Routledge and Keegan Paul, 1978).

2. Henri-Jacques Stiker, *A History of Disability*, tr. William Sayers (Ann Arbor: University of Michigan Press, 1999), 18. Please note that the studies to which I refer in this introduction are mostly journal articles, and where books are referenced they tend to be quotes taken from reviews or fragments available on Google books. I have chosen this practice as a statement of intent since, as a partially sighted scholar, I cannot easily work with texts that cannot be translated by text to voice. I have used some whole books, but only those that are freely and legally given to me as unencrypted electronic text. I have made a policy of not signing disclaimers stating that I will not put such texts online as a hurdle to getting access since this demand expects me to be a criminal first and a partially sighted scholar second. Nor will I read freely given texts by publishers whom I have had to threaten with legal action before a book is sent to me, which every sighted scholar in Britain gets free access to through the copyright deposit system. My practice also means that some of the page numbers I give are inaccurate as they come from (legal) online sources or from pre-publication copies.

3. Susan Burch, "Disability History: Suggested Readings—An Annotated Bibliography," *The Public Historian* 27, no. 2 (Spring 2005): 63–74.

4. Paul K. Longmore and Laurie Umansky, *The New Disability History: American Perspectives* (New York: New York University Press, 2001), 15.

5. David Turner, *Disability in Eighteenth-century England: Imagining Physical Impairment* (New York: Routledge, 2012).

6. Emma Lazarus, 'The New Colossus,' http://www.libertystatepark.com/emma.htm.

7. Lennard J. Davis, *Enforcing Normalcy: Deafness, Disability and the Body* (New York: Verso, 1995), 67.

8. Davis, *Enforcing Normalcy*, 2.

9. Jacques Derrida, *Of Grammatology*, translated by Gayatri Chakravorty Spivak (Baltimore and London: Johns Hopkins University Press, 1987), 158.

10. Jennifer Terry and Jacqueline Urla, eds., *Deviant Bodies: Critical Perspectives in Science and Popular Culture* (Bloomington: Indiana University Press, 1995); Bonnie G. Smith and Beth Hutchison eds., *Gendering Disability* (New Brunswick: Rutgers University Press, 2004); Burch, "Disability History," 70.

11. Chris Mounsey, ed., *Developments in the Histories of Sexualities: In Search of the Normal* (Lewisburg: Bucknell University Press, 2013), 1.

12. Susan Burch, "Disability History."

13. Iain Hutchison, *A history of disability in nineteenth-century Scotland* (Lewiston: Edwin Mellen Press, 2007); L. Linthicum, "Integrative Practice: Oral History, Dress and Disability Studies," in *Journal of design history* 19, no. 4 (2006): 309–318; Susan M. Schweik, "Disability Politics and American Literary History: Some Suggestions," *American Literary History* 20, no. 1–2, (2008): 217–237; Bryan Breed, *From Scorn to Dignity: A brief history of disability* (London: New European, 2008); Julie Anderson and A. Carden-Coyne, "Enabling the Past: New Perspectives in the History of Disability," *European review of history/ Revue europene d'histoire* 14, no. 4 (2007): 447–457;

Anne Borsay, *Disability and social policy in Britain since 1750: a history of exclusion* (Basingstoke: Palgrave Macmillan, 2005); C. F. Goodey, *A history of intelligence and 'intellectual disability': the shaping of psychology in early modern Europe* (Farnham: Ashgate, 2011); Susan M. Schweik, *The ugly laws: disability in public* (New York: New York University Press, 2009); David Wright, *Down's: the history of a disability* (Oxford: Oxford University Press, 2011); Julie Anderson, *War, disability and rehabilitation in Britain: "soul of a nation"* (Manchester: Manchester University Press, 2011); Anne Borsay, "History, Power and Identity," in *Disability Studies Today*, ed. Colin Barnes, Michael Oliver, and Len Barton, 92-119, (Cambridge: Polity, 2002).

14. Teresa Meade and David Serlin, eds., "Disability and History," *Radical History Review* 94, Special Issue, (Winter 2006).

15. Meade and Serlin, *Radical History Review*, 3.

16. https://www.dukeupress.edu/Catalog/ViewProduct.php?productid=16259. Accessed 12 January 2013.

17. *Coming Home*, movie, Hal Ashby, 1987, Los Angeles, CA, United Artists.

18. Meade and Serlin, *Radical History Review*, 8.

19. Kim E. Neilsen, *A Disability History of the United States* (Boston: Beacon Press, 2012).

20. For publication details, see endnote 4.

21. Nielsen's book on googlebooks preview is unpaginated, so I will not note further references.

22. Turner, *Disability in eighteenth-century England*, passim.

23. William Hay, *Deformity: An Essay* (London: George Faulkner, 1754).

24. Turner, *Disability in Eighteenth-Century England*, 117.

25. Sedan-chair carriers: the eighteenth-century equivalent to taxi drivers.

26. Stephen Taylor, "William Hay," in *Oxford Dictionary of National Biography*, ed. H. C. G. Matthew and Brian Harrison (Oxford: Oxford University Press, 2004), http://www.oxforddnb.com/view/article/12739?docPos=5, accessed February 6, 2013.

27. Turner, *Disability in Eighteenth-Century England*, 117.

28. William Hay, *Remarks on the Laws relating to the Poor, with Proposals for their better Relief and Employment* (London: J.Stagg, 1731); William Hay, *An Essay on Civil Government* (London: R. Gosling,1728); William Hay, *Mount Caburn: A Poem* (London: J.Stagg, 1730); William Hay, *Religio Philosophi: or, the principles of morality and Christianity illustrated from a view of the universe, and man's situation in it* (London: R.& J. Dodsley, 1753).

29. Recently discovered and published as part of Stephen Taylor and Clyve Jones, *Tory and Whig* (Woodbridge: The Boydell Press, 1998).

30. Hay, *Deformity: An Essay*, p.29–31.

31. William Hay, *The Works of William Hay* (London: J. Dodsley, 1795).

32. Turner, *Disability in Eighteenth-Century England*, 122.

33. *Martial's Epigrams Selected, Translated and Imitated by William Hay, Esq.* (London: R. & J. Dodsley, 1755).

34. Hay, *Martial's Epigrams*, 3.

35. Hay, *Martial's Epigrams*, 3.

36. Hay, *Martial's Epigrams*, 5.

37. Helen Deutsch, *Resemblance and Disgrace* (Cambridge:, Harvard University Press, 1996), and *Loving Dr. Johnson* (Chicago: University of Chicago Press, 2005). I have not quoted from the Dr. Johnson book as the form in which it was presented to me by the publishers was not amenable to the text to voice technology to which I am accustomed.

38. Deutsch, *Resemblance and Disgrace*, p.4.

39. Deutsch, *Resemblance* and *Disgrace*, p.10.

40. Deutsch, *Resemblance and Disgrace*, p.27.

41. Deutsch, *Resemblance and Disgrace*, p.84.

42. Deutsch, *Resemblance and Disgrace*, p.139.

43. Deutsch, *Resemblance and Disgrace*, p.42.

44. Elizabeth Bredberg, "Writing Disability History: Problems, perspectives and sources," *Disability & Society*, 14, no.2 (1999): 189–201, 191–92.

45. Bredberg, "Writing Disability History," 195.

46. A quick survey of the British Library catalogue for example brings up eleven books on blind history books, sixty-four on deaf history.

47. Peter Jackson, *A Pictorial History of deaf Britain* (Winsford: Deafprint, 2001); and Douglas C. Baynton, *Through Deaf Eyes, A Photographic History of a Deaf Community* (Washington: Gallaudet University Press, 2007).

48. Chris Mounsey, *Being the Body of Christ: Towards a Twenty First Century Homosexual Theology for the Anglican Church* (Sheffield: Equinox, 2012).

49. Listening to this paragraph is very odd for me since only the word in scare quotes at the end sounds right. Try listening to it on your computer's text to voice feature.

50. Robert Jordan, *The Eye of the World* (New York: T. Doherty Associates, 1990).

51. Paul Kelleher has drawn my attention to some similarities in my argument and that of complex embodiment explored by Tobin Siebers in *Disability Theory* (Ann Arbor: University of Michigan Press, 2008), 25, where he writes: The theory of complex embodiment raises awareness of the effects of disabling environments on people's lived experience of the body, but it emphasizes as well that some factors affecting disability, such as chronic pain, secondary health effects, and aging, derive from the body. These last disabilities are neither less significant than disabilities caused by the environment nor to be considered defects or deviations merely because they are resistant to change. Rather, they belong to the spectrum of human variation, conceived both as variability between individuals and as variability within an individual's life cycle, and they need to be considered in tandem with social forces affecting disability. The theory of complex embodiment views the economy between social representations and the body not as unidirectional as in the social model, or nonexistent as in the medical model, but as reciprocal. Complex embodiment theorizes the body and its representations as mutually transformative.

52. "Edvard Munch: The Modern Eye," Tate Modern, Bankside, London, August 12, 2012.

Part One

METHODOLOGICAL

1

"PERFECT ACCORDING TO THEIR KIND"

Deformity, Defect, and Disease in the
Natural Philosophy of Margaret Cavendish

Holly Faith Nelson and Sharon Alker

THOUGH MARGARET CAVENDISH, the Duchess of Newcastle (*c.* 1623–1673), did not suffer from any marked physical or psychological dis/abilities, she was considered mentally deficient by many of her generation who viewed her intellectual pursuits as evidence of her peculiarity, half-wittedness, or even madness. As has been well documented, Cavendish was "diagnosed" by a number of her contemporaries as cognitively or psychologically impaired. While Dorothy Osborne (1627–1695) famously wrote of Cavendish, "There are many Soberer people in Bedlam," Mary Evelyn (1635–1709) presented Cavendish as a monstrous or unnatural creature, an infectious "chimera" of whom she observed: "I was surprised to find so much extravagancy and vanity in any person not confined within four walls."[1] Like many women and men deemed defective in early modern England, Cavendish felt the sting of mockery and contempt. Writing from the intellectual margins, and keenly sensitive to the denigration of those deemed physically or intellectually inferior, Cavendish often defends not only the other-than-human, most notably animals, but also men and women deemed less-than-human because of what we now term a dis/ability. She does so by arguing for the essential similarity yet inevitable peculiarity of every earthly life form, gesturing toward some aspects of Chris Mounsey's notion of "Variability" as defined in the introduction to this volume.[2]

I

As her works of natural philosophy demonstrate, Cavendish was chiefly a theorist of the body or embodiment. Her vitalist or organic materialism led her to focus on self-moving matter rather than on incorporeal spiritual truths which she claimed were the province of churchmen not natural philosophers.[3] Therefore, in *Philosophical and Physical Opinions, Philosophical Letters, Observations upon Experimental Philosophy, Grounds of Natural Philosophy*,[4] and elsewhere, Cavendish dwells on the material nature and operation of both human and nonhuman creation. In the process, she routinely insists that material differences between entities should not inevitably be explained in the language of superiority and inferiority. She perceives differences in mental faculties in the same vein, since the mind and mental operations for Cavendish are wholly material. Therefore, her treatment of those deemed dis/abled resist contemporary notions of such men and women as "wondrous, monstrous, deviant, and pathological"; in fact, she often suggests that their supposed imperfections are normative or potentially so.[5]

This is not to say that Cavendish does not occasionally employ some of the early modern terms used to classify the dis/abled that we now deem deeply offensive; she describes, for example, the mentally challenged as natural or accidental "fools" or "idiots" in *Philosophical and Physical Opinions*.[6] As D. Christopher Gabbard explains, such terms had "a relatively benign appellation" in early modern England: "*idiot* and *idiocy* functioned as legal and medical designations; for example, a distinction between idiocy and lunacy in English law can be traced back to the thirteenth century."[7] Even so, there are moments when Cavendish does appear less progressive than we might like in her representation of those identified as non-normative. However, to read Cavendish's analysis of dis/ability in her philosophical prose is consistently to move away from the notion of the dis/abled body as the precise and fixed opposite of the "able body."[8] It is to confront the fact that almost all humans are imperfect and to understand that perfection itself is a random and even unnatural ontological state.

This essay first situates Cavendish's writings on dis/ability in discussions of the dis/abled mind and body in the mid- to late seventeenth century, the period during which she composed her works of natural philosophy. It then shows why Cavendish's particular brand of vitalist materialism led her to take a more sympathetic or compassionate approach to the dis/abled, relying on the details of her specific theories on material deformity, defect, and disease. In the process, it hopes to identify Cavendish as one of the more enlightened natural philosophers working to understand the diversity of the human mind and body near the end of the seventeenth century.

11

In early modern England, the term disability, as evidenced in the *Oxford English Dictionary*, was used to denote a "physical or mental condition that limits a person's movements, senses, or activities" as early as 1561. Cavendish's fellow natural philosopher Robert Boyle (1627–1691) described his speech impediment in these very terms, writing, in response to a request that he participate in a discussion at a meeting:

> But I conscious to my own Disability's told them resolutely that *I* was as much more willing as more fit to be a hearer then a speaker, among such knowing Persons, and on so abstruse a Subject. And that therefore I beseeched them without necessitating me to proclaim my weaknesses, to allow me to lessen them by being a silent Auditor of their Discourses:[9]

In Cavendish's lifetime the word "disabled" was applied to soldiers injured in the civil wars. In *Two Ordinances of the Lord and Commons Assembled in Parliament* (1647), for example, relief is offered to "every Souldier or Marriner, maimed or disabled in body . . . in the service of the Parliament during these late warres."[10] As in any postwar period, the physically and psychologically impaired were ever in the public eye, bringing the subject of dis/ability to the forefront of society. This desire to cope with and classify the abled or dis/abled body in that period was further intensified by the shift to a more scientific way of knowing and being in the world. As Henri-Jacques Stiker argues in *A History of Disability*, in early modern Europe there was a tendency to find some natural and physical explanation for every known phenomenon. This new focus inspired wholesale reconceptualization of each aspect of the material world, including the essence and operation of human bodies and minds, especially those identified as irregular or aberrant.[11]

To use the word "disability" in the analysis of aspects of early modern society, therefore, is not an anachronistic choice. However, most of the writers of the period, Cavendish among them, employ a range of terms when considering those who would, in present times, be classified as mentally or physically dis/abled. As a result, it is no small feat to establish how the dis/abled were viewed in early modern England, as we try to place in one category those deemed, for instance, diseased, defective, deformed, idiotic, stupid, foolish, mad and monstrous, the most common terms employed at the time for the dis/abled. What David L. Braddock and Susan L. Parish argue about medieval Europe is thus equally true of early modern England: it had "no universal definition or interpretation of disability."[12]

Just as there is no single term by which to identify or define the dis/abled in seventeenth-century England, no lone or stable discourse existed about the dis/abled in the period. Competing points of view of the physically and mentally dis/abled emerged out of a range of contexts—ecclesiastical, spiritual, philosophical, legal, medical, familial, etc.—and even within each of these contexts, perspectives were not single or static. Drawing on the same spiritual sources, for example, some seventeenth-century thinkers linked psychological dis/ability with demon possession while others held that such a dis/ability was an instrument of spiritual growth for both the dis/abled (since suffering could facilitate spiritual development) and those who assisted them (since charitable action purified the soul). A number of physicians also accessed similar medical resources in an attempt to diagnose and cure a given dis/ability, yet often reached radically different conclusions. Such was the case with Lady Anne Conway (1631–1679), who suffered from crippling migraines. Conway received multiple, often competing, diagnoses from the likes of William Harvey (1578–1657), Thomas Ridgley (1576–1656), Thomas Willis (1621–1675), and Francis Mercury Van Helmont (1614–1698), all members of the medical establishment, though committed to different aspects of classical or modern medicine.[13]

So many different discourses surrounded the dis/abled man or woman in the period largely because early modern thinkers, like their modern counterparts, were well aware of the complex etiology of mental and physical dis/abilities.[14] Natural philosophers and physicians often distinguished between hereditary, acquired, and accidental causes of physical, psychological, or intellectual deficits. For example, in his analysis of "stupidity or folly"—that which "signifies the defect of the Understanding and Judgment"—the natural philosopher and physician Thomas Willis explains that if this condition is "originary, or born with a man" it may be "hereditary, as when Fools beget Fools," or it may be "accidental, as it were," caused, for instance, by "[p]arents spend[ing] their Spirits in Study and too much thinking" or "weaken[ing] and enerv[ating] the Body through intemperance, luxury, and ill living." In other cases, Willis claims that the "evil conformation of the Brain" in those considered stupid or fools is "acquired by reason of some Disorders" which prevent the "animal Spirits" from "duely operat[ing]."[15] The physician Thomas Sydenham (1624–1689) is similarly aware of the multiple causes of a physical or mental dis/ability. When discussing different "sorts of Madness," for example, Sydenham differentiates between types of insanity, explaining that while some types of madness "are most commonly cured by large Evacuations, by Bleeding and Purging," a "certain peculiar Madness which follows long Agues, especially Quartans," will not "bear" either of these treatments, and if the patient receives such treatment, he "becomes a Changeling, and continues so as long as he lives."[16] Cavendish and Sydenham agree on the difficulty of identifying the cause and type of a disease and of selecting a suitable treatment, for as she remarks in *Philosophical Letters*, "The disease may vary, and therefore what was good in this temper, may, perhaps, be bad in the variation; insomuch, that one medicine may in a minute prove a Cordial, and Poyson."[17]

An understanding of the multifaceted etiology of most dis/abilities in early modern England is thus matched by an awareness of the complexity of treatment of various mental and physical dis/abilities. As we have demonstrated elsewhere in relation to the neurological illness of Lady Anne Conway, Cavendish's contemporary, Conway's "ailing body becomes an object of speculation, a case study by which noted early modern physicians, surgeons, and chemists test and record the success of new scientific procedures, just as it serves as an object of religious inquiry for spiritual healers seeking to cure her ailment, freeing her from her life as an invalid." Her body, therefore, "becomes a medical space upon which a wide range of established and newly emerging theories of disease and healing collide and are interrogated."[18] Living in a critical time of transition in medicine, marked by an ongoing tension between the ancients and the moderns, dis/abled men and women in the seventeenth-century were routinely offered radically different prognoses and treatment plans.

There was significant debate, for example, over whether intellectually dis/abled individuals were fully human and whether or not they could, through education, improve their intellectual capacity. Gabbard points to the work of Willis who "recommended that idiocy" in many cases "not be regarded as a hopelessly static and permanent condition" and that those considered idiots should "be afforded the chance to develop through education, proposing that their mental faculties be 'amended' by a '*Physician* and a *Teacher*,'" a recommendation with which only a select few early modern physicians would agree.[19] Similar medical debates surrounded the treatment of the deaf and mute. Rene Descartes (1596–1650) had famously argued that those without the ability to hear or produce speech were lacking in reasoning capacities. Others, most notably John Wallis (1616–1703) and William Holder (1615/1616–1698) in England, as Gabbard points out, wrote works on "educating deaf-mutes, a group once presumed to be mentally deficient and therefore, like idiots, uneducable."[20] In his correspondence with Robert Boyle, John Wallis describes his technique for training a young deaf man, Daniel Whaley, to read, write, and speak, tasks he believed he could achieve with some "considerable Success," despite the need to rely on rather basic gestures or signals.[21] In the process, he argued that the hearing must also learn the semiotic systems of the deaf, if progress is to occur: "And we must endeavour to learn their Language, (if I may so call it) in order to teach them ours."[22] Both he and, previously, William Holder taught Alexander Popham linguistic skills, allowing their pupil to express himself in oral and written prose.[23] Definitions, explanations, diagnoses, and prognoses of, and possible treatment plans for, deafness proliferated, as was the case with most dis/abilities in early modern England.

III

The discourses on dis/ability to which Margaret Cavendish would have been exposed and within which she had to work, therefore, were many and varied, and they were embedded primarily in larger religious, philosophical, and (proto) scientific discursive contexts. As we have theorized elsewhere, the philosophical and scientific complexity of Cavendish's works is mainly rooted in the epistemic instability of "the mid-seventeenth century when knowledge formation was in extreme flux," a volatility that "played a part in the onset of the Civil War, which splintered both ideas and bodies, intensifying the climate of uncertainty."[24] Cavendish wished to participate actively in knowledge production at this moment of epistemological fluidity, engaging the subject of dis/ability indirectly by entering debates in the emerging fields of physics, chemistry, and biology and reflecting on the medical significance of the truth(s) discovered in these fields. Cavendish's poetry and treatises on natural philosophy are instruments by which she navigates, authenticates and challenges certain claims made by the likes of Rene Descartes, Thomas Hobbes, Henry More, and Jan Baptista Van Helmont. These and other male intellectuals often addressed humanness and "the failure to be truly human" in their writings, trying to grasp the causes of dis/ability or what they classified in their "Baconian natural histories" as "aberrations of nature."[25] It is these thinkers and ideas with which Cavendish found herself in dialogue.

In tackling these intellectuals and ideas, Cavendish inevitably found herself addressing four overlapping types of dis/ability: intellectual dis/ability, psychological dis/ability, physical dis/ability, and monstrosity. However, though Cavendish recognizes these distinct manifestations of dis/ability, her vitalist and monist materialism, sketched out in the following argument, drives her to see them as inescapably related. Thus, she grapples with them in a similar way, relying on the discourse of matter in motion and variety in nature to account for, and often minimize the significance of, material differences in human beings.

For Cavendish, as noted above, the mind and body are made of the same self-moving "Infinite and Eternal Matter," which is both rational and sensitive, animate and inanimate. As she explains in *Philosophical Letters*, arguing against Cartesian thought,

> [I]n all parts of nature there is a commixture of animate and inanimate matter: and this Life and Knowledg is sense and reason, or sensitive and rational corporeal motions, which are all one thing with animate matter without any distinction or abstraction, and can no more quit matter, then matter can quit motion. Wherefore every creature being composed of this commixture of animate and inanimate matter, has also selfe-motion, that is life and knowledge, sense and reason.[26]

This theory of self-moving matter in which every part of nature—human, animal, plant, and mineral, child and adult, abled and dis/abled—is constituted of identical matter is informed by what we would call Cavendish's hermeneutic of similitude.[27] That is, the interpretive framework that Cavendish places on the natural world leads her to view all things as essentially or substantially alike: "matter, self-motion, and self-knowledge, are inseparable from each other, and make nature one material, self-moving, and self-knowing body."[28] Though some entities in nature, for example, animals, plants, and minerals, lack a nonmaterial soul, this is a supernatural concern, which is not, or only marginally, relevant to the study of the material world, argues Cavendish. What matters to Cavendish is the fundamental similarity between all material objects in nature. This similarity works on both a macrocosmic and a microcosmic level for Cavendish, as the cosmos as a whole and each part or body within it consist of identical rational and sensitive matter, which means that both reason and sense are in every part of each of those bodies. Reason, Cavendish insists, is *not* restricted to one part of the body, such as the brain: "I believe there is sense and reason, or sensitive and rational knowledge, not only in all creatures, but in every part of every particular creature. . . . And therefore, the head or brains cannot engross all knowledge to themselves."[29] Therefore, a defect or deficit in the brain does not remove all of the rational elements from a particular body.

While Cavendish's hermeneutic of similitude ensures that she envisions all entities in nature as composed of the same self-moving and "continuous" matter,[30] it does not negate the beauty of variety or diversity among these entities. Cavendish repeatedly stresses that "Nature delights in variety . . . as it is the propriety of Nature to work variously."[31] In fact, she envisions nature in terms of diversity with a unified, harmonious and ordered whole: "[N]ature is but one body . . . entirely wise and knowing, ordering her self-moving parts with all facility and ease, without any disturbance, living in pleasure and delight, with infinite varieties and curiosities."[32] Variety within species is something that Cavendish values and celebrates, as is evident in her account of nature's "wisdom and liberty" in *Observations upon Experimental Philosophy*, where she writes, "the variety of nature, which is so great, that even in one and the same species, none of the particulars resemble one another so much, as not to be discerned from each other."[33] Variety is so normative to Cavendish that she presents the concept of a perfect being against which all other beings should be measured or to which all other beings should conform as abnormal.

I V

Cavendish's natural philosophy, as briefly outlined here,[34] lends itself to a sympathetic understanding of the dis/abled for four reasons. First, because Cavendish believes that every entity in the natural world is made up of precisely the same self-moving and "continuous" matter, she suggests that humans are far more alike than different, despite variety among them. When challenging other philosophers' claims that non-human animals or deaf and mute humans do not have the capacity to remember because they cannot speak or use language as 'normal' adult humans do, Cavendish writes, "for all other Animals have Memory without the help of Speech, and so have deaf and dumb men, nay more then those that hear and speak: Wherefore, though Words are useful to the mind, and so to the memory, yet both can be without them."[35] While Cavendish recognizes that not all humans have "the like Capacities, Understandings, Imaginations, Wits, Fancies, Passions, &c." she believes that because they are comprised of the identical substance, "all . . . are made by the direction of Reason, and endued with Reason, from the first time of their birth."[36] She continues, "Reason is not in one undivided part, nor bound to one motion, for it is in every Creature more or less, and moves in its own parts variously."[37]

Second, since, for Cavendish, all humans are made of the same substance, each "particular creature" is equally subject to "irregular" or "unnatural" motions of that matter, which is the chief cause of disease, defect, deformity, dotage, and untimely decay.[38] Therefore, all humans are understood as potentially dis/abled. In considering the case of hereditary diseases, for example, Cavendish refuses to accept that certain families are more likely to suffer from specific dis/abling conditions, taking gout as a case study. She contends that all offspring of Adam and Eve can be potentially dis/abled should the self-moving matter of which they are composed move in an irregular or unnatural fashion:

> but every Child has not his Parents diseases, and many Children have such diseases as their Parents never had; neither is any disease tied to a particular Family by Generation, but they proceed from irregular motions, and are generally in all Mankind; and therefore properly there is no such thing as an hereditary propagation of diseases . . . and we consisting of the same natural matter, are naturally subject as well to diseases as to health, according as the Matter moves.[39]

Diseases, Cavendish maintains, are only hereditary inasmuch as "the Scripture it self confirms it, informing us, that disease as well as death, are by an hereditary propagation derived from *Adam* upon all Posterity."[40] This theory of the transmission of disease prevents us from imagining the dis/abled as radically different from abled beings since, ontologically speaking, all humans have one and the same self-moving essence with the potential to experience "irregular" or "unnatural" motions.

Third, because variety within a species is deemed normal and natural, Cavendish often reads difference in terms of potential and possibility rather than absence and lack. In *A Blazing World*, a "science-fiction" novella, Cavendish creates hybrid beings, half men and half beast, who are, without a doubt, differently abled, but it is their very differences that allow them to meet their full potential. The bird men are expert in things relating to the skies, for the Empress (the protagonist) asks them for "a true relation of the two Celestial bodies, *viz.* the Sun and Moon" while the fish men can give information about "the Seas" and the worm men about "the Earth."[41] Moreover, when the Empress makes use of the various creatures during a war at the end of the narrative, she uses each being according to his specialized skills. What might be seen as oddities and differences are part of a complex creature valued for his particularly unique competencies. Variety is not only normal, then, but also useful.

Indeed it is "perfection" and "monstrosity" that Cavendish sometimes classifies as anomalies.[42] In *Philosophical and Physical Opinions*, Cavendish describes perfection thus:

> But it seems to Human sense and reason, that the Cause, that Animate motion Moves or Works so Imperfectly, as seldome to Form any one Creature Exactly . . . so as when any Creature is so Exact, as no Fault can

be found, it seems rather a Work by Chance, than any Design in Motion to Work so Exactly. . . . [I]t would be a Thing or Work above Nature, and to be Accounted a Miracle, if any Creature should be made so Exact as somewhat were not amiss either in Body or Mind.[43]

Monstrosity is described in similar terms, as that which is rarely seen. In *Philosophical Letters*, Cavendish explains that while it is true "[t]hat some parts of Matter may produce another Creature not like to the producer in its species, as for example, Monsters . . . yet it is not usual."[44] And even though monstrous beings, human or otherwise, are generally abhorred, Cavendish does not see them as entirely unlovable: "a Monster . . . is never loved, but for its rarity and novelty, and Nature is many times pleased with changes, taking delight in variety."[45]

Regardless, if perfection and monstrosity are outliers for Cavendish, those considered "normal" would include those who have experienced some kind of dis/ability either through natural or accidental causes.[46] And those who are struck with an intellectual, mental, or physical dis/ability are not, Cavendish proposes, totally diminished. She explains in *Philosophical Letters* that men and women who suffer from mental or intellectual impairment still enjoy a degree of higher-order thinking and feeling:

> a man may become Mad or a Fool through the irregular motions of sense and reason, and yet have still the Perception of sense and reason, onely the alteration is caused through the alteration of the sensitive and rational corporeal motions or actions, from regular to irregular; nevertheless he has Perceptions, Thoughts, Ideas, Passions, and whatsoever is made by sensitive and rational Matter.[47]

And even when a disease or defect is considered "incurable" by Cavendish—a class in which she includes "natural blindness, dumbness, deafness, or lameness"—the "Error of . . . Production" that caused this "Defect" affects only one aspect of life.[48] A person, then, is not defined by a defect. On this point, she remarks in *Grounds of Natural Philosophy*, "If a Man be born Blind, then only his Eyes are Fools; if Deaf, then only his Ears are Fools . . . that is, those Parts have no knowledg of such Properties that belong to such Parts."[49] Cavendish informs us that the rest of the person compensates for such "folly" in one part:

> [A]s for those that are Born Deaf and Dumb . . . they are for the most part very Ingenious to help the Defects of their Body by the Wit of their Minds, for they will Conceive and Inform by signs Ingeniously,

and certainly, were they not only Deaf and Dumb, but Blind also, yet
they would have both Thoughts, Passions, and Conceptions, and those
Thoughts, Passions and Conceptions would be Regular and Rational according to the Kind and Nature of their Figure.[50]

The potential of the dis/abled to compensate for any ontological irregularity is
favorably joined with the possibility for personal happiness, as Cavendish insists
that there is no human so defective that he or she could not attract another and
be loved. Of this she writes in *Philosophical Letters*:

> Again, you may ask me the reason, why a Man seeing two persons to-
> gether, which are strangers to him, doth affect one better then the other;
> nay, if one of these Persons be deformed or ill-favoured, and the other
> well-shaped and handsom; yet it may chance, that the deformed Person
> shall be more acceptable in the affections and eyes of the beholder, then
> he that is handsom. I answer: There is no Creature so deformed, but hath
> some agreeable and attractive parts.[51]

Dis/ability does not, that is, prevent "sympathetical affection."[52] Cavendish here
recognizes that those who do not conform to societal expectations remain a part
of a web of social relations who value and appreciate their difference.

In fact, in some cases, what might be considered a partial deformity is, in
fact, simply a distinct form of humanity, perfect in its own way, according to
Cavendish. In discussing bodily growth and health in *Philosophical and Physical
Opinions*, Cavendish reflects on the fully grown human and, in so doing, finds
perfection in both humans and animals regardless of their size:

> [B]ut do not mistake me, when I say full Growth and Large, as if not
> any Animal were Perfect that were not Tall and Big, no, I mean Large, as
> from the first Degree to the last Degree of their full Growth, for there are
> different Degrees of Sizes amongst one and the same kind, as Mankind,
> for a Little man is as Perfect at full Growth as a Great man, a Pygmy as
> Perfect as a Giant. . . . [S]ome Little men may be Stronger than men
> of a Greater size, as also a Little man may have more Wit, Knowledge
> or Understanding than a Greater man, for neither strength of Body nor
> Mind lie in the Bulk of Inanimate matter, but in the Regularity and
> Strength of Sensitive and Rational Motions.[53]

For Cavendish, a little person is no less perfect than a man of average size or a
giant because difference among "the same kind" or species in such a case should

be regarded simply as evidence of variation in nature rather than as proof of the diminished value of certain atypical human beings. The tendency to evaluate people against a specific standard of perfection, therefore, is continually found to be unsound in Cavendish's writings.

Finally, because Cavendish strives to situate religious matters outside the realm of natural philosophy, given God's immaterial nature, she never assigns spiritual causes to deformities, defects, or diseases; [54] that is, she never suggests that intellectual, psychological, or physical afflictions are the consequences of, or punishment for, sin. She neither presents the dis/abled as spiritually weak and vulnerable nor associates them with a lack of moral worth.[55] In the case of those diagnosed with the "disease" or "distemper" of madness, for example, Cavendish does not even consider the possibility that the mentally ill are demon-possessed, morally depraved, spiritually menacing, or wholly or permanently marred. Claiming that madness is caused by "irregular motions" in either the rational or sensitive animate matter, or both, Cavendish advocates highly compassionate treatment of the mad that will enable the matter of which they are composed to "keep" its proper "Time" and "Measure." This can best be accomplished by "Harmonious musick" in conjunction with "Gentle perswasions . . . [and] Kind expressions."[56] Cavendish's compassionate treatment plan is not merely a direct result of her scientific mindset. There were some in the religious establishment who advocated that the mad be treated in an equally humane fashion and other materialists who were far less sympathetic to the mentally ill. Though Willis, for example, "approved treatment by soothing and pleasurable activities," unlike Cavendish, he "showed little interest in the more sensitive and caring attitudes that began to emerge in his day," "advising beatings and restraints" for the mentally ill if he felt them necessary.[57] Though the healthcare plan proposed by Cavendish for the mad is not a direct result of her theory of self-moving matter, it does accord with her overarching scientific vision which seeks, as Lisa T. Sarasohn rightly argues, to defend and authorize those with limited access to power who are often subject to, and victimized by, the "confining categories" established by those who would dominate them. While Sarasohn has women and animals chiefly in mind when making this claim, we would include the dis/abled in this group.[58]

V

It would be inaccurate to see Cavendish as a radical figure in the history of dis/ability studies. Her work was not ultimately influential on this topic and her understanding of the human body and the social rights of, and responsibilities toward, the differently abled was far from ours. Yet the hermeneutic of similitude that she developed in her works of natural philosophy produced a voice of resistance against emergent binaries that deemed those who did not conform to a predetermined ontological state wholly abnormal and deficient. Rather than organize the multiple discourses on dis/ability available to her into a tidy system in which difference could be easily identified and catalogued, Cavendish chose a far messier and complex knowledge system, one that made it harder to classify and thus stigmatize the dis/abled and one more in tune with the idea that all beings are "Variable" or "the same only different" as theorized by Mounsey.[59] Her scientific vision is that in essence human creatures—despite their differences—cannot simply be categorized based on their physical, psychological, or intellectual differences; that is to say, their differences do not define them in any way but are merely a reflection of natural variety and thus should not predefine or ordain their place in society. Naturalizing superficial differences within similitude of substance leaves far less room for ethical, spiritual, or scientific hierarchies, and puts her concepts in opposition to the patriarchal medical power systems that, as Michel Foucault has noted (and perhaps overstated), would classify and ultimately contain the human body deemed different over the next few centuries.

Notes

1. Dorothy Osborne to William Temple, 8 May 1653, *Letters to Sir William Temple* (Harmondsworth: Penguin, 1987), 79; Mary Evelyn to Ralph Bohun, *c.* 1667, in *Paper Bodies: A Margaret Cavendish Reader*, ed. Sylvia Bowerbank and Sara Mendelson (Peterborough: Broadview, 2000), 91–92.

2. See Chris Mounsey's introduction to this collection, "Variability: Beyond Sameness and Difference."

3. As Holly Faith Nelson has argued elsewhere, though Cavendish largely avoids spiritual matters in her philosophical prose, she does on occasion address them: for example, when writing of the nature of the human soul. Cavendish is variously considered an animist materialist, vitalist materialist, or organic materialist; on this subject, see, for example, Lisa T. Sarasohn's *The Natural Philosophy of Margaret Cavendish: Reason and Fancy during the Scientific Revolution* (Baltimore: Johns Hopkins University Press, 2010), Eileen O'Neill's introduction to her edition of Cavendish's *Observations upon Experimental Philosophy* (Cambridge: Cambridge University Press, 2001), and John Rogers's chapter on Cavendish in *The Matter of Revolution: Science, Poetry and Politics in the Age of Milton* (Ithaca: Cornell University Press, 1996).

4. Margaret Cavendish, *Philosophical and physical opinions written by . . . the Lady Marchioness of Newcastle* (London: William Wilson, 1663); *Philosophical letters, or, Modest reflections upon some opinions in natural philosophy maintained by several famous and learned authors of this age, expressed by way of letters / by the thrice noble, illustrious, and excellent princess the Lady Marchioness of Newcastle.*

(London: 1664); *Observations upon experimental philosophy to which is added, The description of a new blazing world / written by . . . Princesse, the Duchess of Newcastle* (London: A. Maxwell, 1668); *Ground of natural philosophy divided into thirteen parts: with an appendix containing five parts / written by the . . . Dvchess of Newcastle* (London: A. Maxwell, 1668).

5. Allison P. Hobgood, "Caesar Hath the Falling Sickness: The Legibility of Early Modern Disability in Shakespearean Drama," *Disability Studies Quarterly* 29, no.4 (2009), accessed May 1, 2013, http://www.dsq-sds.org/article/view/993/1184.

6. Margaret Cavendish, *Philosophical and Physical Opinions*, 333.

7. D. Christopher Gabbard, "From Idiot Beast to Idiot Sublime: Mental Disability in John Cleland's *Fanny Hill*," *PMLA* 123, no.2 (2008): 375–89 (376, 375).

8. Allison P. Hobgood and David Houston Wood, "Introduction: Disabled Shakespeares," *Disability Studies Quarterly* 29, no.4 (2009), accessed May 1, 2013, http://www.dsq-sds.org/issue/view/42.

9. Robert Boyle, *The Sceptical Chymist* (London: J.Cadwell, 1661), 8.

10. *Two Ordinances of the Lords and Commons Assembled in Parliament* (London, 1647), 4.

11. Henri-Jacques Stiker, *A History of Disability*, trans. William Sayers (Ann Arbor: University of Michigan Press, 1999), 91–94.

12. David L. Braddock and Susan L. Parish, "An Institutional History of Disability," in the *Handbook of Disability Studies*, ed. Gary L. Albrecht, Katherine D. Seelman, and Michael Bury (Thousand Oaks: Sage, 2001), 21.

13. Holly Faith Nelson and Sharon Alker, "Conway: Dis/ability, Medicine, and Metaphysics," in *The New Science and Women's Literary Discourse: Prefiguring Frankenstein*, ed. Judy A. Hayden (New York: Palgrave Macmillan, 2011), 65–83.

14. For ease of reference, we differentiate here between mental and physical dis/abilities. However, these were not (and are still not) clearly defined categories. Many early modern natural philosophers and physicians attributed intellectual or psychological aberrations to physical or material causes.

15. Thomas Willis, "Of Stupidity or Folly," in *The London Practice of Physick: Or the whole Practical Part of Physick Contained in the Works of Dr. Willis* (London, 1685), 489–90.

16. Thomas Sydenham, *The Whole Works of that Excellent Practical Physician, Dr. Thomas Sydenham* (London, 1734), 54.

17. Cavendish, *Philosophical Letters*, 353; Cavendish, *Grounds of Natural Philosophy*, 85.

18. Nelson and Alker, "Conway: Dis/ability, Medicine, and Metaphysics," 65.

19. Gabbard, "From Idiot Beast to Idiot Sublime," 380.

20. Gabbard, "From Idiot Beast to Idiot Sublime," 380.

21. Quoted in Jan Branson and Don Miller, *Damned for their Difference: The Cultural Construction of Deaf People as Disabled* (Washington, DC: Gallaudet University Press, 2002), 80–81. As Branson and Miller note, the attempt to teach the deaf to read, write, and speak began at least as early as the medieval period, often in monastic settings.

22. Quoted in Branson and Miller, *Damned for their Difference*, 81.

23. Branson and Miller, *Damned for their Difference*, 81–82.

24. Holly Faith Nelson and Sharon Alker, "Writing 'Science Fiction' in the Shadow of War: Bodily Transgressions in Cavendish's *Blazing World*," in *Travel Narratives, the New Science, and Literary Discourse, 1569–1750*, ed. Judy Hayden (Aldershot: Ashgate, 2012), 103, 105.

25. Erica Fudge, *Brutal Reasoning: Animals, Rationality, and Humanity in Early Modern England* (Ithaca: Cornell University Press, 2006), 47; Peter Anstey, "Literary Responses to Robert Boyle's Natural Philosophy," in *Science, Literature and Rhetoric in Early Modern England*, ed. Juliet Cummins and David Burchell (Aldershot: Ashgate, 2007), 150.

26. Cavendish, *Philosophical Letters*, 14, 99–100.

27. In using the phrase "the hermeneutic of similitude" to characterize the interpretive lens through which Cavendish reads all created matter, we are indebted to Michel Foucault's theory of epistemic frameworks, in particular to the "hermeneutics of resemblance" he assigns to Renaissance thought prior to the Scientific Revolution (Michel Foucault, *The Order of Things: An Archaeology of the Human Sciences*, trans. Alan Sheridan [New York: Harper and Rowe, 1973], 30). That Cavendish's natural philosophy shares characteristics with earlier epistemological paradigms has been noted by, for example, John Rogers and Lisa T. Sarasohn in *The Matter of Revolution* and *The Natural Philosophy of Margaret Cavendish* respectively.

28. Cavendish, *Observations*, 137.

29. Cavendish, *Observations*, 151, 152.

30. As O'Neill explains in her introduction to *Observations*, while Cavendish formerly subscribed to atomism, she later believed that "instead of being atomic in structure," the material of which nature is made is "continuous" (xxi).

31. Cavendish, *Philosophical Letters*, 416. Cavendish distinguishes here between "variety," which nature "delights in," and "confusion," in which nature "doth not delight" (416).

32. Cavendish, *Observations*, 48. To explain further, Cavendish writes, "And thus nature may be called both 'individual,' as not having single parts subsisting within her, but all united in one body: and 'dividable,' by reason she is partible in her own several corporeal figurative motions" (48).

33. Cavendish, *Observations*, 139.

34. For a comprehensive account of Cavendish's natural philosophy, see Sarasohn's groundbreaking monograph *The Natural Philosophy of Margaret Cavendish*. We have not detailed here the law or principle behind self-motion in Cavendish's system since it is not especially relevant to her treatment of dis/ability. See O'Neill's fine introduction to *Observations* (esp. xxi–xxxv) and Sarasohn's monograph on this and other related subjects.

35. Cavendish, *Philosophical Letters*, 35.

36. Cavendish, *Philosophical Letters*, 37, 36.

37. Cavendish, *Philosophical Letters*, 36.

38. Cavendish, *Philosophical Letters*, 345; Cavendish, *Philosophical and Physical Opinions*, 333. In *Philosophical and Physical Opinions*, Cavendish differentiates between the causes of dis/abilities thus: "Madness is onely an Irregularity of some Sorts of Sensitive and Rational motions, and Mistempered matter; but to be a Natural fool is by Unnatural motions, or a Defect in Creation

and Birth, either caused by the Sensitive motions in the Architecture of the Body, or a Scarcity of Rational matter, or Irregularity of motions in the Creation or Beginning. . . . Dotage . . . is caused by the Weakness and Decay of the Body, and so of the Mind; for though a Man in Age have all the Parts of his Body Sound, and nothing Diminished, yet the Sensitive motion is working this Body to some other Figure, which causes his Senses to be Imperfect, and his Body Weak. . . . As for those Idiots or Fools that are made so by Hurts in the Head, the Violent motions must of necessity Change or Alter these Rational Natural motions that belong to the Head; and those that are made Fools by great Frights or Fears, are so, by reason in that Excessive Passion, the Rational matter and motions were so put out of Order, as this Disorder caused such a Change, as to Alter their Natural motions to Unnatural motions. . . . the like in Some Sorts of Sickness" but in that case "the Sensitive motions have Disordered the Rational" (333–34).

39. Cavendish, *Philosophical Letters*, 400.

40. Cavendish, *Philosophical Letters*, 400.

41. Margaret Cavendish, *A Blazing World, Paper Bodies*, ed. Bowerbank and Mendelson, 165, 174.

42. Elsewhere in her writings, Cavendish does use the word "perfect" when, for example, attempting to describe those beings whose development does not involve any irregular or unnatural motions and who attain "full Growth" (*Philosophical and Physical Opinions*, 35). However, these occasional statements do not detract from her overarching conception of most beings as flawed or faulty in some way.

43. Cavendish, *Philosophical and Physical Opinions*, 248.

44. Cavendish, *Philosophical Letters*, 424–25.

45. Cavendish, *Philosophical Letters*, 294. Cavendish again references monsters or changelings as liminal beings in *Grounds of Natural Philosophy*: "for, the Sense may be a Natural Fool as well as the Reason; as we may observe in those sorts of Fools whom we name *Changelings*, whose Body is not only deformed, but all the Postures of the Body are defective, and appear as so many fools" (85). But Cavendish quickly moves on to the compensatory strategies of those who have only one or two defective parts and she ends this section of the work by emphasizing that "only *some* particular sorts of Deformity, or Defects, are Foolish" (87).

46. By "accidental," natural philosophers of the period draw on Aristotle's meaning, "relating to or denoting properties which are not essential to something's nature" (*OED* accidental *adj.* A.I.2), which is opposed to "natural," "Existing or present by nature; inherent in the very constitution of a person or thing" (*OED* natural *adj.* A.I.1).

47. Cavendish, *Philosophical Letters*, 153–154.

48. Cavendish, *Observations*, 242; Cavendish, *Grounds*, 85.

49. Cavendish, *Grounds*, 85.

50. Cavendish, *Philosophical and Physical Opinions*, 335. In *Grounds of Natural Philosophy*, Cavendish also notes, "That when the Body is defective, but not the Mind then the Mind is very industrious to find out Inventions to Art, to help the Defects that are natural" (86–87).

51. Cavendish, *Philosophical Letters*, 294; Cavendish states that the exception to this rule is the "Monster," which "is never loved" except "for its rarity and novelty," as cited above (294).

52. Cavendish, *Philosophical Letters*, 294.

53. Cavendish, *Philosophical and Physical Opinions*, 35–36.

54. Cavendish stresses that she is an orthodox Christian. However, she argues that because "God is an Immaterial and Spiritual Infinite Being," and thus radically different from the "infinite and Eternal Matter" of which nature is made, God is outside of and "not tied to Natural rule." She states, therefore, that the natural philosopher should only study nature "by the Light of Reason onely" (*Philosophical Letters*, 14, 16, 17). However, as earlier noted, spiritual reflections appear here and there in her works of natural philosophy.

55. Unfortunately, in striving to separate religion from natural philosophy, Cavendish does not have access to the spiritual discourses often employed in support of the dis/abled in early modern England. For example, the language of religion was used to suggest that the dis/abled were also made in God's image, since their bodies and minds were shaped by God. As Stiker explains, some early modern intellectuals claimed that dis/ability was caused by "aberrant germs," arguing that these "germs are as ordained as any others and come from his [God's] wisdom. Aberrations and deformities are equally rational: in their structure they are just as functional as normal organisms and, moreover, they are part of that immense intelligence of the world that is beyond our ken" (93).

56. Cavendish, *Philosophical and Physical Opinions*, 329, 330, 331; see also Cavendish, *Grounds*, 124–29.

57. Theodore Millon, with contributions from Seth D. Grossman and Sarah E. Meagher, *Masters of the Mind: Exploring the Story of Mental Illness from Ancient Times to the New Millennium* (Malden: Wiley Blackwell, 2004), 74.

58. Sarasohn, *The Natural Philosophy of Margaret Cavendish*, 13, 194

59. Mounsey, introduction to this volume.

2

WHAT'S THE MATTER WITH MADNESS?

John Locke, the Association of Ideas,

and the Physiology of Thought

Jess Keiser

I N   T H E   C O U R S E   O F   D R A F T I N G   the fourth edition of the
Essay concerning Human Understanding, John Locke found himself contemplating
madness. As he had in previous versions of that work, Locke described madness
in the new edition of the *Essay* as a disease that made the mind doubly deranged.
First, madness confuses the mind's ideas. It occurs, Locke explains, when "*Ideas*
that in themselves are not at all of kin, come to be so united in some Mens
Minds, that 'tis very hard to separate them."[1] Second, madness creates a kind of
internal blindness. More specifically, it makes the mind incapable of perceiving
and thereby rectifying the aforementioned ideational confusions. In this respect,
madness is the "most dangerous" of "the Errors in the World . . . since so far as it
obtains, it hinders Men from seeing and examining" their thoughts.[2] According to
Locke, reason, argument, and evidence have no effect on the false associations of
madness. Indeed, while we can observe madness in others, we are ignorant of this
malady when it affects us.

But in addition to recapitulating past theories, the fourth edition of the *Es-say* also added something new to Locke's thoughts on madness—something that
seemed to depart radically from the stated aims of that work. For the first time,
Locke argued that the root of madness could be located in the body and brain.
More specifically, Locke contended that madness's propensity to both blind and
confuse the understanding was a result of animal spirits carving smooth pathways
into the corporeal mind.[3] In another new chapter in the *Essay*—one that dealt
specifically with religious madness—he pointed to a "warmed or over-weening
Brain" as the probable cause of false enthusiasm.[4] These claims, perhaps unsurprising at first glance, become more striking in the context of the *Essay* as a whole.

Locke explains plainly in the second paragraph of that work that he "shall not at present meddle with the Physical Consideration of the Mind."[5] As we will see, Locke took this stricture seriously. Besides for the new additions to the *Essay*, Locke's remaining references to physiology and brain anatomy are cautious (even apologetic); in other instances, Locke simply ridicules such explanations.[6] Even more importantly, as a number of scholars have recently shown, Locke's refusal to "meddle" with the physical and material structure of the mind makes the *Essay*'s project—examining the work of consciousness and recording its labors in a "history" of the understanding—possible in the first place.[7] Given Locke's rejection of such explanations, then, how can we account for his turn to physiology and pathology when describing the bodily errors of madness?[8]

My goal in the following essay is not to explain away this inconsistency. Strictly speaking, Locke's claims about the physiology of madness in the fourth edition of the *Essay* exceed the strict epistemological guidelines that the remainder of that work lays down. Nevertheless, despite their obvious dissimilarities, Locke's writings *against* physiology and his writings *about* the physiology of madness have more in common than may be evident at first glance. As I demonstrate, Locke's cautious empiricism and his speculative pathology point to a more general anxiety in the *Essay*: an anxiety about our blindness to the ways in which body and brain affect the conscious mind.

Before contending with the *Essay*'s curious lapses into otherwise disavowed neurophysiology, I first explore Locke's reasons for denying such theories of mind in the first place. Locke argues that, due to the frailty of human faculties, we can never perceive how matter affects mind. He therefore maintains that we should attend solely to the interactions of conscious ideas rather than guessing at their more fundamental material nature. I next turn to Locke's writings on madness in the fourth edition of the *Essay*, a moment in that work where Locke fails to heed his own advice. Here Locke explains that animal spirits produce ideas in the conscious mind (or in the very least are responsible for the misassociations that trouble rational thought). In this instance, the brain tricks the mad into perceiving otherwise irrational connections in the mind's ideas. In both instances, the body's impact on mind remains a blind spot for rational thought. Just as Locke's cautious empiricism dictates that we must remain blind to the manner in which the matter of the brain produces conscious ideas in the mind, Locke's speculative neuro-pathology contends that the mad are similarly blind to whether or not those ideas are produced by rational means or by the flux of misbehaving matter.

The Enlightened and Dark Parts

It is implied early on in the *Essay* that there is a great deal at stake in circumventing physiology. If the purpose of the Locke's work is, as he puts it, "to enquire into the Original, Certainty, and Extent of humane Knowledge,"[9] then this project only gets off the ground once the weighty conjectures of materialist philosophy of mind have been jettisoned from the *Essay's* pages. Locke writes:

> I shall not at present meddle with the Physical Consideration of the Mind; or trouble my self to examine, wherein its Essence consists, or by what Motions of our Spirits, or Alterations of our Bodies, we come to any Sensation by our Organs, or any *Ideas* in our Understandings; and whether those *Ideas* do in their Formation, any, or all of them, depend upon Matter, or no. These are Speculations, which, however curious and entertaining, I shall decline, as lying out of my Way, in the Design I am now upon.[10]

With questions concerning the corporeality of the mind put aside, the *Essay* can attend to its real subject: not the human brain seen as a piece of dead matter that somehow produces ideas and sensations, but rather the mind understood as an active and alive entity, one that grapples with objects in the world as well as ideas in the psyche. The above passage continues:

> It shall suffice to my present Purpose, to consider the discerning Faculties of a Man, as they are employ'd about the Objects, which they have to do with: and I shall imagine I have not wholly misimploy'd my self in the Thoughts I shall have on this Occasion, if, in this Historical, plain Method, I can give any account of the Ways, whereby our Understandings come to attack those Notions of Things we have.[11]

To the modern reader, weaned on a heady blend of materialist philosophy and cognitive neuroscience, the above passages might seem to enact a curious reversal. For one thing, the physical mind appears oddly insubstantial in the first quotation. Under Locke's cautious gaze, the corporeal mind in its messy, vibrant reality—the brain as organ or body cut through with animal spirits and pulsing with strange atomic motions—dissolves into the stuff of uncertain rumor and speculation. In its place, the seemingly more abstract model of the understanding as it is "employ'd" with various mental objects—Locke calls this sort of employment "consciousness" elsewhere in the *Essay*[12]—becomes a fitter object of study. Locke explains that it is only thanks to observing this non-physiological model of mind that he finally can "set down any Measures of the Certainty of our Knowledge," a task that relegates speculations on neurophysiology to "curious and entertaining" but ultimately idle anatomy lessons.

That Locke consigns the "Physical Consideration of the Mind" to obscurity might surprise those critics who have read him as a kind of mistaken materialist.[13] Nevertheless, claims like this are of a piece with the larger aims of his work and more specifically of a piece with the "empirical" nature of his philosophy. As Locke explains in the above passage, the *Essay* is written according to the rules of the "Historical, plain Method." In the late seventeenth century, the phrase served as a term of art, one loosely adapted from the distinction between "natural philosophy" and "natural history."[14] "Natural philosophy" sought to build complete metaphysical systems that could account for a host of phenomena, while "natural history" took on the more modest task of observing and cataloguing a set of facts without speculating into their underlying nature. To borrow an example from Michael Ayers: Robert Boyle's sincere but unconfirmed conviction that the nature of reality could be explained by the motion and texture of invisible atoms or "corpuscles" is an example of "natural philosophy," while Boyle's insight into the inverse relationship of pressure and volume in a gas (i.e., "Boyle's Law") operates as a "natural history," since this law merely records an observable fact rather than speculating upon its underlying cause.[15]

For Locke's *Essay* to read as a "history," then, it too must confine itself to observing and cataloguing the available facts of consciousness. This means attending solely to the ideas that populate the conscious mind rather than guessing at their more fundamental material nature. As Locke puts it:

> [M]y present purpose being only to enquire into the Knowledge the Mind has of Things, by those *Ideas*, and Appearances, which *God* has fitted it to receive from them, and how the Mind comes by that Knowledge; rather than into their Causes, or manner of Production, I shall not, contrary to the Design of this Essay, set my self to enquire philosophically into the peculiar Constitution of Bodies, and the Configuration of Parts, whereby they have power to produce in us the *Ideas* of their sensible Qualities.[16]

In other words, the precise nature of the mind's ideas, their physical constitution, and the disposition of the organs that receive and retain them—all of these things lie outside the more limited purview of Locke's "history." They form a dark background to the starker images that draw the *Essay*'s attention: ideas as they are immediately present and perceptible to the conscious mind.[17]

We should be careful, though, when stressing the limits of Locke's project since doing so can give the sense that the *Essay* is a more modest, more cautiously superficial undertaking than it really is. In fact, the *Essay*'s self-imposed constraints in one area usually unloose possibilities in another. If Locke cuts off ideas at their roots, leaving accounts of their material and physical causes to wither away in dark conjectures, he does so in the hope of seeing them bloom all the more brightly in the mind. This curious strategy—transforming moments of apparent limitation or obscurity into secret strengths and more abundant sources of clarity—occurs throughout the *Essay*, but it is especially evident in a markedly figurative passage in its first chapter. Building on earlier admonitions against neurophysiology, this passage strengthens the case for abandoning epistemologically unsteady ground. Moreover, this passage conveys this point by drawing on images of light and darkness in order to cast an epistemological warning in a dramatic chiaroscuro. Locke writes:

> For I thought that the first Step toward satisfying several Enquiries, the Mind of Man was very apt to run into, was, to take a Survey of our own Understandings, examine our own Powers, and see to what Things they were adapted. Till that was done I suspected we began at the wrong end, and in vain sought for Satisfaction in a quiet and secure Possession of Truths, that most concern'd us, whilst we let loose our Thoughts into the vast Ocean of *Being*, as if all that boundless Extent, were the natural, and undoubted Possession of our Understandings, wherein there was nothing exempt from its Decisions, or that escaped its Comprehension. . . . Whereas were the Capacities of our Understanding well considered, the Extent of our Knowledge once discovered, and the Horizon found, which sets the Bounds between the enlightned and dark Parts of Things; between what is, and what is not comprehensible by us, Men would perhaps with less scruple acquiesce in the avow'd Ignorance of the one, and imploy their Thoughts and Discourse, with more Advantage and Satisfaction in the other.[18]

Although this quotation does not mention the rejection of "Physical Consideration[s] of Mind" that worried Locke earlier in the *Essay*, it nevertheless repeats a similar lesson: one must hew away areas of ambiguity and uncertainty in order to clear a more stable and certain place for human understanding. More striking still, though, is the manner in which this passage imparts that message. For a moment, Locke ornaments his "historical, plain Method" with a series of images that turn mind and world into topographically (and tropologically) distinct zones—spaces marked by their relative degrees of light and darkness. Thanks to these figures, the mind appears in the *Essay* as an illuminated, surveyed space, a site where our knowledge of things can be certain and evident (at least in principle). Beyond the confines of the psyche, however, stretches a vast, illimitable, and obscure waste, a realm where we at best reside in stupefied skepticism and at worst suffer in frustrated ignorance. In fact, a single phrase in the above passage—Locke's plea that we must set "the Bounds between the enlightned and dark Parts of Things; between what is, and what is not comprehensible by us"—makes epistemology into a matter of sight. According to the logic of this phrase and its figure, what we can see, we can know, but what we cannot perceive, we cannot understand.[19] The purpose of such images, of course, is to direct our attention toward the "enlightned . . . Parts of Things" (like the conscious mind), which we can perceive and know with certainty, and away from the "dark Parts" (like metaphysical considerations of the nature of reality or "being"), which only lead to darkness and doubt. In doing so, such figures illustrate what Cathy Caruth has called Locke's "philosophical humility topos:" a moment when the apparent "limitation of reason, really tells of a new and unbounded power over its own territory."[20]

At least in principle, then, the internal mental territory that the *Essay* explores can be perceived and therefore mapped in its entirety. For Locke, the conscious mind has no unconscious, no dark corner or obscure vestibule where an idea or thought might lurk unseen and disregarded. Locke's epistemology closes the gap between having an idea somewhere within the mind (for example, carried to the understanding by the senses) and being able consciously to perceive that idea: "For if these Words (*to be in the Understanding*) have any Propriety, they signify to be understood. So that, to be in the Understanding, and, not to be understood; to be in the Mind, and, never to be perceived, is all one, as to say, any thing is, and is not, in the Mind or Understanding."[21] Locke is well aware, of course, that we do not have an immediate and intuitive perception of all the thoughts and images that populate the understanding—that particular ability belongs perhaps only to angels or some higher beings.[22] Nevertheless, the *Essay* promises its readers that, should they take the time to survey properly their internal worlds, then nothing will be hidden from view. This process of self-discovery is frequently portrayed as a kind of labored or purposeful in-sight. "The Understanding, like the Eye, whilst it makes us see, and perceive all other things, takes no notice of it self: it takes Art and Pains to set it at a distance."[23] Hence, gaining knowledge of our own mind is a twofold process. First, we must force our inner eye to focus on the thoughts within the psyche; second, we must set to work on perceiving and thereby understanding this newly revealed internal mental territory.

I want to suggest that Locke's refusal to countenance physiology and neuroanatomy—his insistence that conjectures into the constitution of bodies and ideas must be cordoned off from the natural history of the *Essay*—is of a piece with this quest to gain certain knowledge of the mind by banishing uncertainty from its confines. We can better survey human knowledge, Locke argues, by first marking off its boundaries. Once we have cleared away obscure places of confusion, we then can set to work exploring this new territory. The same logic applies to consciousness itself: we can better illuminate the conscious mind by keeping the roots of consciousness out of sight. Hence, "the peculiar Constitution of Bodies, and the Configuration of Parts" that are the "Causes, or manner of Production" of the ideas that flicker before the inner eye must themselves remain obscure and unknowable. No amount of work will bring certain facts of consciousness (for example, how matter produces thought) to light. The implication here is that physiology and neuroanatomy belong, along with other equally speculative topics, to that great sea of metaphysical doubt that licks the shores of enlightened certainty.

The Body and the Abyss

One reason Locke refuses to "meddle with the Physical Consideration of the Mind," then, has to do with the *Essay*'s strategy for identifying and thereby cordoning off intractable questions about the ways in which matter relates to mind. But this strategy raises a series of questions in turn: why did Locke insist that such questions are unanswerable in the first place? Why does the *Essay* contend that neurology, rather than aiding the "history" of the understanding, would only obscure such efforts? Why must Locke put matter out of mind before he can concentrate on the thoughts within the mind? Furthermore, why does Locke insist that the body and brain's effect on the mind stands in an epistemological blind spot? In order to answer these questions, I want to consider some facts about Locke's medical education before turning to a fuller consideration of the *Essay*'s rejection of neurology.

Locke's attitude toward neurology is hardly borne out of an ignorance of contemporary physiology or brain anatomy. As historians like Kenneth Dewhurst and Patrick Romanell have shown, Locke's early medical training at Oxford exposed him to a number of advancements in science and medicine.[24] During his time at Oxford, Locke met and corresponded with experimentalists like Robert Boyle, Robert Hooke, and Richard Lower; he performed anatomical experiments of his own in order to better understand the mechanics of respiration; he wrote a treatise on the same topic and another on the nature of disease and contagion; and—perhaps most important for our purposes—he attended a series of lectures by the physician and neurophysiologist Thomas Willis.[25] I'll have more to say about Willis and his lectures—and their possible influence on Locke's thinking—below, but for now it's worth noting that these lectures drew on Willis's recently published work *Cerebral Anatomy*, the text that coined the term "neurology" and perhaps the fullest account of brain anatomy available at the time. In Willis's lectures, Locke heard a number of theories about the manner in which the seemingly obscure matter of the brain produced the more readily apparent occurrences in conscious life.[26]

Nevertheless, by the time Locke left Oxford in 1667, his capacious medical pursuits had changed direction considerably. Locke rejected his earlier experiments in anatomy along with his speculations into the nature of respiration and disease. In their place, he adopted a stance of epistemological modesty that would survive into his more mature work. The impetus for this turn is usually traced to the influence of one man: Dr. Thomas Sydenham.[27] An important physician in his own right, Sydenham's energy seemingly focused on two pursuits: composing detailed case histories of his patients' maladies and writing treatises decrying anatomy and natural philosophy. Sydenham doubted that physicians could ever understand the precise nature and causes of the diseases they encountered. The best they could do was observe the disease carefully, register its effects on a patient, and record successful treatments if any could be found. Nature and the frailty of our human faculties kept everything else hidden from view. Sydenham writes:

> It is in accordance with immutable laws, and by a scheme known to herself only, that Parent Nature accomplishes the generation of all things; and though many thing she may bring forward from the abyss of cause into the open daylight of effect, it is in deepest darkness that she veils their essences, their constituent differentiae, their inherent natures; and hence it is, that each species of malady, even as each species of animal and each species of vegetable, hath taken as its portion its own state: proper, permanent, unequivocal, derivative from its essence.[28]

Sydenham's argument anticipates Locke's later warnings about the futility of prying into the hidden essence of matter. Moreover, Sydenham's striking claim

that "Parent Nature" "veils" the workings of bodies and matter in "deepest darkness"—only sometimes allowing an errant appearance to slip into "the open daylight of effect"—prefigures Locke's troping on the epistemology of darkness and
light, blindness and insight. These borrowings are unsurprising since Locke clearly
admired the older physician, even going so far as to name him in the *Essay*, along
with Boyle, Newton, and Huygens, as one of the four "Master-Builders, whose
mighty Designs, in advancing the Sciences, will leave lasting Monuments to the
Admiration of Posterity."[29]

Sydenham's influence on Locke's thought is perhaps most evident in a
short piece entitled *Anatomia*. Composed in 1668, the argument of *Anatomia* is
a halfway point between Sydenham's earlier admonitions against peering beneath
Parent Nature's veil and Locke's later writings on epistemology and empiricism in
the *Essay*.[30] The goal of this early essay is to demonstrate that anatomy is not likely
"to afford any great improvement to the practice of physic."[31] Anatomy, according
to Locke, lacks practical benefits: understanding more about the body's organs or
the nature of a disease is not useful in healing those organs or in eradicating that
disease. Locke explains that "[a]ll that Anatomie can doe is only to shew us the
gross and sensible parts of the body, or the vapid and dead juices all which, after
the most diligent search, will be noe more able to direct a physician how to cure a
disease than how to make a man."[32] This claim might strike the modern reader—
beneficiary of centuries of medical excursions into the recesses of the body—as
odd, but Locke insists that dissection will not reveal knowledge about how the
structures of the body actually work (or fail to work should a disease or malady
afflict them). The problem with anatomy is that we cannot perceive (and are hence
ignorant of) the mechanisms that make bodies work: "Now it is certaine and
beyond controversy that nature performs all her operations on the body by parts
so minute and insensible that I thinke noe body will ever hope to pretend, even
by the assistance of glasses or any other invention, to come to a sight of them."[33]

Even in this early piece, then, Locke frames his discussion of the body, and
our knowledge of it, in terms of darkness and light. Locke claims in *Anatomia* that
even though dissection can uncover heretofore hidden structures in the body, the
"operation" of these structures remains obscure, even on a well-lit operating table.
At best we can observe the "vapid and dead" body under the knife—but observing the dead body is no assurance that we will be able to comprehend its lively
mechanisms. In fact, we cannot discover the mechanisms of the body because the
real source of those mechanisms remains just out of sight. Even with the best technology or training—the sharpest knife, the keenest eyesight, or perhaps a newly

developed microscope—the stuff that anatomy reveals is only the "gross and sensible" body. The real source of the body's operations, however, are those "minute and insensible" structures that are by definition inaccessible (because invisible) to human faculties. These structures languish in Sydenham's "abyss of causes," never making their way into the "open daylight of effect" that is the proper provenance of human knowledge. With this in mind, *Anatomia* hopes to train the physician's gaze on precisely those bodily effects that are most readily observable, a project that will hopefully lead to more pragmatic and practical medical knowledge: "How [should the physician] regulate his dose, to mix his simples and to prescribe all in a due method? All this is only from history and the advantage of a diligent observation of these diseases, of their beginning, progress, and ways of cure."[34]

As its call for a pragmatic "history" of disease nicely illustrates, *Anatomia* is a rehearsal for the "Historical, plain Method" of the later *Essay concerning Human Understanding*. In fact, much of that later work appropriates and augments language from Locke's earlier medical writing. As in *Anatomia*, Locke insists in the *Essay* that, due to the weakness of human faculties, we are condemned to experience only the superficies of things. Lurking beneath exterior appearances is not some hidden depth of knowledge but yet another surface, one that mocks our best efforts to observe and to understand the real constitution of bodies. As Locke explains in the *Essay*: "[S]ince we having but some few superficial *Ideas* of things, discovered to us only by the Senses from without, or by the Mind, reflecting on what it experiment in it self within, [we] have no Knowledge beyond that, much less of the internal Constitution, and true Nature of things, being destitute of Faculties to attain it."[35] Moreover, like *Anatomia*, the *Essay* further contends that the real mechanisms by which bodies produce certain observable effects are simply too minute for proper observation. We cannot see or understand those "insensible Corpuscles, [that are] the active parts of Matter, and the great Instruments of Nature."[36] As Locke goes on to explain:

> Did we know the Mechanical affections of the Particles of *Rhubarb*, *Hemlock*, *Opium*, and a *Man*, as a Watchmaker does those of a Watch, whereby it performs its Operations, and of a File which by rubbing on them will alter the Figure of any of the Wheels, we should be able to tell before Hand, that *Rhubarb* will purge, *Hemlock* kill, and *Opium* make a Man sleep; as well as a Watch-maker can, that a little piece of Paper laid on the Balance, will keep the Watch from going, till it be removed . . . But whilst we are destitute of Senses acute enough, to discover the

minute Particles of Bodies, and to give us *Ideas* of their mechanical Affections, we must be content to be ignorant of their properties and ways of Operations; nor can we be assured about them any farther than some few Trials we make, are able to reach.[37]

The argument here extends the skeptically informed pragmatism of *Anatomia* to all knowledge (although it interestingly retains the medical examples that were the subject of Locke's earlier work). Once again, Locke's point is that the mechanisms by which cause leads to effect—why it is, for example, that one kind of thing heals while another hurts—remain hidden from view. Unlike watches or geometric figures, which can be anatomized in order to better understand their workings and constitutions, physical bodies hide their clockwork from even the deepest dissections. Hence, we can observe that hemlock kills and that rhubarb heals, but we will be forever disappointed in our efforts to explain precisely why these drugs—or for that matter bodies in general—behave in this manner.

Given our superficial knowledge about the workings of natural bodies, it is no wonder that Locke refuses to "meddle with a Physical Consideration of the Mind" in the *Essay*. If we cannot observe how the healing effects of rhubarb spring from "the abyss of causes," then we also cannot hope to perceive how the "Motions of our Spirits, or Alterations of our Bodies" produce "any *Ideas* in our Understandings."[38] To be sure, we can experience matter and mind interacting. Thought influences matter (Locke calls this "willing" or "volition") just as matter seems to affect thought.[39] Nevertheless, what remains hidden from us, what really stands outside the otherwise well-illuminated confines of the conscious mind isn't matter or body as such but the knowledge of how body affects mind. Locke writes:

> How any thought should produce a motion in Body is as remote from the nature of our *Ideas*, as how any Body should produce any Thought in the Mind. That it is so, if Experience did not convince us, the Consideration of the Things themselves would never be able, in the least, to discover to us.[40]

Hence, Locke's official view on the relationship between thought and matter is best described as a kind of agnosticism. We know that things think (as our own thinking amply illustrates), but we cannot be sure what the precise nature of a thinking things is. Likewise, we can observe matter affecting mind, but since our weak and limited faculties cannot pry into the substance of thinking things we must refrain from speculating into how it does so.

The Origins of Insanity

Now that we've gotten a sense why Locke refuses to speculate upon the physical mind, I next want to turn to a moment in the *Essay* where he does just that: specifically, in his writings on the association of ideas and madness. If much of the *Essay* implores its readers to ignore the workings of body and brain in order to focus on what we can see and know (the play of ideas in our conscious mind), then Locke's writings on madness tell a different story. Not only do these writings force the reader to recognize that conscious thought is embodied in flesh and nerves, they also compel one to face the epistemological blind spot that attends all attempts to think through the relation of body and mind. One thing that we certainly cannot see, according to Locke, is how brain and body creates the mind. Most of the *Essay* explains that we should disregard the "minute and insensible" mechanisms underlying material substance so as to draw our attention to the "enlightned . . . Parts of Things." But Locke's writings on madness place our ignorance of these mechanisms front and center. These writings reveal that perhaps behind our thoughts is a physical process—the creation of conscious ideas by fully material entities in the brain—that we cannot see and therefore understand.

At first glance, much of Locke's writing on the association of ideas puts emphasis on the *cultural* origins of madness rather than on bodily derangement. According to Locke, education, custom, and in particular early childhood trauma play a key role in mental derangement.[41] Nevertheless, Locke also explains that culture only partially explains the peculiar madness of association. There is another, deeper mechanism at work here:

> This sort of Unreasonable [i.e., madness] is usually imputed to Education and Prejudice, and for the most part truly enough, though that reaches not the bottom of the Disease, nor shews distinctly enough whence it rises, or wherein it lies. Education is often rightly assigned for the Cause, and Prejudice is a good general Name for the thing it self: But yet, I think, he ought to look a little farther who would trace this sort of Madness to the root it springs from, and so explain it, as to shew whence this flaw has its Original in very sober and rational Minds, and wherein it consists.[42]

Attributing "prejudice" to education and custom, then, cannot exhaust all the symptoms of madness. In particular, it cannot explain how otherwise reasonable minds become mad. In order to examine the root cause of this malady, Locke looks beyond kinds of thinking and considers instead the physiology of thought.

After introducing a distinction between "natural" and "unnatural" association—between those trains of ideas that have a "natural Correspondence and Connexion" and those that have been sundered together irrationally—Locke goes on to trace the latter to the animal spirits within the brain:

> This strong Combination of *Ideas*, not ally'd by Nature, the Mind makes in it self either voluntarily, or by chance, and hence it comes in different Men to be very different, according to their different Inclination, Educations, Interests, *etc.* Custom settles habits of Thinking in the Understanding, as well as of Determining in the Will, and of Motions in the Body; all which seems to be but Trains of Motion in the Animal Spirits, which once set a going continue in the same steps they have been used to, which often treading are worn into a smooth path, and Motion in it becomes easy and as it were Natural. As far as we can comprehend Thinking, thus *Ideas* seem to be produced in our Minds; or if they are not, this may serve to explain their following one another in an habitual train, when once they are put into that tract, as well as it does to explain such Motions of the Body.[43]

In other words, education and custom are at the origin of false association, but they are only the first link in a chain of causes that leads irrevocably to madness. On the other end of the chain is the body and more specifically the animal spirits within the corporeal mind. According to Locke, society or some chance trauma suggests a wrong association of ideas; habitual thinking reproduces and repeats this misassociation; the movement of animal spirits then inscribes this disorder directly onto the flesh. Thus, education, custom, and habit literally carve certain ways of thinking into the body. The animal spirits in turn ensure that superstition and whim become part of brain anatomy.

It's worth underlining just how curiously un-Lockean these passages are. For one thing, Locke abandons his medical pragmatism when he deals with madness and the association of ideas. We'll remember that Locke, following the example of Thomas Sydenham, abjures dark speculations into the hidden workings of the body in order to focus on a more empirical "natural history" of disease. Since we can never observe directly the "minute and insensible" bodies that produce disease, Locke and Sydenham recommend that physicians attend to the "superficial" effects of their patients' maladies and abandon the hunt for hidden and obscure causes. Yet, faced with the disease of madness, Locke himself gazes directly into what Sydenham called "the abyss of cause." Education and prejudice—the most readily observable sources of madness—"reach not bottom of the Disease, nor shew distinctly enough whence it rises." In order to understand false association, one must "trace this sort of Madness to the root it springs from," namely, to the body and brain.

This deviation from Locke's official stance on medical matters points to yet another divergence in his thought. In the *Essay*, Locke's medical pragmatism shades into a more general call for a cautious empiricism: just as we cannot observe how cause leads to effect in disease, we also cannot observe how matter in the body makes thoughts in the mind. Given our ignorance, Locke refuses to comment on precisely how matter influences our thinking. Nevertheless, in the case of madness, matter evidently outthinks faculties like will and reason. The smooth paths of the animal spirits—the result of random moments of confusion burnt into the brain—produce conscious thought. As Locke puts it plainly in the above passage: "As far as we can comprehend Thinking, thus *Ideas* seem to be produced in our Minds."

While these claims may sound less like the John Locke who was influenced by the epistemological modesty of Thomas Sydenham, they are nevertheless similar to a host of contemporary writings on madness and mental derangement. As Michael Ayers and John P. Wright have both stressed, Locke's writings on madness are indebted to Cartesian thinkers and in particular Nicolas Malebranche. Like the Cartesians, the Locke who wrote "Of the Association of Ideas" attributes madness to the body and brain. As Ayers notes, much of what Locke has to say about mental derangement in the *Essay* is "consonant with Cartesian physiological explanations of error (especially prominent in Malebranche's *Search after Truth*) which attribute irrationality and delusion to the influences of the corporeal imagination."[44]

While I agree that Malebranche was an important influence on Locke's thought, it's also worth noting that Locke would have heard similar remarks about madness—and in greater physiological detail—while attending Thomas Willis's lectures. Indeed, Willis's lectures, with their emphasis on the role of the diseased brain in the creation of mental pathologies, serve as a fitting parallel for Locke's own writings on the subjects. Furthermore, it is Willis who suggests the connection between blindness and madness that suffuses Locke's thoughts concerning madness. These lectures marked a turning point in Willis's career. Having just completed *Cerebral Anatomy*, his first major work, Willis was in the process of extending the insights of that work into questions of disease and mental pathology. The result was *Two Discourses concerning the Souls of Brutes*, a text that provided perhaps the most complete physiological account of mental derangement in the seventeenth century.

Willis argues in this later work that human beings possess two souls: a higher, immaterial soul and a lower, corporeal counterpart comprising nerves, animal spirits, chemical reactions, blood, and bodily organs. The corporeal soul, according to Willis, is responsible for the body's autonomic functions and for mental faculties like sensation, memory, and imagination. The incorporeal soul allows humans to engage in higher forms of reasoning (like mathematics and art), to discourse with one another, and to freely will their actions. Willis contends that the souls are "knitted" together in the corporeal imagination, an organ that serves as clearinghouse for the body's sense impressions.[45] From its vantage point within the imagination, the rational soul can view the physical world as if it were gazing through a window, and it can steer the body accordingly. As Willis puts it: "In Man indeed it is obvious to be understood, that the Rational Soul, as it were presiding, beholds the Images and Impressions represented by the Sensitive [Corporeal], as in a looking Glass, and according to the Conceptions and notions drawn from thence, exercise the Acts of Reason, Judgment, and Will."[46] Hence, in a healthy mind and body, the two souls work in unison. The corporeal soul feeds its immaterial counterpart sensible images; the immaterial soul in turn, perceives, deliberates, and acts upon the sensible information it receives from the body.

However, in a diseased brain—one made mad by fever, drunkenness, or melancholic reflection—the souls "differ among themselves" and "sometimes are wont to dissent and move more than Civil Wars."[47] Because the corporeal and rational souls are joined in the imagination, their battle mainly unfolds there. Willis explains:

> For if at any time the Imagination is so disturbed, or perverted, that it falsly conceives, or evilly composes or divides, the species and notions brought from the Sense or Memory; presently for that reason the intellect beholds or forms conceptions and thoughts only deformed, distracted one from another, and very confused: Which indeed are represented to it from the Brain evilly affected, and as it were monsters from a multiplying or distorted Glass.[48]

In other words, if the imagination normally serves as the incorporeal soul's window to the world, then the fancy of a diseased and rebellious body blinds this soul with images that rearrange sense experience into incongruous shapes. More troubling still, because the incorporeal soul—obscurely ensconced somewhere within the corporeal imagination—no longer receives reliable sensory information from the body, it takes the confused images of the deranged imagination for truth and acts madly as a result. As Willis notes, when the imagination "represents the images of sensible things distorted, double, or incoherent; [then] hence the mind and the will, choose or pick out nothing but ridiculous and impertinent conceptions and passions; and cause the actions of the body to become almost irregular."[49]

We can recognize in Willis's vision of the corporeal soul in revolt the outlines of Locke's own thoughts on madness. Willis, like Locke, also describes mental derangement as a twofold process. First, in a diseased brain, ideas that ought to remain separate and distinct become unmoored and soon mix. For example, in "phrensie," a variety of madness marked by high fever,

> the Animal Spirits beings at first very much irritated in the whole Brain, are driven into inordinate, very confused, and also impetuous motions . . . and at the same time, very many Ideas of things being raised up out of the memory, the old are confounded with the new, and some evilly joined, or wonderfully divided, are confounded with others, the imagination suggests manifold *Phantasms*, and almost innumerable, and all of them incongruous.[50]

Second, since the rational soul still relies on the corporeal imagination for its view of the world, it is blind to the fact that it receives false information. The incorporeal soul acts on this false information, thereby perverting the intellect and will:

> [W]hilst the various images of the imagination and memory being excited at once, are confounded together, they object only incongruous and absurd *phantasies* of the rational Soul, and so both the acts of the intellect and the will, are only inordinately chosen or drawn forth.[51]

Madness and Insight

Locke's theory of mental derangement always had one thing in common with Willis and other seventeenth-century physiologists: a fear that madness would confuse and blind an otherwise rational mind. Where Locke differed from his teacher and fellow physicians—at least until the fourth edition of the *Essay* appeared—was in his uncertainty about whether or not the mutable matter of the body and brain could be the source of this disease. For example, in a passage that appeared in the second edition of the *Essay* (and survived into later versions of that work), Locke hedges on the precise cause of madness. He notes that the mad "do not appear

. . . to have lost the Faculty of Reasoning: but having joined together some *Ideas* very wrongly, they mistake them for Truths; and they err as Men do, that argue right from wrong Principles."[52] "Reasoning," in Locke's technical use of the term, is the process of tracing out the connections (or the agreement and disagreement) of the mind's idea. In madness, then, the work of reason continues unabated, though it now works with faulty materials. Because ideas have been "wrongly" joined in the mind, reason is forced to follow false connections.

What remains unclear in this passage, though, is precisely why the mind's ideas are wrongly joined in the first place. Willis, as we saw, accounts for this sort of mental confusion by positing a war between mind and body: the corporeal soul blinds its incorporeal counterpart by confusing or falsely joining ideas that ought to have remained separated, an act which leaves the immaterial soul to pick out "nothing but ridiculous and impertinent conceptions and passions." Locke's reflection on madness in the early versions of the *Essay* similarly portrays the mind as riven by an internal war. But in abandoning speculations into the interaction of mind and body in this instance, Locke stages a war without combatants. He attributes both reason and the unreasonable misassociation of ideas to mad men. But how is that mad men themselves join ideas wrongly when their reason (the faculty charged with properly observing the agreement and disagreement of the mind's ideas) continues its work as usual? Why is an otherwise intact reason insensible to the fact that it is being duped?

It's only in the fourth edition of the *Essay* that we receive an answer to these questions. It's in that edition of the *Essay* that the body emerges as the source of this curious blindness. Consider "Of Enthusiasm," a chapter Locke added to this later edition of the *Essay*. Locke maintains that, far from being guided by the hand of God, enthusiasts are in fact led astray by "the ungrounded Fancies of a Man's own Brain."[53] He writes:

> Enthusiasm, which though founded neither on Reason, nor Divine Revelation, but rising from the Conceits of a warmed or over-weening Brain, works yet, where it once gets footing, more powerfully on the Perswasions and Actions of Men, than either of those two, or both together: Men being most forwardly obedient to the impulses they receive from themselves; And the whole Man is sure to act more vigorously, where the whole Man is carried by a natural Motion. For strong conceit like a new Principle carries all easily with it, when got above common Sense, and freed from all restraint of Reason, and check of Reflection, it is heightened into a Divine Authority, in concurrence with our own Temper and Inclination.[54]

Here body and brain serve as mechanisms that circumvent the work of reason. Enthusiasm makes the mind "obedient" to the "impulses" of the body. Indeed, the body's impulses—its "Natural motion"—carries the mind away from reason and reflection, thereby forcing the understanding to heed otherwise senseless matter as if it were divine authority. Thanks to the brain's repression of reason and truth, the false thoughts that flood the mind are not examined or corrected; they are simply obeyed: "whatsoever odd Action [enthusiasts] find in themselves a strong Inclination to do, that impulse is concluded to be a call or direction from Heaven, and must be obeyed; 'tis a Commission from above, and they cannot err in executing it."[55]

We saw a similar dynamic at work in the chapter on the association of ideas. In this case, the random flux of matter, rather than rational thinking, determines the connection of the mind's thoughts. Thanks to the repetition of custom and habit, the animal spirits carve confusion directly into the brain as they create smooth paths in the corporeal mind. In a striking claim—one that overturns much of the *Essay*'s careful strictures against speculating upon the impact of matter on mind—Locke contends that these paths give rise to misassociated ideas in the conscious mind. Thus, the minds of mad men, blind to the source of their own ideas, "are filled with false Views, and their Reasonings with false Consequences."[56] Indeed, when made mad, the brain's ideas have a mind of their own: "When this Combination [i.e., false association] is settled and whilst it lasts, it is not in the power of Reason to help us, and relive us from the Effects of it. *Ideas* in our Minds, when they are there, will operate according to their Natures and Circumstances."[57] By bringing to light the physiological underpinnings of madness in this chapter of the *Essay*, then, Locke also makes it clear that the brain itself "hinders Men from seeing and examining" their errors and misconceptions. After all, the trick of madness is that we can never tell if the ideas in our mind are the result of conscious, controlled, and rational deliberation or the consequence of errant animal spirits. In the case of the mad, Locke writes, it is the body and brain "that blinds [the mad's] Understandings, and makes them not see the falshoods of what they embrace for real Truth . . . [and that] leads Men of Sincerity blindfold from common Sence."[58]

Conclusion

I began this essay by asking why Locke, in bald contradiction to the stated aims of the *Essay*, turned to neurophysiology in order to account for madness. We can now recognize that, in one respect at least, Locke's writings on the physiology of madness and his writings *against* physiology share a common theme. Locke the cautious empiricist explains that, while we can observe matter affecting mind, we cannot know precisely how it does so. We are blind to the mechanisms by which the nerves, flesh, and animal spirits of the brain give rise to conscious thought. Locke the speculative neurologist ignores these strictures in order to present an account of mental pathology that relies on the animal spirits creating confusion in the mind. And yet, in the course of doing so, he makes a claim about our ignorance of the interactions of body and mind that parallel the more cautious passages of the *Essay*. The mad, Locke the neurologist explains, are blind to the confusing effects of matter on the mind.

Hence, what appears at first as a major inconsistency in Locke's *Essay* is, upon second glance, simply the same point made from different perspectives. Locke's normative epistemology asks us to ignore the body that subtends our thoughts so as to focus instead on the ideas in our conscious mind. Because we cannot perceive the mechanisms by which matter creates thought, we should instead overlook this blind spot and train our inner eye on only the conscious thoughts themselves. But Locke's writings on madness, because they trace this malady to body and brain, force us to see this blind spot. For Locke, the recognition of madness (in others if never in ourselves) challenges us to acknowledge an alarming point: namely, that our body and brain can determine our thought—even though we can never know precisely when it does so.

Notes

1. John Locke, *An Essay concerning Human Understanding*, 4th ed., ed. P.H. Nidditch (Oxford: Oxford University Press, 1975), 2.33.5.

2. Locke, *Essay* 2.33.18.

3. Locke, *Essay* 2.33.6.

4. Locke, *Essay* 4.19.7.

5. Locke, *Essay* 1.1.2.

6. See Locke, *Essay* 2.1.15: "*Perhaps it will be said*, that in a waking Man, the materials of the Body are employ'd, and made use of, in thinking; and that memory of Thoughts is retained by the impressions that are made on the Brain" (my emphasis); Locke, *Essay* 2.8.4: "*If* it were the design of my present Undertaking, to enquire into the natural Causes and manner of Perception, I *should* offer this as a reason *why a privative cause might . . . produce a positive idea, viz.* That all Sensation being produced in us, only by different degrees and motion in our animal Spirits" (my emphasis); Locke, *Essay* 2.10.5: "How much the constitution of our Bodies, and the make of our animal Spirits, are concerned in [memory loss] . . . I shall not here enquire, though it may seem probable, that the Constitution of the Body does sometimes influence the Memory." After speculating upon the ways in which external bodies cause perceptions in the mind—a discussion that draws on the

physiology of perception and sensation—Locke apologizes to his reader for this "little Excursion into Natural Philosophy" (Locke, *Essay* 2.8.22). In Locke, *Essay* 3.4.10 and 3.9.16, he points to Cartesian theories of perception and debates about the fluid within nerves, respectively, as examples of linguistic abuse.

7. See especially Jonathan Walmsley, "Sydenham and the Development of Locke's Natural Philosophy," *British Journal for the History of Philosophy* 16, no.1 (2008): 65–83; Charles T. Wolfe, "Empiricist Heresies in Early Modern Thought" in *The Body As Object and Instrument of Knowledge: Embodied Empiricism in Early Modern Science*, eds. Charles T.Wolfe and Ofer Gal, (Dordrecht: Springer, 2010), 333–344; and Stephen Gaukroger, "The Role of Natural Philosophy in the Development of Locke's Empiricism," *British Journal for the History of Philosophy* 17, no.1 (2009): 55–83.

8. This question has received little critical attention. John P. Wright and Michael Ayers are two of the few scholars who have remarked upon this inconsistency (much less offered an explanation). Both Wright and Ayers stress the influence of Malebranche on Locke's theories of madness. As they note, Malebranche, like Locke in the fourth edition of the *Essay*, traces madness to the corporeal mind. While I draw on both Ayers's and Wright's work for this essay (see Section IV below), I nevertheless take a different approach to this question by providing a fuller account of this inconsistency on the *Essay*'s own terms. See Michael Ayers, *Locke: Epistemology and Ontology* (London: Routledge, 1993), 112, and John P. Wright, "Association, Madness, and the Measures of Probability in Locke and Hume," in *Psychology and Literature in the Eighteenth Century*, ed. Christopher Fox (New York: AMS Press, 1987), 113.

9. Locke, *Essay* 1.1.2.

10. Locke, *Essay* 1.1.2. In this passage, Locke refuses to countenance what we would refer today as the "hard problem" of consciousness. The "hard problem" asks how consciousness (the feeling of "what it is like" to have certain thoughts or feel certain emotions) arises from seemingly unconscious stuff like matter. For a fuller explanation of the problem see David Chalmers, *The Conscious Mind: In Search of a Fundamental Theory* (New York: Oxford University Press, 1996); for an account of how the "hard problem" plays out in eighteenth-century literature and thought more generally—and in Locke's philosophy more particularly—see Jonathan Kramnick, *Actions and Objects from Hobbes to Richardson* (Stanford: Stanford University Press, 2010), esp. 64–71.

11. Locke, *Essay* 1.1.2.

12. Locke defines "consciousness" in the *Essay* as "the perception of what passes in a Man's own mind," Locke, *Essay* 2.1.19.

13. I am thinking in particular of Richard Rorty's writings on Locke—though as Rorty notes his reading of Locke stretches back to the *Essay*'s earliest interpreters (Thomas Reid in the eighteenth century; T.H. Green in the nineteenth). Reid, Green, and Rorty argue that the key metaphor of mind in Locke's work is the *tabula rasa*, and that this metaphor allows Locke to waver between describing the mind with epistemological terms (as something filled with conscious ideas) and with physiological terms (as a substance or surface—a blank slate—that receives physical impressions from the senses). See Richard Rorty, *Philosophy and the Mirror of Nature*. (Princeton: Princeton University Press, 2009), 139–148.

14. For a fuller account of these terms see Katharine Park and Lorraine Daston, "Introduction" in *Early Modern Science*, eds. Katherine Park and Lorraine Daston, (Cambridge: Cambridge

University Press, 2006), 4. The distinction between "natural history" and "natural philosophy" became more familiar in the eighteenth century as "experimental philosophy" and "speculative philosophy," respectively. On this later terminology see Peter R. Anstey, "The Experimental History of the Understanding from Locke to Sterne," in *Eighteenth-Century Thought*, vol. 4, (New York: AMS Press, 2009), 143–69. Because Locke uses "natural history" and "natural philosophy" within the *Essay*—e.g., the *Essay* itself follows the "Historical, plain Method"; a digression on the physiology of perception is a "little Excursion into Natural Philosophy" (Locke, *Essay* 2.8.22)—I have maintained these terms.

15. Ayers, *Locke*, 17–18.

16. Locke, *Essay* 2.21.73.

17. In other words, Locke refuses to say whether or not ideas have some physical presence in the mind; they may not be "corporeal ideas"—a view that caused some controversy for the first readers of the *Essay*. See Emily Michael and Fred S. Michael, "Corporeal Ideas in Seventeenth-Century Psychology," *Journal of the History of Ideas* 50, no.1 (1989): 31–48.

18. Locke, *Essay* 2.21.73.

19. For an even more explicit connection between knowledge and sight in Locke's writings, see the companion piece to the *Essay*, *Of the Conduct of the Understanding*, where Locke states plainly: "Knowing is seeing" (Section 24).

20. Cathy Caruth, *Empirical Truths and Critical Fictions: Locke, Wordsworth, Kant, Freud* (Baltimore: Johns Hopkins University Press, 1991), 5.

21. Locke, *Essay* 1.2.5: 50–51.

22. Locke, *Essay* 4.3.6: 543.

23. Locke, *Essay* 1.1.1: 43.

24. For Locke's medical background see Kenneth Dewhurst, *John Locke, 1632–1704, Physician and Philosopher: A Medical Biography with an Edition of the Medical Notes in His Journals* (London: Wellcome Historical Medical Library, 1963) and Patrick Romanell, *John Locke and Medicine: A New Key to Locke* (Buffalo, N.Y: Prometheus Books, 1984).

25. On Willis's anatomical experiments see Carl Zimmer, *Soul Made Flesh: The Discovery of the Brain and How It Changed the World* (New York: Free Press, 2004) and Robert G. Frank, "Thomas Willis and His Circle: Brain and Medicine in Seventeenth-Century Medicine" in *The Languages of Psyche: Mind and Body in Enlightenment Thought: Clark Library Lectures, 1985-1986*, ed. Rousseau (Berkeley: University of California Press, 1990), 107–46.

26. Thomas Willis, Kenneth Dewhurst, John Locke, and Richard Lower, *Thomas Willis's Oxford Lectures* (Oxford: Sandford Publications, 1980).

27. This is a common story in accounts of Locke's medical education see David E. Wolfe, "Sydenham and Locke on the Limits of Anatomy," *Bulletin of the History of Medicine*, 35, no. 3 (1961):193–220; Jonathan Walmsley, "Sydenham and the Development of Locke's Natural Philosophy"; Kenneth Dewhurst, *John Locke Physician and Philosopher: A Medical Biography*; Patrick Romanell, *John Locke and Medicine* (Buffalo: Prometheus, 1984).

28. Thomas Sydenham, *Methodus curandi febres*, 177; qtd. in Walmsley, "Sydenham and the Development of Locke's Natural Philosophy," 18–19.

29. Locke, *Essay* Epistle, 9.

30. This piece appears in Kenneth Dewhurst's edition of Thomas Sydenham's writings, though Locke was established recently as the sole author. See G. G. Meynell, "Locke as the Author of *Anatomia* and *De Arte Medica*," *The Locke Newsletter* 25 (1994): 65–73.

31. Kenneth Dewhurst, *Dr. Thomas Sydenham, 1624-1689: His Life and Original Writings* (Berkeley: University of California Press, 1966), 85.

32. Dewhurst, *Dr. Thomas Sydenham,* 85.

33. Dewhurst, *Dr. Thomas Sydenham,* 86.

34. Dewhurst, *Dr. Thomas Sydenham,* 86.

35. Locke, *Essay* 2.23.31.

36. Locke, *Essay* 4.3.25.

37. Locke, *Essay* 4.3.25.

38. Locke, *Essay* 1.1.2.

39. See Locke, *Essay* 4.3.28–29.

40. Locke, *Essay* 4.3.28.

41. For example, Locke explains that if a child eats too much honey and is made nauseous as a result, he or she will forever associate sweetness and sickness; likewise, if a nurse scares a child with stories of goblins in the night, the child will falsely associate darkness and danger. See Locke, *Essay* 2.33.7 and 2.33.20, respectively.

42. Locke, *Essay* 2.33.3.

43. Locke, *Essay* 2.33.6.

44. Ayers, *Locke*, 47.

45. Thomas Willis, *Two Discourses Concerning the Soul of Brutes: Which Is That of the Vital and Sensitive of Man*, tr. Samuel Pordage, (Gainesville, Fla: Scholars' Facsimiles & Reprints, 1971), 38.

46. Willis, *Two Discourses*, 32.

47. Willis, *Two Discourses*, 38.

48. Willis, *Two Discourses*, 179.

49. Willis, *Two Discourses*, 182.

50. Willis, *Two Discourses*, 182.

51. Willis, *Two Discourses*, 179.

52. Locke, *Essay* 2.11.13.

53. Locke, *Essay* 4.19.3.

54. Locke, *Essay* 4.19.7.

55. Locke, *Essay* 4.19.6.

56. Locke, *Essay* 2.33.18.

57. Locke, *Essay* 2.33.13.

58. Locke, *Essay* 2.33.18.

3

DEFECTIONS FROM NATURE

The Rhetoric of Deformity in
Shaftesbury's *Characteristics*

Paul Kelleher

THIS ESSAY PRESENTS the first part of a larger investigation into the presence and pervasiveness of the rhetoric of deformity in the corpus of British moral philosophy.[1] I have written these pages with two, often overlapping, audiences in mind: scholars working in the field of eighteenth-century studies and those working in disability studies. The existing connections between these two constituencies owe much, of course, to the pioneering work of scholars such as Lennard Davis, Felicity Nussbaum, and Helen Deutsch and the more recent contributions of David M. Turner, Simon Dickie, and D. Christopher Gabbard, among others.[2] However, as others have noted, the historical purview of disability studies at-large still remains largely focused on the nineteenth through twenty-first centuries, and its intellectual repertoire draws heavily on the conceptual language and political strategies of twentieth-century theory and contemporary activism. There are good reasons for this, of course—historical, political, intellectual, and (not least) personal reasons that catalyzed the formation of disability studies as a field of inquiry and continue to define its critical itinerary. To be sure, my own work draws inspiration from these various contexts and motivations; at the same time, though, my aim is to expand the archive and diversify the strategies of disability studies by demonstrating how British moral philosophy of the eighteenth century embodies a vital element in the genealogy of Western notions of disability.

Disability studies have paid relatively little attention to the history of philosophy, whereas science and medicine, literature and popular culture, have proven rich sites for understanding and critiquing how disabled minds and bodies have been made the objects of (mis)representation, pathologization, correction, and exclusion.[3] But the history of philosophy, without a doubt, has had an enormous impact on how disability has been conceptualized and experienced in modern Western culture. Consider, for instance, the intellectual ambitions and objectives of the branch of philosophy that is my concern here. Broadly speaking, moral philosophy addresses the fundamental question of what constitutes the good life: what is a life well lived, it asks, and how is such a life conducted in a world shared by others (both human and non-human) and sustained in a world comprised of materials and objects (both "natural" and "man-made")? Any answers to these questions—and indeed, the needs and desires that prompt such questions—necessarily implicate those who, at different times, have been regarded as monstrous, deformed, freakish, deviant, or disabled.

As even a cursory glance reveals, the pages of moral-philosophical treatises are replete with invocations—or more accurately, deprecations—of "deformity." The phrase "physical deformity" remains current in contemporary culture, but we have become much less familiar with what eighteenth-century British philosophers referred to as "moral deformity." Moral deformity was understood as a deviation from the good, virtuous, and true that could be variously manifested in our thoughts, passions, motives, or actions. And turning to the work of the so-called sentimental school of British moral philosophy (Shaftesbury, Hutcheson, Hume, and Smith, among others), we discover that their interest in grounding morality in the "natural" capacities of the body—the senses, the affections, the passions—leads them to posit a strong analogy between the moral and the corporeal. The relationship thus forged between morality and the body expresses itself in the language and according to the logic of aesthetic perception and evaluation. Thus, just as eighteenth-century critics would judge an artist's excellence or failure of execution according to the standards of the "beautiful" and the "deformed," a philosopher such as Shaftesbury self-consciously appropriates "beauty" and "deformity" as categories for judging a moral subject's affections and actions. Deformity, though, is not only in the eye of the philosophical beholder; in Shaftesbury's and other like-minded thinkers' estimation, every human creature is understood to be naturally predisposed to regard the world according to the criteria of the beautiful and the deformed. As I argue in this essay, the rhetoric of deformity not only pervades the discourse of eighteenth-century moral philosophy, but more importantly, it makes possible the articulation of moral systems as such. Anthony Ashley Cooper, the Third Earl of Shaftesbury's *Characteristics of Men, Manners, Opinions, Times* (1711) will serve as my primary example. Shaftesbury draws heavily on what appear to be, at first, quite conventional notions of the deformed; however, as he presses deformity into philosophical service in order to articulate his ideas regarding natural affection and virtue, his writing steadily reveals the power of deformity to problematize and reimagine the form and the substance of the "good life."

Sensing Deformity

Of the diverse texts collected in *Characteristics*, Shaftesbury's *An Inquiry Concerning Virtue or Merit* is unquestionably where he presents his ideas in the most systematic fashion. An apt epigraph from Horace ("Putting play aside, let us turn to serious things") prepares us for what is also the least ironic and playful, the least formally experimental text in *Characteristics*. Divided into two books, each of which is further divided into parts and sections, and rounded off with a conclusion, the very look of the *Inquiry* on the page intimates what Shaftesbury both performs and advocates in his philosophical argument: namely, a harmonious correlation between form and content, between the pleasing shape of a body, thought, or action and the moral beauty that inheres within such an orderly, well-proportioned shape. The first book of the *Inquiry* sets out to define the nature of "goodness" and "virtue" and determine to whom the terms "good" and "virtuous" may be applied. The second book considers what induces moral agents to embrace virtue and shun vice, and moreover, what rewards and what punishments are respectively allocated to the virtuous and the vicious.

Shaftesbury carefully arranges his arguments and signals how they progress and build on one another; and yet, in some sense, the *Inquiry* is less argument than assertion. In the opening pages of the first book, Shaftesbury gives away the ending, so to speak, of his "inquiry": one paragraph summarizes the bulk of the arguments to come and concludes with the brief pronouncement, "[a]nd thus virtue and interest may be found at last to agree."[4] By quickly reaching the end before we hardly have begun, we learn something about the design—in more than one sense—of Shaftesbury's moral system. The *Inquiry* presents a worldview in which beauty, truth, goodness, and virtue are indissociable from one another; each reflects the others in a philosophical hall of mirrors, and no one conceptual element can be shifted or removed without distorting the mutually ratifying correspondences that comprise this vision of the world. It is appropriate, then, that the agreement of virtue and interest should be announced so decisively near the beginning of the text. Throughout the *Inquiry*, we encounter appeals to self-evident truths, to circular, nearly tautological moral observations. For some readers, these tendencies bespeak Shaftesbury's lack of philosophical rigor, his naïve understanding of human nature, or his ideological elitism disguised as moral optimism (or a combination of all three).[5] Without delving further into these (often persuasive) critiques, I would suggest that what may appear to be Shaftesbury's philosophical weaknesses also can be understood as the performative discursive embodiment of his central belief that the universe is, as J. B. Schneewind phrases it, a "harmonious whole, a harmonious system of harmonious systems."[6]

Nevertheless, the relationship between part and whole, individual and humankind, must still be posed as a task for thought, even if unity and harmony inform Shaftesbury's text from beginning to end. As he observes, "When we reflect on any ordinary frame or constitution, either of art or nature, and consider how hard it is to give the least account of a particular part without a competent knowledge of the whole, we need not wonder to find ourselves at a loss in many things relating to the constitution and frame of nature herself."[7] The difficulty of comprehending "nature herself" would certainly pose a problem for an inquiry into the moral life of the individual, especially given Shaftesbury's assumption that the individual is "naturally" linked to and oriented toward this inviting, elusive, somewhat opaque—that is, ideologically feminized—nature. But even if the ultimate ends of nature remain unknown, Shaftesbury assures us that "study and observation" will demonstrate "with great exactness" "to what end the many proportions and various shapes of parts in many creatures actually serve."[8] The assumption of the unity and intelligibility of "nature herself" as necessary givens authorizes an inquiry into the individual, one that will implicitly circle back on itself and confirm the supposed dictates of nature. With nature firmly in place conceptually, Shaftesbury can then freely invoke the modalities of "natural" relations and processes. "We know that there is in reality a right and a wrong state of every creature," he observes, "and that his right one is by nature forwarded and by himself affectionately sought. There being therefore in every creature a certain interest or good, there must be also a certain end to which everything in his constitution must naturally refer."[9]

With the opening premises of the *Inquiry* established, Shaftesbury turns to a more detailed account of the inner workings of his moral system. As we will see, at several crucial moments early in his philosophical exposition, Shaftesbury conjures up images of monstrosity, illness, and deformity in order to bring into sharper relief what—at least according to the tenets of his own philosophy—should require little or no demonstration, given the immediate and irresistible bond that ostensibly obtains between nature and humankind. In the first moment I have in mind, the problem of defining the individual is addressed once again. The problem, though, poses no serious intellectual challenge, but rather allows the philosopher to indulge in a bit of fiction-making. Shaftesbury offers the following speculation: "Should a historian or traveller describe to us a certain creature of a more solitary disposition than ever was heard of—one who had neither mate nor fellow of any kind, nothing of his own likeness towards which he stood well-affected or inclined, nor anything without or beyond himself for which he had the least passion or concern—we might be apt to say perhaps, without much hesitation, that this was doubtless a very melancholy creature, and that in this unsociable and sullen state he was like to have a very disconsolate kind of life."[10] The two paths "without or beyond" the individual are a mate or a fellow, each of whom represents a kind of salutary limit to individuality, a breaching of the individual's self-enclosure through the pleasures of likeness, affection, and passion. A mate points the way toward the reproductive order of family, generations, and ultimately, the "race or species," while a fellow signals the ties of affection and sociability that, though not responsible for the literal reproduction of the species, maintain at least a minimum amount of peaceful association among individuals.[11] Bereft of those ties to others that make life worth living, that make life something more than mere biological existence, the remarkably solitary creature that Shaftesbury imagines must surely face a life of misery. But what if this creature in fact enjoyed life? "[I]f we were assured that, notwithstanding all appearances, the creature enjoyed himself extremely, had a great relish of life and was in nothing wanting to his own good, we might acknowledge, perhaps, that the creature was no monster nor absurdly constituted as to himself. But we should hardly, after all, be induced to say of him that he was a good creature."[12] Shaftesbury is willing to entertain the thought that this creature is—*perhaps*—not a monster. Yet the indulgent qualification "perhaps" leaves the monstrous potential of this creature in reserve—and for good reason. The truest monster is what Shaftesbury's moral system cannot fully recognize or flesh out, namely, a creature who finds no likeness of himself and still has the audacity to relish life and to flourish, or perhaps a creature who finds no likeness of himself and discovers a way to passionately relate to and be concerned about those who are *unlike* him.

The fiction of the solitary creature underscores the impossibility of radical individuality giving rise to a moral life, and thereby it opens the way to a discussion of what constitutes "goodness." Whether monster or no, Shaftesbury asserts that this creature cannot be good, for goodness arises from an individual's contributing toward the well-being of what the *Inquiry* frequently refers to as his "kind." Serving the best interests of one's kind, however, is not enough to guarantee a claim to goodness. Motive and intention are essential. Thus, a "good creature" is one whose "real motive" for an action is a "natural affection for his kind," and "*such a one as by the natural temper or bent of his affections is carried primarily and immediately, and not secondarily and accidentally, to good and against ill.*"[13] In order to make his point more concrete, Shaftesbury offers some striking examples: "We do not . . . say of anyone that he is an ill man because he has the plague spots upon him, or because he has convulsive fits which make him strike and wound such as approach him. Nor do we say, on the other side, that he is a good man when, having his hands tied up, he is hindered from doing the mischief he designs or (which is in a manner the same) when he abstains from executing his ill purpose through a fear of some impending punishment or through the allurement of some exterior reward."[14] Given the *Inquiry's* general tendency to read physical anomalies as figures for more metaphysical kinds of moral depravity, these plague-spotted and convulsive men stand out as exceptions to the general rule that governs this moral system. They further stand out by simply being human. This passage appears in the midst of a discussion pertaining to all "sensible creatures," in which Shaftesbury describes how one "kind" providentially serves another "kind." The fly's "heedless flight, weak frame and tender body" is in "perfect" relation to the spider's "rough make, watchfulness and cunning." Thus, the "web and wing are suited to each other," much as "in our own bodies, there is a relation of limbs and organs."[15] These appeals to the body—be they human or nonhuman—are at once rhetorically captivating and conceptually problematic. On the one hand, images of corporeal disability are recruited to distinguish between bodily appearances or gestures that are unintended and unwilled and what Shaftesbury considers to be the morally "ill." Corporeal difference, therefore, is not culpability. On the other hand, the ease with which Shaftesbury posits an analogy between the perfect fit of one animal to another, and the intricate connections among the limbs and organs of the human body, reminds us how often the *Inquiry* will collapse one kind of "illness" into another. Like the creature who only *perhaps* is not a monster, within Shaftesbury's moral system, the disabled body only *perhaps* is not a moral aberration.

The next moment I want to consider, in which an early mention of bodily difference marks an important turn in Shaftesbury's exposition, appears immediately after his discussion of creaturely goodness. Here we find the first invocation of "deformity" in the *Inquiry*. The subject of goodness, as we have seen, comprehends both human and nonhuman creatures; indeed, everything from vegetables and other "inferior" things to planets, suns, and galaxies find their place within the all-encompassing dominion of "universal nature."[16] In this moral universe, a crucial difference sets the human apart from other "sensible creatures," however "good" they may be: namely, a capacity for virtue. Given that goodness and virtue are closely allied in everyday thought and, outside of a more specialized philosophical discourse, might very well be seen as interchangeable, Shaftesbury pauses to outline how virtue is formed within the human subject and consequently how it distinguishes itself from mere goodness. The human, we are told, is the sole "creature capable of forming general notions of things."[17] Through the senses, external objects become "objects of the affection." But the power to form "general notions" means that another kind of perception also takes place within the human mind. As Shaftesbury describes it, the "very actions themselves and the affections of pity, kindness, gratitude and their contraries, [by] being brought into the mind by reflection, become objects. So that, by means of this reflected sense, there arises another kind of affection towards those very affections themselves, which have been already felt and have now become the subject of a new liking or dislike."[18] The notion of "reflected sense" offers us a glimpse of the first stirrings of rational thought, as it apprehends and assesses moral objects, thereby enabling the human creature to recognize virtue, and by recognizing virtue, ideally strive to become virtuous. Importantly, in keeping with the holistic ethos of Shaftesbury's thought, reason in the *Inquiry* remains very much in the realm of the senses and affections. Reason and understanding, in fact, are understood as modifications of sense, sense taken to a higher power, as Shaftesbury makes clear when he later observes how "man . . . from several degrees of reflection has risen to that capacity which we call reason and understanding."[19]

The rationalizing power of reflected sense is synonymous with what may be called the power of *moral objectification*. Actions and affections are apprehended as "objects"; these objects are then subjected to a reflexive process whereby affection-as-object becomes the object of a new affection. This new affection operates as a moral evaluation, as a "new liking or dislike" that is at once a feeling felt and a judgment delivered. Having woven this intricate conceptual web, Shaftesbury is ready to turn explicitly to a favorite subject in *Characteristics*—that is, aesthetic experience—and render a description of the "moral sense," the influential concept on which his fame rests to this day. The philosophical articulation of the moral sense, we find, is grounded in the rhetoric of deformity:

> The case is the same in the mental or moral subjects as in the ordinary bodies or common subjects of sense. The shapes, motions, colours and proportions of these latter being presented to our eye, there necessarily results a beauty or deformity, according to the different measure,

arrangement, and disposition of their several parts. So in behaviour and actions, when presented to our understanding, there must be found, of necessity, an apparent difference, according to the regularity or irregularity of the subjects.

The mind, which is spectator or auditor of other minds, cannot be without its eye and ear so as to discern proportion, distinguish sound and scan each sentiment or thought which comes before it. It can let nothing escape its censure. It feels the soft and harsh, the agreeable and disagreeable in the affections, and finds a foul and fair, a harmonious and a dissonant, as really and truly here as in any musical numbers or in the outward forms or representations of sensible things.[20]

According to Shaftesbury, the "common and natural sense of a sublime and beautiful in things," our "natural moral sense,"[21] distinguishes between right and wrong, just as surely and immediately as we sense the difference between a beautiful statue and an ugly statue, a pleasing musical score and a grating one. A similar passage in his philosophical dialogue, *The Moralists, a Philosophical Rhapsody*, describes the immediacy of "an inward eye distinguish[ing] and see[ing] the fair and shapely, the amiable and admirable, apart from the deformed, the foul, the odious or the despicable," whether this inward eye beholds a "figure" or an "action."[22] Immediacy, for Shaftesbury, implies necessity and inevitability—which, in turn, imply the workings of "nature herself." A rhetorical question is thus warranted: "How is it possible therefore not to own that as these distinctions have their foundation in nature, the discernment itself is natural and from nature alone?"[23]

Faced with the absolute distinction that divides beauty and deformity, we cannot help but recall the *Inquiry*'s earlier discussion of bodies marked by plague spots and wracked by convulsive fits. True, these passages that describe the moral sense do not explicitly mention a body touched by disease or otherwise perceived as visually anomalous. And as I noted earlier, Shaftesbury does concede that plague spots and convulsions, to the extent that they are unintentional bodily manifestations, are not to be considered forms of moral "illness." Nevertheless, the accumulated weight of Shaftesbury's rhetorical invocations of deformity, I would argue, makes itself felt, and human disability—be it mental or physical—always implicitly figures in the background of his philosophical discourse. Differently put, Shaftesbury's aestheticization of morality—or what comes to the same, his *moralization of aesthetics*—does not overtly argue that what we today refer to as "disability" is synonymous with "moral deformity." But as we will see, his penchant for upholding strict binaries (good versus ill, right versus wrong, beautiful versus deformed), combined with his tendency to conflate any number of experiential realms (aesthetics, morality, politics), makes it exceedingly difficult to distinguish one sort of "deformity" from another and to imagine a kind of "deformity" that is not, in the end, simply ill and wrong.

Discriminating Deformity

After outlining how the process of "reflected sense" allows the beauty or deformity of moral objects to become immediately and naturally apparent to the understanding, the task of virtue is described as a "new trial or exercise of the heart."[24] Virtue requires more than a merely creaturely gravitation toward the good; it requires, rather, the self-conscious practice of choosing what is "naturally" felt to be morally good and right, and shunning what, just as "naturally," is felt to be morally ill and wrong. The capacity for becoming "worthy or virtuous" is thus reserved for humans only, and virtue is within reach for any human creature, provided that "it can have the notion of a public interest and can attain the speculation or science of what is morally good or ill, admirable or blameable, right or wrong." Shaftesbury does not hesitate, though, to exclude—in advance—certain creatures from the realm of virtue: "For though we may vulgarly call an ill horse vicious, yet we never say of a good one, nor of any mere beast, idiot, or changeling, though ever so good-natured, that he is worthy or virtuous."[25] The eighteenth-century prized "good nature" as an attribute of one's moral character, and so in some sense, Shaftesbury's mention of the good-natured dispositions of the "beast, idiot, or changeling" extends to these creatures a compliment of sorts. However, once we consider the context, this compliment amounts to very faint praise. Shaftesbury regards the beast, idiot, and changeling, each in its respective way, as mentally deficient—that is, either devoid of human reason (the beast) or lacking a sufficient amount of human reason (the idiot and changeling). He gathers together these different creatures—an animal, a human, and a human child with possibly other-worldly affiliations—to underscore the point that virtue depends on "a knowledge of right and wrong and on a use of reason sufficient to secure a right application of the affections."[26] Without reason, or without enough reason, there is no access to the experience of moral beauty; without the ability to perceive the moral beauty of another's (or one's own) thoughts, affections, or actions, no virtue is possible. Shaftesbury presumably assumes that his grouping of beast, idiot, and changeling more clearly illuminates the necessary relation between reason and morality. But the conspicuous diversity of these examples begs the question of whether or not diversity might be read differently. As we linger over the examples of beast, idiot, and changeling, we might wonder if Shaftesbury's vast moral universe might accommodate more diverse—that is, differential, plural, even perhaps as yet unimagined—incarnations of reason, beauty, and virtue.

An instructive counterpoint to these creatures of diminished reason appears elsewhere in *Characteristics*. While the *Inquiry* articulates the moral relationship between the individual creature and the "universal nature" in which it resides, Shaftesbury's *Soliloquy, or Advice to an Author* offers a seemingly more practical moral lesson. The *Soliloquy* begins with a playful meditation on the difficulty of giving advice to anyone, and quickly turns to the especially difficult task it will address at length: namely, the task of one author giving advice to another author. For the moment, I will leave aside a detailed consideration of the *Soliloquy*, and move instead to those moments where, as compared to his thoughts in the *Inquiry*, Shaftesbury reveals a less ideologically nuanced—which is to say, a less forgiving—perspective on deformity. As one author advises another, the former may feel somewhat awkward, just as the latter may feel somewhat resistant. Shaftesbury thus smoothes the way with a hyperbolic description of the truly excellent poet. After casting a few aspersions on modern poets, an "insipid race of mortals" whose claim to fame is having "attained the chiming faculty of a language with an injudicious random use of wit and fancy," he declares a true poet to be "a second Maker, a just Prometheus under Jove":

> Like that sovereign artist, or universal plastic nature, he forms a whole, coherent and proportioned in itself, with due subjection and subordinacy of constituent parts. He notes the boundaries of the passions and knows their exact tones and measures, by which he justly represents them, marks the sublime of sentiments and action and distinguishes the beautiful from the deformed, the amiable from the odious. The moral artist who can thus imitate the Creator and is thus knowing in the inward form and structure of his fellow creature, will hardly, I presume, be found unknowing in *himself* or at a loss in those numbers which make the harmony of a mind.[27]

The human creature examined in the *Inquiry* is understood as naturally inclined to register the difference between beauty and deformity. With enough reason and some moral exertion, such a creature can harness these natural perceptions and make them the foundation of a virtuous life well lived. Shaftesbury's poet takes the practice of morality to a higher level. Unlike everyday moral subjects, who only perceive and judge the beautiful and the deformed, the poet perceives, judges, and then, in near-divine fashion, *(re)produces* beauty and deformity. Further, knowing the "inward form and structure of his fellow creature" bespeaks the poet's knowledge of his own interior composition. The harmony that reigns within his mind enables the poet's imitation of the Creator's sovereign artistry. At the same time, with a nod to the teachings of the ancients, the poet exemplifies the Delphic moral injunction that Shaftesbury invokes throughout *Characteristics*: "Know thyself."

Given the *Soliloquy's* particular objective—an author's advice to authors—it seems fitting to return to (and extend) our earlier discussion of how the *Inquiry's* form and content mirror and performatively authorize one another. Shaftesbury relies on a similar strategy in the *Soliloquy*. When he asserts that "there can be no kind of writing which relates to men and manners where it is not necessary for the author to understand poetical and moral truth, the beauty of sentiments, the sublime of characters," we inevitably recall that the full title of *Characteristics* promises a consideration of *Men, Manners, Opinions, Times*.[28] And when Shaftesbury goes on to add that the author who "naturally" has "no eye or ear for these interior numbers" will be unlikely to correctly "judge" the "exterior proportion and symmetry of composition which constitutes a legitimate piece," we recognize how the *systematicity of moral systems* is fashioned through a circular, self-authorizing and self-legitimating interplay between form and content.[29] While the *Soliloquy* offers a less philosophically systematic exposition than the *Inquiry*, its somewhat looser form reveals more explicitly its ideological use of the rhetoric of deformity. Shaftesbury's authorial advice regarding what is required to produce a "legitimate piece" functions simultaneously as prescription and (self-)description. A proper perception of the morally beautiful and morally deformed enables an author to imaginatively reproduce moral beauty and moral deformity—as represented objects and philosophical subjects. Deformity, then, is both morally suspect and discursively necessary. Accomplished authors distinguish themselves by maintaining a morally correct relationship to deformity; evidence of this correct moral disposition is embodied in the beautiful—the undeformed—formal characteristics of their texts. Deformity may be addressed *within* a piece of writing, but it must never insinuate itself into the form itself. Needless to say, the porous boundary between form and content ensures that an author always must be attuned to—and thus, always must be invested in and dependent on—the subject of deformity.

Dedicated to the aesthetic trinity of beauty, truth, and virtue, but continually compelled to contemplate deformity, it comes as no surprise when Shaftesbury momentarily reveals his moral distaste for unintentional and unwilled bodily anomalies: *"in the very nature of things there must of necessity be the founda-tion of a right and wrong taste, as well in respect of inward characters and features as of outward person, behaviour and action."*[30] In the *Inquiry*, no moral stain was associated with plague spots or convulsions. And earlier in the *Soliloquy*, Shaftes-bury imagines reuniting with an "intimate friend" who has endured "many sick-nesses and run many ill adventures" while traveling in "the remotest parts of the East and the hottest countries of the South"; despite the physical toll exacted by his friend's travels, which have so "altered his whole outward figure" that, at first glance, he might not be taken for the "same person," Shaftesbury assures us that his intimate friend would remain essentially unchanged, undeformed, so long as his mind, passions, and manners had remained the same. This hypothetical scenario illustrates the following point: "[I]t is not certainly by virtue of our face merely that we are ourselves. It is not we who change when our complexion or shape changes."[31] The disfigured "person" of the imagined traveler poses no moral difficulty. Why then, some pages later, is the "outward person" of an individual rendered the object of moral taste and distaste? One answer would be that Shaft-esbury "really" or "secretly" harbored an aversion to, or a prejudice against, bodily anomalies, be they acquired or "natural." This answer, to my mind, is less interest-ing than another: given his unwavering dedication to elaborating a philosophy of moral aesthetics, a philosophy that renders all things physical the objects of moral judgment, even Shaftesbury himself could not always practice accurately the principle of discriminating between the moral and the accidental, between an outward sign of malicious intent and an outward sign of the unavoidable vicis-situdes of human embodiment.

The Inward Part

Shaftesbury's philosophical discourse points in two directions: the carefully—in-deed, intensely—cultivated attention to outward form is intended to heighten and sharpen our perception of inner worth and beauty. Further, according to the neo-Platonic itinerary articulated in *Characteristics*, the journey from outer to in-ner ultimately leads to the *higher*. But as with so many other idealizing intellectual projects, which ground themselves in the material, only with a view to transcend it, Shaftesbury's penchant for *anatomizing* the moral life of human creatures often makes it difficult for him to detach discursively from the body as such. The pas-sages I have considered thus far all concern themselves with the ways that external phenomena register within the human subject, and how the internal workings of sense, reason, and affection apprehend and then morally judge external phenomena of various sorts. Shaftesbury certainly devotes a good deal of time to describing how the human mind morally perceives the affections and conduct of others. He is equally concerned, though, with tracing the features of the moral landscape within the human mind. As we will see, the rhetoric of deformity articulates the depths of the moral subject, and it is only through bodily figures that Shaftesbury's moral philosophy can represent and understand "what passes within ourselves."[32]

With the nature of goodness and virtue established in the first book of the *Inquiry*, the second book undertakes a closer examination of the inner life of morality. More specifically, in the second book Shaftesbury schematizes the affections into three classes—the "*natural affections*, which lead to the good of the public"; the "*self affections*, which lead only to the good of the private"; and the "*unnatural affections*," which contravene the good of both the public and the private—and demonstrates how these three classes of affections interrelate in the moral system sketched out in the *Inquiry*.[33] Shaftesbury's prime objective in this portion of the *Inquiry* is to refute the potential counterargument that, no matter how well-ordered and well-proportioned the universe may be, there will be occasions when the private good will conflict with the public good, when self-affection will go one way while natural affection beckons in another. Following in the tradition of Cicero's *On Duties*, Shaftesbury posits the harmony of the private and the public, the beneficial and the virtuous, and suggests that what might look like possible moral contradictions are merely misperceptions on the part of the critic.

In order to affirm and defend his vision of moral harmony, Shaftesbury describes what we now refer to as human "interiority" in strikingly physical terms: "The parts and proportions of the mind, their mutual relation and dependency, the connection and frame of those passions which constitute the soul or temper, may easily be understood by anyone who thinks it worth his while to study this inward anatomy. It is certain that the order or symmetry of this inward part is, in itself, no less real and exact than that of the body."[34] The orderliness of this "inward anatomy" reiterates *within* the exactness of our bodily composition; likewise, mind and body materially emblematize the orderliness of the universe beyond. The figurative turn, whereby the mind assumes the shape of the body, affords Shaftesbury a power rhetorical device. To his potential critics, he implicitly can say: my conception of the mind is the mind "as it really is,"[35] as real and legible as any of the faces you see around you. Another advantage of this figurative turn: if the mind and its moral disposition are understood as analogues of the body and its functional coherence, then Shaftesbury opens the way toward a contemplation of how and why the moral mind becomes "ill" and depraved. He rhetorically arms himself, in other words, to *moralize*.

Just as he earlier argued that moral goodness and illness depend on the "real motive" behind an affection or action, here Shaftesbury again contemplates moral agency and considers those instances when human subjects willfully and unreasonably inflict moral wounds upon themselves. Unlike most other thinkers, he tells us, *he* acknowledges the existence of the "inward anatomy" and recognizes the philosophical importance of truly understanding its strengths and weaknesses. With some irony, given his own perspective, Shaftesbury declares, "We never trouble ourselves to consider thoroughly by what means or methods our inward constitution comes at any time to be impaired or injured. The *solutio continui* [interruption of continuity], which bodily surgeons talk of, is never applied in this case by surgeons of another sort. The notion of a whole and parts is not apprehended in this science. We know not what the effect is of straining any affection, indulging any wrong passion or relaxing any proper and natural habit or good inclination."[36] Place alongside this passage an apposite one from his *Miscellaneous Reflections*, where Shaftesbury describes the "physician's way" of apprehending beauty and truth. "Natural health," he writes, "is the just proportion, truth and regular course of things in a constitution. It is the inward beauty of the body. And when the harmony and just measures of the rising pulses, the circulating humours and the moving airs or spirits are disturbed or lost, deformity enters and, with it, calamity and ruin."[37] The human mind, naturally inclined to perceive the beautiful and the deformed, must turn its "inward eye" upon itself, behold its own beautiful (though deformable) composition, and thus renew its moral vigilance. The passage from the *Miscellaneous Reflections* continues thus: "Should not this, one would imagine, be still the same case and hold equally as to the mind? Is there nothing there which tends to disturbance and dissolution? Is there no natural tenor, tone or order of the passions or affections? No beauty or deformity in this moral kind? Or allowing that there really is, must it not, of consequence, in the same manner imply health or sickliness, prosperity or disaster? Will it not be found in this respect, above all, that what is beautiful is harmonious and proportionable, what is harmonious and proportionable is true, and what is at once both beautiful and true is, of consequence, agreeable and good?"[38]

Having invoked images of injury and sickness, in the *Inquiry* Shaftesbury also will use, somewhat strangely, images of architecture, animal reproduction, and childbirth. If the mind represents a "moral kind of architecture," it obeys principles of structure and design similar to those used to fashion a building.[39] The metaphor of a well-built house sits alongside his assertion that "in every different creature and distinct sex there is a different and distinct order, set or suit of passions, proportionable to the different order of life, the different functions and capacities assigned to each." Architecture and biology then are conjoined in the following observation: "The inside work is fitted to the outward action and performance. So that where habits or affections are dislodged, misplaced or changed, where those belonging to one species are intermixed with those belonging to another, there must of necessity be confusion and disturbance within."[40] Anyone who doubts this insight is invited to "compar[e] the more perfect with the imperfect natures, such as are imperfect from their birth by having suffered violence within in their earliest form and inmost matrix."[41] Shaftesbury's earlier speculations on a solitary creature who may or may not be a monster now take on a more concrete—and more pernicious—form. "We know how it is with monsters," he writes matter of factly, "such as are compounded of different kinds or different sexes. Nor are they less monsters who are misshapen or distorted in an inward part."[42] Even "ordinary" animals may be regarded as "unnatural and monstrous" when they "lose their proper instincts, forsake their kind, neglect their offspring and pervert those functions or capacities bestowed by nature."[43] According to Shaftesbury, if the most legible sign of monstrosity manifests itself as bodily anomaly, a perversion of the affections is equally a characteristic of the monster. And so another rhetorical question is called for: "How wretched must it be, therefore, for man, of all other creatures, to lose that sense and feeling which is proper to him as a man and suitable to his character and genius?"[44] Instead of attempting to provide a real answer to this question, we might ask a question in return: if Shaftesbury wishes to stress the importance of "exercising" our affections in the correct manner, which necessarily implies a measure of intentionality, to what extent do these peculiar examples of buildings, animals, and monsters undermine—not to say, deform—the consistency and coherence of his philosophical logic?

The figurative interplay between mind and body, as we have seen, inspires another metaphorical transformation, which Shaftesbury has learned from Socratic and Stoic philosophy: the philosopher becomes an anatomist, physician, and surgeon.[45] No longer content to simply entice or exhort his reader to adopt the moral aesthetics on display in *Characteristics*, Shaftesbury is ready to intervene into—to figuratively operate on—the moral mind. And why not, he might ask, when we consider humankind's perverse inclination to turn away from the morally beautiful and embrace—and thus, become—the morally vicious? Given the "fabric of the mind or temper . . . as it really is," removing one good affection or introducing one bad, is the first step toward bringing on a completely "dissolute state"; indeed, when one intentionally warps his own affections, and thereby undermines his "integrity, good nature or worth," he acts with "greater cruelty towards himself than he who scrupled not to swallow what was poisonous or who with his own hands should voluntarily mangle or wound his outward form or constitution, natural limbs or body."[46] No one presumably would mangle or wound his own body—why then would someone mangle and wound his "inward anatomy"? Shaftesbury offers an extreme case in point. A man who, in a fit of passion, has murdered his companion might immediately feel remorse and begin to hate himself, or he might rationalize his rash action by "idoliz[ing] some false species of virtue and affect as noble, gallant or worthy that which is irrational and absurd."[47] According to Shaftesbury, though, this perverse state of moral rationalization can only last so long, for the "economy of the passions" will exact its revenge in the end.[48] "The more he engages in the love or admiration of any action or practice as great and glorious, which is in itself morally ill and vicious, the more contradiction and self-disapprobation he must incur." It is absolutely "certain" that once a natural affection is "contradicted," or an unnatural affection "advanced," "inward deformity" will grow greater and greater.[49] The endpoint of this degenerative process is the condition of utter "moral deformity," which he glosses as a "total apostasy from all candour, equity, trust, sociableness or friendship" and as a "moral delinquency" that signals a "most horrid, oppressive and miserable" "defection from nature."[50] The vehemence of his rhetoric here, and its strong religious ("apostasy") and political ("defection") connotations, is somewhat at odds with the image we typically have of Shaftesbury: the elite Whig intellectual who counseled politeness, decorum, and good-natured raillery and advocated for moderation in matters of religion and politics. A critic of zealotry of all stripes, he cannot help but allow himself a moment or two of zealous moralizing. Inspired by the vision of moral beauty, and stirred to defend against the encroachments of deformity under the guise of "false species of virtue," Shaftesbury promulgates a philosophy that is at once lesson, advice, correction, and cure.

In this essay, I have tracked how the rhetoric of deformity is essential to Shaftesbury's philosophical project in *Characteristics of Men, Manners, Opinions, Times*. At almost every turn, deformity enables him to articulate his concepts and demarcate his moral distinctions. By way of conclusion, I briefly turn from Shaftesbury's public persona to his more private writing self. The recent publication in unabridged form of the *Askêmata*, his philosophical notebooks, provides a salutary glimpse of another aspect of Shaftesbury's thought. Although a full analysis of the *Askêmata* is not possible here, I want to indicate how these private philosophical exercises cast a different light on his relationship to the concept of deformity.

In a section of his notebooks dedicated to the subject of the "Passions," Shaftesbury's first entry (dated from Rotterdam in 1698) meditates on two kinds of joy. One kind of joy brings with it an unwholesome fierceness and inconstancy, leaving the moral subject's mind susceptible to the vagaries of external events. The second kind of joy is "soft, still, peaceable, serene"; the moral subject animated by this joy remains stoically tranquil, firm, and disciplined, no matter what calamities or reversals ensue.[51] Whatever may have occasioned such a marked change in tone, the next entry on the passions (dated from St. Giles House in 1699) begins with these words: "How happy had it been with Thee, hadst thou kept to these Rules! Now see! whither a certain Lightness & Transport has led Thee! & what Passions are grown from those wrong Indulgencyes [*sic*] in Friendship! Wretch!" After this self-condemnation we find an extended—and extraordinarily disconcerting—metaphorical transformation of his troublesome passions into festering sores. "If Thou canst not think of these as *Sores*," Shaftesbury tells himself, "all is Corruption & Sore to the Bottom of thy Mind."[52] A graphic description of how sores are treated—including incisions, cauterization, and bandaging—leads him to ask, "[W]ilt thou spare thy Flesh, & fly from the Fire, the Steel, the Operations & sharper Remedyes? [*sic*] or are the other Wounds something, but these Nothing? is it no matter how it is *within*, or whether thou liv'st allways [*sic*] with a Macerated corrupted Mind? Would'st thou willingly go out of the World because of such a Body that is incurable; & not because of such a Mind?" "Either, therefore, thou art curable, or not," he concludes. "But if Curable; remember in what Way, and what belongs to one who is A Patient, & under Cure."[53]

The task ahead recalls those moments in *Characteristics* when the philosopher dons the persona of the surgeon. But now, the knife is turned against the self: "Well may the [Principles] be so compar'd to the Surgeon's Instruments. [F]or consider the *Wounds* which they are to cure."[54] Shaftesbury ventriloquizes the anxious self-questionings of a patient suffering from a bodily ailment, but only in order to reinforce within himself the knowledge that a moral illness poses an even greater threat to the human subject. "Is it not thus with One who has but a common Sore? and for fear of what? for fear of being Lame; for fear of a Deformity of Person; for fear of being offensive by an ill smell. What Solicitude! what anxiouse [*sic*] Care! what Concern & Thoughtfullness! [*sic*] . . . But what is this Distemper in comparison with another? is this the only proper *Distemper*? are other Sores less felt within? is there not a wors [*sic*] Lameness, a wors [*sic*] Deformity, & Filth?"[55] No doubt, the experience of encountering these private meditations, especially after a reading of *Characteristics*, is both poignant and disarming. It is necessary to recall here that during his relatively short life, Shaftesbury (1671–1713) endured and was increasingly debilitated by respiratory disease (severe asthma, and then possibly tuberculosis).[56] Therefore, when he addressed the notion of deformity, in both *Characteristics* and *Askêmata*, he did not have the luxury to forget entirely his own bodily predicament. To suggest that Shaftesbury fashioned an aestheticized moral philosophy in order to escape or transcend his own fears of, and corporeal struggles with, "lameness," "deformity," and "filth" perhaps would assume too much about the pressure biography exerted on philosophy in his life. We might do better, then, to respect the ambiguities of any body of thought, and say simply that Shaftesbury was the eighteenth century's greatest philosopher of deformity.

Notes

1. For their generosity, both intellectual and practical, I would like to thank Chris Mounsey, George Haggerty, Helen Deutsch, Rosemarie Garland-Thomson, Ben Reiss, and Erwin Rosinberg.

2. See Lennard J. Davis, *Enforcing Normalcy: Disability, Deafness, and the Body* (New York and London: Verso, 1995) and *Bending over Backwards: Essays on Disability and the Body* (New York: New York University Press, 2002); Felicity Nussbaum, "Feminotopias: The Pleasures of 'Deformity' in Mid-Eighteenth-Century England," in *The Body and Physical Difference: Discourses of Disability*, edited by David Mitchell and Sharon L. Snyder (Ann Arbor: University of Michigan Press, 1997), 161–73; Felicity Nussbaum, *The Limits of the Human: Fictions of Anomaly, Race and Gender in the Long Eighteenth Century* (Cambridge: Cambridge University Press, 2003); Helen Deutsch, *Resemblance and Disgrace: Alexander Pope and the Deformation of Culture* (Cambridge: Harvard University Press, 1996); Helen Deutsch and Felicity Nussbaum, eds., *"Defects": Engendering the Modern Body* (Ann Arbor: University of Michigan Press, 2000), which, in addition to the editors' introduction, includes many fascinating contributions from eighteenth-century scholars; David M. Turner, *Disability in Eighteenth-Century England: Imagining Physical Impairment* (New York and London: Routledge, 2012); Simon Dickie, *Cruelty and Laughter: Forgotten Comic Literature and the Unsentimental Eighteenth Century* (Chicago: University of Chicago Press, 2011); D. Christopher Gabbard, "From Idiot Beast to Idiot Sublime: Mental Disability in John Cleland's *Fanny Hill*," *PMLA: Publications of the Modern Language Association of America* 123.2 (2008): 375–89.

3. For work that considers questions of disability with reference to the history of philosophy, see the following: C. F. Goodey, *A History of Intelligence and "Intellectual Disability": The Shaping of Psychology in Early Modern Europe* (Burlington: Ashgate, 2011); Nancy J. Hirschmann, "Freedom and (Dis)Ability in Early Modern Political Thought," in *Recovering Disability in Early Modern England*, ed. Allison P. Hobgood and David Houston Wood (Columbus: Ohio State University Press, 2013), 167–86; Martha C. Nussbaum, *Frontiers of Justice: Disability, Nationality, Species Membership* (Cambridge: Harvard University Press, 2006); Simo Vehmas, "What Can Philosophy Tell Us about

Disability?" in *Routledge Handbook of Disability Studies*, ed. Nick Watson, Alan Roulstone, and Carol Thomas (New York: Routledge, 2012), 298–309.

4. Anthony Ashley Cooper, Third Earl of Shaftesbury, *Characteristics of Men, Manners, Opinions, Times*, ed. Lawrence E. Klein (Cambridge: Cambridge University Press, 1999), 167.

5. For critiques of Shaftesbury's ideological pretensions, see Robert Markley, "Sentimentality as Performance: Shaftesbury, Sterne, and the Theatrics of Virtue," in *The New Eighteenth Century: Theory, Politics, English Literature*, ed. Felicity Nussbaum and Laura Brown (New York: Methuen, 1987), 210–30; Terry Eagleton, *The Ideology of the Aesthetic* (Oxford: Blackwell, 1990); John Barrell, "'The Dangerous Goddess': Masculinity, Prestige, and the Aesthetic in Early Eighteenth-Century Britain," *Cultural Critique* 12 (Spring 1989): 101–31; Ronald Paulson,

6. J. B. Schneewind, *The Invention of Autonomy: A History of Modern Moral Philosophy* (Cambridge: Cambridge University Press, 1998), 308.

7. Shaftesbury, *Characteristics*, 167.

8. Shaftesbury, *Characteristics*, 167.

9. Shaftesbury, *Characteristics*, 167.

10. Shaftesbury, *Characteristics*, 167–68.

11. Shaftesbury, *Characteristics*, 168.

12. Shaftesbury, *Characteristics*, 168.

13. Shaftesbury, *Characteristics*, 171; original emphasis.

14. Shaftesbury, *Characteristics*, 169.

15. Shaftesbury, *Characteristics*, 168.

16. Shaftesbury, *Characteristics*, 169.

17. Shaftesbury, *Characteristics*, 172.

18. Shaftesbury, *Characteristics*, 172.

19. Shaftesbury, *Characteristics*, 208.

20. Shaftesbury, *Characteristics*, 172–73.

21. Shaftesbury, *Characteristics*, 173, 180.

22. Shaftesbury, *Characteristics*, 326.

23. Shaftesbury, *Characteristics*, 326–27.

24. Shaftesbury, *Characteristics*, 173.

25. Shaftesbury, *Characteristics*, 173.

26. Shaftesbury, *Characteristics*, 175. The changeling, to Shaftesbury's mind, is most likely a human child with developmental disabilities. At the same time, folkloric traditions depict the changeling as the offspring of fantastical creatures, or in the words of the *OED*, "a child (usually stupid or ugly) supposed to have been left by fairies in exchange for one stolen."

27. Shaftesbury, *Characteristics*, 93; original emphasis.

28. Shaftesbury, *Characteristics*, 149.

29. Shaftesbury, *Characteristics*, 150.

30. Shaftesbury, *Characteristics*, 150; original emphasis.

31. Shaftesbury, *Characteristics*, 127.

32. Shaftesbury, *Characteristics*, 229.

33. Shaftesbury, *Characteristics*, 196; original emphasis.

34. Shaftesbury, *Characteristics*, 194.

35. Shaftesbury, *Characteristics*, 195.

36. Shaftesbury, *Characteristics*, 194–95.

37. Shaftesbury, *Characteristics*, 415.

38. Shaftesbury, *Characteristics*, 415.

39. Shaftesbury, *Characteristics*, 215.

40. Shaftesbury, *Characteristics*, 215.

41. Shaftesbury, *Characteristics*, 215.

42. Shaftesbury, *Characteristics*, 215.

43. Shaftesbury, *Characteristics*, 215.

44. Shaftesbury, *Characteristics*, 215.

45. For a nuanced consideration of ancient notions of philosophy as medicine, see Martha C. Nussbaum,

46. Shaftesbury, *Characteristics*, 195.

47. Shaftesbury, *Characteristics*, 210.

48. Shaftesbury, *Characteristics*, 198.

49. Shaftesbury, *Characteristics*, 210.

50. Shaftesbury, *Characteristics*, 211, 194, 230.

51. Anthony Ashley Cooper, Third Earl of Shaftesbury, *Askêmata*, vol. 2, no. 6, of *Standard Edition: Complete Works, Correspondence and Posthumous Writings*, ed. Wolfram Benda, Christine Jackson-Holzberg, Patrick Müller, and Friedrich A. Uehlein (Stuttgart: Frommann-Holzboog, 2011), 244.

52. Shaftesbury, *Askêmata*, 247.

53. Shaftesbury, *Askêmata*, 248; original emphasis.

54. Shaftesbury, *Askêmata*, 249; original emphasis.

55. Shaftesbury, *Askêmata*, 249; original emphasis.

56. Robert Voitle suggests that, based on the biographical evidence, Shaftesbury suffered from tuberculosis; see Robert Voitle, *The Third Earl of Shaftesbury, 1671–1713* (Baton Rouge: Louisiana State University Press, 1984), 226.

4

THOMAS REID

Power as First Philosophy

Emile Bojesen

T HOMAS REID (1710–1796), replacement for Adam Smith's professorial chair in moral philosophy at Glasgow University and founder of the Scottish School of Common Sense, argued that animate beings have the capacity for power and that their actions are free within the constraints of that power. Power, for Reid, is the resource of the will. Power and weakness are contradictory as "weakness or impotence are defects or privations of power."[1] This same logic can be applied to ability and disability. Disability is frequently conceived as the opposite to ability: the "able bodied" being grouped differently to the "disabled." If disability were instead conceived as contradictory to ability, the power of the individual agent would be conceived of separately to their subjection to certain physical or mental disabilities. Power is what differentiates beings with a "will" from those without; their power is, in a sense, what makes them the author of their actions and their life. This essay will argue that to be defined by one's limitations rather than by one's actions is consistent with the philosophies of scepticism and empiricism. It is only when, as in Reid's philosophy, power in general as well as specific powers are separated out from the will and its experiential intertwinement that it becomes possible to conceive of disabilities as having nothing to do with power *or* the will; the will being subject to many different powers. The will can act in response to a disability but it is not subject to its "power" as it has none, which is to say that the agent has power over their dis/ability rather than their dis/ability having power over them.

This essay will aim to explore what exactly Reid's definition of power is, the significance of the difference of this notion of power in relation to those given by Locke and Hume, and, finally, offer suggestions for how this conception of power effects on a thinking of capability and disability.

I. What is Power?

Although Reid does discuss specific powers these are not the particular subject of interest for this essay, instead it is his more general and primary notion of *power* which will be elaborated on. The definition he gives in *Essays on the Intellectual Powers of Man* is helpful because of the complexity he gives to the subject:

> The words power and faculty, which are often used in speaking of the mind, need little explication. Every operation supposes a power in the being that operates; for to suppose any thing to operate which has no power to operate is manifestly absurd. But, on the other hand, there is no absurdity in supposing a being to have power to operate when it does not operate. Thus, I may have power to walk when I sit, or to speak when I am silent. Every operation, therefore, implies power; but the power does not imply the operation.[2]

Thus power is the prerequisite of every active or passive faculty and their operation. The implication of power in the operation but not the reverse highlights an inactive (although *not* passive) power can be called upon by operation but exists regardless of its being called upon. As long as a will is possible then it must be predicated by the existence of power, regardless of various limitations imposed on an individual by internal, external or corporeal states. This is significant in that "power," as Reid conceives it, is outside the empirical realm at every instance when it is not an active in causing an empirically perceivable effect. Empiricism is not sufficient to the task of conceiving of power in Reid's terms. It is embodied power rather than embodied perception that is afforded primacy in Reid's philosophy That, for him, power exists even when it is not active or perceivable, puts him firmly against the empirical or sceptical schools of philosophy prevalent in the mid-eighteenth century. Instead it might place him more in the context of philosophers such as Rousseau, Nietzsche and Dewey, for whom the body and its capacity for liberty *as* power prior to action, is of primary importance.

The more general conception of power, which is not related to specific faculties but underlies them all, is introduced in his late and only recently published essay, "Of Power," where it is defined as being antecedent not only to an event but also to the will which produces an event:

> Every voluntary exertion to produce an event seems to imply a persuasion in the agent that he has power to produce an event. A deliberate exertion to produce an event implies a conception of the event, and some

belief or hope that his exertion will be followed by it. This I think cannot be denied. The consequence is that a conception of power is antecedent to every deliberate exertion of will to produce an event.[3]

Several faculties might be called upon to conceive of an event before acting toward its realization, however, each of these faculties and, of course, the will required to produce it through action are all dependent on sufficient power to do so. What interests Reid, perhaps particularly because of his emphasis on common sense, is that the *conception* of power precedes action; this is a conception of a general capacity as well as specific capability afforded by individual faculties. Power precedes the operation of every individual faculty and every wilful action undertaken by an agent. Our conception of our own power, generally or specifically, is dependent on our faculties and therefore, for a gamut of reasons, we may vastly under or overestimate our power. We may be particularly prone to underestimating our power, for example, if we have learned to read certain aspects of our constitution as directive or limiting of our action. Disability, gender, class, and sexuality may be examples of perceivable qualities being operative in defining our ability to act, whereas, in Reid's terms, these would be considered subject to the agent's power and therefore nothing to do with the faculties capable of utilising power. Reid's location of the primacy of power in experience and action is the key to considering the agency available to us in its direction:

> We are conscious that we have power to produce certain events by our will and exertion. The conviction of this power is implied in the very voluntariness of exertion, for no man makes an exertion to do what he does not think to be in his power. In our own voluntary actions, therefore, we have a conviction and consequently a conception of efficient or productive power in ourselves. And this conception we had so early that it must be the work of nature.[4]

Power is therefore not something that we invent or gain from outside but rather the basis of all understanding and action as well as the very *capacity* for future understanding or action. "Efficient or productive power" is a predicate of a will and the action of the will is the only perceivable measure of that power even though will and power are not assimilable. Reid goes further, writing in *Active Powers* that not only does the will depend on power but that, in fact, the will is *in* man's power:

> "In common life, when men speak of what is, or is not, in a man's power, they attend only to the external and visible effects, which only can be

perceived, and which only can affect them. Of these, it is true, that nothing is in a man's power, but what depends upon his will, and this is all that is meant by this common saying. But this is so far from excluding his will from being in his power, that it necessarily implies it. For to say that what depends upon the will is in a man's power, but the will is not in his power, is to say that the end is in his power, but the means necessary to that end are not in his power, which is a contradiction.[5]

This significantly limits any conception of the primacy of the will in human action, making the will subject not only to power in general but also to the complex relation between the various faculties afforded power prior to its event. For example, I may want to lift a 100kg weight in a complex compound exercise such as a power clean but I will not have sufficient power to do so if I am not yet or anymore strong enough to lift this weight; my central nervous system is insufficiently prepared; my nutrition has been poor the preceding week; or, my mind is distracted by things outside of the gym or by occurrences in the gym. I may then reflect on my insufficient power and direct my will elsewhere accordingly. The same is true in terms of disability. Disability is, in these terms, the location of an absence of power. However, that is not to define an agent as being without power in general. In fact, Reid's methodology for the understanding of power is much more clearly focused on the power of an agent (whether they are disabled or not: Reid himself was deaf at the time of these writings) rather than its absence. Power is Variable according to the peculiar power of faculties. Power dictates the direction of the will and locates the will as being subject to these various bodily faculties: emphasising the Variable experience of the body and mind before the direction of the will. This conception of "power" as being separate from the will and its effects is at once inside and outside the consideration of metaphysics, especially that of empiricism. Our very ability to have the power to conceive of power implies its existence. Reid's conception of power is subject to this paradox because it is only *implied* in the "voluntariness of exertion," it does not consist in it. Power *is* but is only measurable by its effects rather than in itself.

By attempting to reduce "power" to the logic of empiricism or metaphysics more generally and read it as just yet another "will" we enter the territory of infinite regress which is therefore not applicable to Reid's philosophy. As Timothy O'Connor argues, power precedes volition but is not itself volition because, "We needn't have performed a prior act of will in order to have determined the action-initiating volition. We simply exert active power (a conception of which we form through its effects) in so determining it—that is, we determine the will directly. *The exertion of active power is not itself a type of volition*."[6] As such, active power is not will but it *is* what makes will possible. O'Connor goes on to suggest correctly that "an exertion of active power, according to Reid, is not any kind of event at all. Rather, it is the instantiation of a causal relation between agent and volition, and Reid does not consider this to be an event."[7] Reid himself argues that:

> But it is said, "That nothing is in our power but what depends upon the will, and therefore the will itself cannot be in our power." I answer, That this is a fallacy arising from taking a common saying in a sense which it never was intended to convey, and in a sense contrary to what it necessarily implies.[8]

This is why I would argue that Gideon Yaffe is incorrect to state that Reid has "a well-developed conception of the metaphysics of power" despite the fact that he suggests Reid "is able to tolerate the mysterious metaphysics that our linguistic practices imply and which bar us from analyzing the efficient causal relation in any way which could count as a reduction."[9] It is not the "metaphysics of power" that Reid seems to be describing at all but rather the *experience* or *sense* of power. Of course at least one aspect of that experience is related to the faculty of reason but power is not limited to that faculty, nor is it subject to it. The danger for Reid is not just the reduction of the causal relation but, rather more importantly, the insistence of the reduction of power to metaphysics or specifically to the faculty of reason. We are able to relate the faculty of reason to power but power also enables that faculty, as well as many others, and is not the same as it.

II. Reid on Locke and Hume's Concepts of Power

Reid reads Locke as suggesting that power is a form of potentiality, which is preceded by a reflection influenced by sensory experience of the effects of power. This not only excludes power's primacy but also reduces the sphere of human action to that of perception. Furthermore, it precludes the possibility of the conception of complex subjectivity as underpinning our understanding as well as our action. As such, Reid works towards unpacking Locke's conception of a limited subjectivity and agency by beginning with an exposition and analysis of the philosopher's conception of power:

> The sum of it is, That observing, by our senses, various changes in objects, we collect a possibility in one object to be changed, and in another a possibility of making that change, and so come by that idea which we

call power. Thus we say the fire has a power to melt gold, and gold has power to be melted; the first he calls active, the second passive power. He thinks, however, that we have the most distinct notion of active power, by attending to the power which we ourselves exert, in giving motion to our bodies when at rest, or in directing our thoughts to this or the other object as we will. And this way of forming the idea of power he attributes to reflection, as he refers the former to sensations.[10]

In Reid's reading, everything for Locke is reduced to sensation and reflection, with no sense that both are subject to faculties, which are themselves subject to sufficient power. The conflation of power to will or even basic physical action also leaves no room for a freedom prior to the application of the will. For Locke there is no power to reflect, only power in the actions that reflection results in. Most unsettlingly for Reid, power seems for Locke to be the potential to be effected on, as well as to effect, present in any object:

> Whereas he distinguishes power into active and passive, I conceive passive power is no power at all. He means by it, the possibility of being changed. To call this power, seems to be a misapplication of the word. I do not remember to have met with the phrase passive power in any other good author. Mr Locke seems to have been unlucky in inventing it; and it deserves not to be retained in our language.[11]

Reid cannot come to terms with Locke's use of the term "passive power" because the idea that power is simply potentiality significantly reduces identity to perceivable traits or qualities and thereby to the logic of an empirical consciousness. For Locke, consciousness (as reflection on sensation) becomes an objective subjectivity with determinable potential. More importantly, the complexities of individual agency become secondary to empirically perceived reality. To understand fully the repercussions of this requires an inversion: if one's subjective agency is primarily advanced through its relation to empirically determined reality then one is understood to be more or less able to perceive or engage in that "reality." If, instead, primacy is afforded to power rather than Variable sense perception then everything that follows in a conception of subjective agency would focus on the empowerment of Variable ability rather than the limitations of disability. Equally, the primacy of power escapes from the reduction of "reality" to reason, as power cannot itself be reduced to reason, nor can the faculties that it empowers, including that of the faculty of reason. For Reid, the primacy of power frees agency from the constraints of determinable potential altogether. Potential is empirically determinable, power is not. Every faculty is grounded in power and thus every idea is the product of the faculties that power engenders.

Locke's reduction of the derivation of ideas to what is empirically perceived is challenged by Reid as revealing the contradiction implicit in Locke's philosophical thinking on how power is perceived:

> the account which Mr Locke himself gives of the origin of our idea of power, cannot be reconciled to his favourite doctrine, That all our simple ideas have their origin from sensation or reflection; and that, in attempting to derive the idea of power from these two sources only, he unawares brings in our memory, and our reasoning power, for a share in its origin.[12]

It is with the scattered origin of power in the very faculties used to derive it that Reid enables the agent's reflection on their own power beyond the confines of empirical and metaphysical thought.

Reid continues his reading of Locke through his reading of Hume, who he rejects even more vehemently. Reid begins by outlining the latter's arguments that "we have no idea of substance, material or spiritual; that body and mind are only certain trains of related impressions and ideas; that we have no idea of space or duration, and no idea of power, active or intellective."[13] After making it clear that he only wishes to engage with what he disagrees with in Hume's rejection of the popularly conceived conception of power, he writes:

> I observe, that whether this popular opinion be true or false, it follows from mens having this opinion, that they have an idea of power. A false opinion about power, no less than a true, implies an idea of power; for how can men have any opinion, true or false, about a thing of which they have no idea?[14]

This very basic argument acts as a strategically placed platform from which Reid is able to further and more carefully critique Hume's (non)conception of power through the latter's reading of Locke:

> The first of the very obvious principles which the author opposes to Mr Locke's account of the idea of power, is, That reason alone can never give rise to any original idea. This appears to me so far from being a very obvious principle, that the contrary is very obvious. Is it not our reasoning faculty that gives rise to the idea of reasoning itself? As our idea of sight takes its rise from our being endowed with that faculty; so

does our idea of reasoning. Do not the ideas of demonstration, of probability, our ideas of a syllogism, of major, minor and conclusion, of an enthymeme, dilemma, sorties, and all the various modes of reasoning, take their rise from the faculty of reason? Or is it possible, that a being, not endowed with the faculty of reasoning, should have these ideas? This principle, therefore, is so far from being obviously true, that it appears to be obviously false.[15]

The analogical significance Reid gives to faculties of perception as well as the faculty of reason is not simply an analogy and, in fact, clarifies the grounding of both forms of faculty in power. Reid conceives of faculties as being generative of specific ideas and systems of though through the general power afforded by them to specific ends. This argument works in (at least) two directions at once; first, power is conceived of as being that which enables the operation of faculties; second, that the idea of power is generated or realised through the operation of these faculties, perhaps primarily (for Reid, at least) through their very operation.

After Reid's refutations of Hume's suggestion that reason cannot give rise to original ideas, the latter's form of scepticism as whole comes specifically under attack. Here it is Reid's humility with regard to philosophical truth that allows him a position from which to attack Hume. Philosophy for Reid seems perfectly valuable even if it is only able to afford provisional truths, which may later be refuted or come into question:

> If we had experience, ever so constant, that every change in nature we have observed, actually had a cause, this might afford ground to believe, that, for the future, it shall be so but no ground at all to believe that it must be so, and cannot be otherwise. Another reason to shew that this principle is not learned from experience is, That experience does not shew us a cause of one in a hundred of those changes which we observe, and therefore can never teach us that there must be a cause of all. Of all the paradoxes this author has advanced, there is not one more shocking to the human understanding than this, That things may begin to exist without a cause. This would put an end to all speculation, as well as to all the business of life.[16]

Not only does Reid here outline what he perceives as the unphilosophical character of scepticism through the limits it imposes on provisional philosophical thought and speculation but also its irrelevance to his own philosophical programme. As such, Reid moves away from Locke by suggesting a far more complex subjectivity, which precedes specific actions or events whereas Hume is helpful to Reid in allowing him to demonstrate that the power of faculties is separate to their action, even if this is not conceivable within the confines of sceptical philosophy, which Reid rejects.

III. Power, Liberty and Dis/ability

Reid's discussion of power is explicitly directed towards an elaboration of what he calls "the liberty of moral agents." He defines the latter in the following way:

> By the liberty of a moral agent, I understand, a power over the determinations of his own will. If, in any action, he had power to will what he did, or not to will it, in that action he is free. But if, in every voluntary action, the determination of his will be the necessary consequence of something involuntary in the state of his mind, or of something in his external circumstances, he is not free; he has not what I call the liberty of a moral agent, but is subject to necessity.[17]

Will, as already discussed, is not only dependent on sufficient power but also different from it. Power is outside of necessity and therefore is the only vestige of freedom and capacity for moral liberty. Moral actions cannot be measured in terms of involuntary states or circumstances, such as physical or mental disabilities, but must rather be understood in terms of the power available to the individual outside of necessity. The difficulty therein is that power is only perceivable through its effects on actions and events. However, it is to undermine the power of any agent to focus more on their subjection to necessity than on their wilful actions. Despite Reid's primary focus being on power he is also sensitive to actions or ways of being which seem to involve no specific power as well as the influence of necessities such as illness. Equally there is little credit to be afforded to the action of an individual's moral liberty if, as he argues in the case of Cato, their goodness is simply part of their constitution:

> What was, by an ancient author, said of Cato . . . He was good because he could not be otherwise. But this saying, if understood literally and strictly, is not the praise of Cato, but of his constitution, which was no more the work of Cato, than his existence. On the other hand, if a man be necessarily determined to do ill, this case seems to me to move pity, but not disapprobation. He was ill, because he could not be otherwise. Who can blame him? Necessity has no law.[18]

Reid's insistence on the absolute difference between necessity and power is significant in separating influences on agency from limits on agency. It is therefore clearly possible to have a positive or enabling influence on an individual's conception of their power, just as it is possible to engage (consciously or not) in disabling an individual's agency through an education or culture where the perception of "weaknesses" is given primacy. The role cultures and societies play in enabling rather than labelling otherwise "free agents" becomes a very particular kind of moral question when then individual moral action of an individual is suppressed or they are not educated in such a way as to be aware of their own power and its concomitant liberty.

Reid's conception of a "free agent" is extremely nuanced and puts into question the concept of a "reasonable agent," the faculty of reason being only one of many influencing the actions of man:

> We call man a free agent in the same way as we call him a reasonable agent. In many things he is not guided by reason, but by principles similar to those of the brutes. His reason is weak at best. It is liable to be impaired or lost, by his own fault, or by other means. In like manner, he may be a free agent, though his freedom of action may have many similar limitations. The liberty I have described has been represented by some Philosophers as inconceivable, and as involving an absurdity.[19]

Liberty, for Reid, is not freedom of the will (reasonable or not) but rather the freedom afforded to the individual by their power, which may or may not become realized in the will. It is the freedom of power to be able to act by instinct or habit as well through conscious will. It is only within this freedom of power that his conception of moral liberty can be of significance, precisely because the freedom is much greater and more complex than simply the freedom of the will (to be well or ill according to an external or internal rational schema). The presumed absurdity he locates is that of infinite regress of will, however, as Reid conceives of it, this regression ends in power. The specific effects of power on moral liberty are defined as being limited and frequently completely absent—most actions perhaps being conceivable as amoral:

> This moral liberty a man may have, though it do not extend to all his actions, or even to all his voluntary actions. He does many things by instinct, many things by the force of habit without any thought at all, and consequently without will. In the first part of life, he has not the power of self-government any more than the brutes. That power over

the determinations of his own will, which belongs to him in ripe years, is limited, as all his powers are; and it is perhaps beyond the reach of his understanding to define its limits with precision. We can only say, in general, that it extends to every action for which he is accountable.[20]

As such power seems to develop with age and is presumably educable. It is therefore perhaps also possible to create a context where the enabling of individual powers is of primary educative value. This would replace a context where power is read as secondary to perceivable objective potential and limited by a focus on limitation itself rather than personal and social facilitation of Variable and particular power. Power over the determination of will is achieved through the complex relations of the specific powers of the various faculties. But as long as there is power there is freedom and it is in that freedom, rather than in our limitations, that we may begin to act.

Notes

1. Thomas Reid, *Essays on the Active Powers of Man* (Edinburgh: John Bell, 1788), 11–12.

2. Thomas Reid, *Essays on the Intellectual Powers of Man* (Edinburgh: John Bell, 1785), 6. Reid's texts, particularly *Essays on the Active Powers of Man*, will be quoted from extensively as his texts are rarely read now, and not in common consciousness as Locke's and Hume's.

3. Thomas Reid & John Haldane, "An essay by Thomas Reid on the conception of power." *Philosophical Quarterly* 51 (2002):1–12, 3.

4. Thomas Reid & John Haldane, "An essay by Thomas Reid," 7.

5. Thomas Reid, *Essays on the Active Powers of Man*, 274.

6. Timothy O'Connor, *Person and Causes: The Metaphysics of Free Will* (Oxford· Oxford University Press, 2000), 46.

7. Timothy O'Connor, *Person and Causes*, 47

8. Thomas Reid, *Essays on the Active Powers of Man*, 273.

9. Gideon Yaffe, *Manifest Activity: Thomas Reid's Theory of Action* (Oxford: Oxford University Press, 2004), 157. As O'Connor argues, 'Reid's view is not subject to any *internal* problem that forces him to choose between an infinite regress of mental acts and an uncaused event at the core of every free action. Reid never squarely addresses the further question of why the obtaining of a causal relation between agent and volition (an exertion of active power) doesn't qualify as a kind of event. It is not, to be sure, a prior event that produces the willing.' in Timothy O' Connor, *Person and Causes,* 48

10. Thomas Reid, *Essays on the Active Powers of Man*, 23.

11. Thomas Reid, *Essays on the Active Powers of Man*, 23.

12. Thomas Reid, *Essays on the Active Powers of Man* (Edinburgh: John Bell, 1788), 26.

13. Thomas Reid, *Essays on the Active Powers of Man*, 27.

14. Thomas Reid, *Essays on the Active Powers of Man*, 30.

15. Thomas Reid, *Essays on the Active Powers of Man*, 30.

16. Thomas Reid, *Essays on the Active Powers of Man*, 32.

17. Thomas Reid, *Essays on the Active Powers of Man*, 267.

18. Thomas Reid, *Essays on the Active Powers of Man*, 269.

19. Thomas Reid, *Essays on the Active Powers of Man*, 271.

20. Thomas Reid, *Essays on the Active Powers of Man*, 270.

Part Two

CONCEPTUAL

5

"AN HOBBY-HORSE WELL WORTH GIVING A DESCRIPTION OF"

Disability, Trauma, and Language in *Tristram Shandy*

Anna K. Sagal

WORDS ARE UNSTABLE in the best of novels, and in *Tristram Shandy*, delightfully so. The power of words in *Tristram Shandy*—legislative, philosophical, political, sexual, and religious—shapes both narrative and form, as language is perpetually in danger of misinterpretation and subject to unconventional deployment. The physical and psychological consequences of unstable language are particularly crucial in a narrative whose main characters are all disabled in some way—individuals who Felicity Nussbaum argues, "display disability *as* character."[1] While that is not to say that Tristram is only his consumption or that Toby is no more than his ambiguous groin injury,[2] is it necessary to note that this novel is among the few eighteenth-century texts, and perhaps the first, to invest figures of disability in positions of central importance.[3] Given the value of a disability-sensitive interpretation of this novel, I argue that when we talk about language in *Tristram Shandy*, we have to talk about disability.

Tristram himself is the master linguist, the virtuoso with a pen who fears no limits except the final one—an unsurprising talent, perhaps, given his eccentric upbringing. Yet just as the text is inscribed with the unparalleled eloquence of its narrator, so, too, is it infused with the frustrated language of his uncle Toby. Rather than existing merely as a foil for the verbosity and vivacity of the narrator, however, Toby's struggles with language are the foundation for Laurence Sterne's experiment with communicative possibilities outside of language. For scholars invested in reading the disability of Toby Shandy as more than a quirk of character (or even additional proof of nothing "well hung" in the family), Sterne's experiment with Toby's hobby-horse has the potential to be a radical mode of communication—a method of meaning-making not restricted to the able-bodied.

Toby Shandy has captured the imaginations of countless scholars in the centuries after Sterne first created the character of which he himself avowed, "I have got soused over head and ears in love."[4] William Hazlitt's comment remains one of the most well-known assessments of Toby's character, as he declares him "one of the finest compliments ever paid to human nature."[5] Yet a great disservice has been done to his character in much criticism and popular review, as he is all too often relegated to the position of an amiable but effeminate eccentric who exists to balance Walter's acerbic neuroses with gentle sentiment.[6] While Toby necessarily functions as a comic character in a novel that Chinmoy Banerjee calls "a comedy of the mind as it is,"[7] Sterne has written a level of complexity in this figure that is often overlooked, or undervalued. Toby Shandy's story is a unique story of a body suffering from trauma that defies expression, and a disabled man who adapts to his new life through unconventional methods. Toby's hobby-horse, that infamous fixation on warfare and its "accoutrements,"[8] represents not an emasculating fascination with a lost military past (and the lost whole body), but rather a way of engaging with and communicating that pain and trauma of his war experience. By acknowledging Toby's disability as not merely comically emasculating (in the same way that, say, Tristram's circumcision is) but as crucial to an understanding of his character, we must adjust our assessment of his relationship to language. Employing the psychological formulation of trauma as an often unspeakable experience, I want to reconsider Toby's hobby-horse as the creation of a new system of meaning-making and communicative function: these objects, maps, scale-models, and accessories become the vehicle by which his unspeakable narrative can be told.

In the first section of this chapter, I outline the parameters of my discussion on disability, the ways in which eighteenth-century notions of disability pertain to Uncle Toby's character, and the extent to which our modern critical investment in a disability-sensitive reading can be a rewarding mode of reading *Tristram Shandy*. In the second section, I evoke contemporary theories of trauma and the experience of pain to foreground Toby's disability as more than just impairment. By working within a framework that fruitfully pulls from both disability studies and trauma theory, I hope to arrive at a more nuanced understanding of Toby's character—a character who is, after all, a disabled veteran suffering from what modern psychology would term post-traumatic stress. That is not to ignore the comic or sentimental dimensions of his character, but to argue for the benefit that this reading may have to the expanding discussion on eighteenth-century disability studies. Then, in the third section, I position my argument within the existing body of criticism on language and its failures (intentional or otherwise) in the novel. What I hope to demonstrate are the ways in which previous critical analyses of Toby's relationship to language did not take into account his disability and his traumatic experience as "game-changing factors," so to speak. That is, the interpretative implications of trauma and disability radically alter our understanding of Sterne's play with language, as both experiences bear an acknowledged alien relationship with language that able-bodiedness does not. Finally, in the fourth section, I read Toby's narrative in light of these theoretical parameters; from the point of his injury to the expansion of his bowling-green, into his "amors" with the Widow Wadman, I look at his shifting relationship with language as he navigates a recovery from trauma and searches for a sort of equilibrium with his disability.

As one last point of preface, I evoke Philoctetes, one of the most bitterly memorable figures in classical tragedy—a man whose body cannot heal as long as he remains incapable of confronting and negotiating the pain of his injuries. For Sophocles's tragic hero, his inability to express that pain compromises his individual identity, and so "Philotectes" becomes a metonym for pain. I see a shadow of this figure in the background of Sterne's work because I see the problem of Philoctetes re-embodied in Toby Shandy: re-embodied and transcended, as Toby frees himself from that discursive relegation to bodily pain through the development a revolutionary method of communication—his hobby-horse.

(I)

While modern socio-medical discourse makes the distinction between physical impairment—"loss or abnormality of physiological or anatomical structure and function"—and disability—"the restriction on a person's ability to undertake certain tasks or functions which may be caused by social and environmental factors"[9]—the terms in the eighteenth century often encompassed facets of both definitions. Johnson's *Dictionary* (3rd edition) primarily defined "disability (n)" as "want of power to do any thing; weakness," and "disable (v)" as "(1) to deprive of natural force; to weaken," "(2) to impair; to diminish," and (4) "to deprive of usefulness or efficacy."[10] Many of these definitions have physical connotations, which align more closely with our own delineation of "impairment." That fourth option, however, the erasure of "usefulness or efficacy," gets at something crucial about both eighteenth-century codifications of disability and at Toby's situation— disability removes that which makes a man "worth something" in a social context. There is certainly a component of frustration at an early retirement, as well as a sense of powerlessness, that Toby redresses through his re-enactments—to say

nothing of his unconfirmed-but-highly-likely castration. It is precisely his identification as a disabled veteran[11] that makes his linkage to disability particularly
notable: here is a figure that both Sterne's contemporaries and the modern critical
audience would recognize as disabled.

We can assume contemporary recognition because the term "disabled" was
often used to describe those injured in battle in the eighteenth century. Soldiers
and sailors with wounds sustained in service which "rendered them unfit for
service"[12] were considered medically "disabled" and subsequently discharged.
As part of a larger social activist movement on behalf of veterans' rights, the
image of the disabled serviceman was one of the most common "objects of
compassion"[13] among the spectrum of eighteenth-century depictions of disability. In part, this sympathy comes from a distinction between "disability" and
"deformity," where the latter often applied to bodily abnormalities a person was
born with, rather than those he acquired;[14] a man born with a bad leg elicits less
sympathy than a man who loses his leg, especially if the second man loses his leg
in service.[15] Sterne therefore evokes the most sympathetic representation of the
disabled body for his Uncle Toby, as most critics have recognized.[16] However,
what David Turner calls the "mixture of pathos and patriotism that attended
representations of disabled servicemen at the end of the eighteenth century"[17]
is certainly part of the picture, but not all. By largely separating the "pathos" of
Toby's character from his injury (and affixing it firmly to his amors and his moments of sentimental excess), Sterne does not seek to evoke sympathy for Toby's
character strictly on Turner's grounds.

Although the usage of the term "disabled" in the eighteenth-century context
does not entirely comport with our own, Toby's injury and his subsequent physical
impairment renders him subject to both contemporary and modern significations
of the term. Those with maimed or missing limbs were commonly called "lame" or
"crippled."[18] "Lame," the more ambiguous of the two terms, was commonly used
to "refer to all kinds of impairment, whether temporary or permanent," and seems
to have been somewhat less derogatory.[19] "Cripple," on the other hand, "described
a more 'pitiable,' all-encompassing state of incapacity,"[20] and was often applied to
objects of scorn or derision, especially in the type of fiction in which disability is
aligned with monstrosity. While Sterne does not use the term "cripple" to refer to
Toby for obvious reasons, he also curiously avoids the word lame: Toby is referred
to as "lame" only three times in the novel.[21] This is a pertinent observation for a
few reasons. Firstly, the fact that "lame" is nebulous word both in terms of location
(what precise injury renders the subject "lame"?) and duration or state of perma-

nence (a temporary physical impairment or permanent one?) makes the epithet especially applicable to Toby's physical condition. We know neither the precise location of his wound, nor to what extent it continues to trouble him during the period in his life that Tristram recounts. Secondly, the evasion of referring to a markedly lame man as such points to the kind of rewriting of physical disability that Sterne seems to be doing in the novel—although, of course, this might also be because the injury Sterne is more interested in depicting (or not depicting) lies in Toby's groin, not his leg. The ambiguity of the term "lame," as well as Toby's tentative linkage to the label, substantiates a reading of Toby as a character with a particularly unstable relationship with words as meaning-bearing signs, as well as with his own body. And that, perhaps, is the most crucial experiential component of disability—the unstable relationship the disabled subject has with his own body.

Though varying terms and labels were used, most notions of deformity and disability in the eighteenth century were rooted in evolving philosophical conceptions of the body. In the previous century, the idea of categorical physical abnormality (what would become the concept of disability) emerged in response to codifications of normative physicality. Writers such as Baldassarre Castiglione addressed bodily abnormality as part of his rhetoric of deportment (in which standards of appropriate behavior are explicitly linked to normative or attractive physical appearance),[22] as did Locke in his own way regarding mental normativity. However, in moving away from the early modern conception of the abnormal body as monstrous and somehow linked to morality, British thinkers involved in the rise of the New Science were more concerned with bodily abnormality as a subject for scientific and philosophical evaluation. For example, Bacon's brief essay "Of Deformity"[23] wrote of disability as a physical condition with significant psychological impact, rather than the corporeal manifestation of a monstrous spirit: "Whosoever hath anything fixed in his person, that doth induce contempt, hath also a perpetual spur in himself, to rescue and deliver himself from scorn."[24] Disability—especially a life-long condition—inspired bitterness of spirit as a defense mechanism, but did not always indicate bad character. Bacon also leaves room for what would become the heroic figure of the suffering disabled, proposing of some disabled men that "they will, if they be of the spirit, seek to free themselves from scorn; which must be either by virtue or malice; and therefore let it not be marveled, if sometimes they prove excellent persons."[25] This ability to belie the temperament suggested by physical appearance demonstrated a kind of transcendence of biology that many sentimental authors evoked in the latter half of the eighteenth century. In such a paradigm, the disabled body is capable of arousing sympathy, rather than scorn. Sterne, for one, is entirely uninterested in the fictional device of the bitter cripple.

By the time Sterne was writing, physical disability could serve a number of potentially conflicting purposes in fiction, as the difference between innate and acquired disability also took on new significance. Lennard J. Davis notes that the eighteenth century was a transitional period in the perception of disability, during which there were "two opposing, historically divergent readings of disability—deformity as sign or punishment versus disability as impersonal affliction randomly assigned throughout the population."[26] While this positioned real disabled men and women at the nexus of conflicting notions of how disability dictated their place in society, it also provided fodder for new depictions of disability in literature. Davis observes, "What we do see in the second half of the eighteenth century is a remarkable appearance of the disabled person in print as author and character."[27] As in Bacon's formula, a disabled man might be abnormal or even repulsive, but also sympathetic—a trope that was often deployed in sentimental fiction. Davis identifies these sympathetic characters as "the deserving literary disabled," a category that included "women, children, [and] older people,"[28] and presumably, wounded soldiers.[29] It is moreover imperative to note that these "deserving" disabled men and women are often those who either occupy positions of *conditional* disability (the impoverished, or the temporarily ill, who are disabled only conditionally, rather than intrinsically) or those who *become* disabled after birth through accident or illness. The congenitally disabled, however, were often relegated to the category of "undeserving characters," as birth defects and the like retained connotations of monstrosity.[30]

Scholars of the period also emphasize the importance of visible disability. As Nussbaum, Sharon L. Snyder, David T. Mitchell, and others have demonstrated, the conversations about disability in the eighteenth century often concerned noticeably different bodies across a spectrum of physical difference, which included race, gender, and sexuality, as well those individuals with marked deformities—the deaf, the pock-marked, the unnaturally short. The lame, the nose-less, and the impotent characters of *Tristram Shandy* clearly meander somewhere along that spectrum of disability, but unlike the figures of ridicule of which Simon Dickie[31] or Roger Lund[32] write, they are not intended to be read as grotesque in the same way as Fielding's Mrs. Slipslop,[33] for example. However, neither are they intended to explicitly evoke sympathy. Toby, Walter, and Tristram are all some manifestation of "the deserving literary disabled," but their disabilities are not particularly physically noticeable, and more often than not, are contingent upon that which remains hidden as the defining factor of disability (Toby's groin, Tristram's genitals, et. al.). To recall the Nussbaum quote with which I opened this chapter, Sterne uniquely evokes disability as a defining character trait, rather than solely a restrictive physical one. By reading Toby as a unique manifestation of disability in literature, we expand our critical understanding of eighteenth-century notions of disability to encompass a greater degree of nuance in how disability was constituted and depicted.

(11)

I turn to trauma theory for a foundational concept of this argument: the proposition that the experience of pain and suffering can be inexpressible through language, and that this inexpressibility inevitably damages the body in pain. Elaine Scarry formulates this incompatibility of experienced pain and language as an antithetical relationship: physical pain is that which "does not simply resist language but actively destroys it," an antagonism that "is not simply one of [pain's] incidental or accidental attributes but is essential to what it is."[34] Pain by its very nature is outside the spectrum of that which is linguistically expressible. Scarry emphasizes this essential problem of representation when she remarks that "physical pain—unlike any other state of consciousness—has no referential content. It is not *of* or *for* anything."[35] That is, pain inhabits a body, or part of a body, and is perceived in a corporeally geographic sense by the body experiencing that pain, but pain is not linguistically framed in such a way as to take an object. Pain can be located, but it cannot be related in such a way as to make it comprehensible to others. As Stanley Cavell elaborates, "The fundamental importance of someone's having pain is *that* he has it; and the nature of that importance—namely, that he is suffering, that he requires *attention*—is what makes it important to know where the pain is, and how severe and what kind it is."[36] Yet there is an unbridgeable "gap" between the person in pain and the person who pays attention, as Cavell questions the possibility of truly knowing another's pain: that is "the sense in which we can have the same feeling is insufficient for knowing whether another person feels what I feel, or feels anything at all."[37] There is something intrinsic in the experience of felt pain that makes it unrelatable, linguistically and empathetically.

The fact that *un-locatability* of bodily pain has a direct correlation with the *un-relatability* of the experience of injury creates one of the most basic problems of post-traumatic recovery: the inability to process the traumatic experience in a meaningful way. As Dori Laub remarks about his observations of Holocaust survivors,[38] "There is, in each survivor, an imperative need to *tell* and thus to come to *know* one's story, unimpeded by ghosts from the past against which one has to protect oneself. One has to know one's buried truth in order to be able to live one's life."[39] The longer that this traumatic memory remains irreconcilable with what psychologists call normal, "narrative memory," the more damaging it becomes to the individual's psyche. I find the idea of "normal" memory linked to the concept of narrative critically useful, because it allows us to read the experience of posttraumatic individuals in fiction as being in search for their own comprehensible narratives within a larger narrative—with regards to Sterne's work, a larger narrative that is itself of uncertain comprehensibility.[40] This need for a coherent narrative as the foundation for the healing process likewise informs a nuanced reading of Toby's convalescence.

The vocabulary of Toby's recovery is moreover the vocabulary of trauma, as the internal experience of trauma is often articulated as one of violence and confusion. Kai Erickson succinctly defines trauma as "a blow to the tissues of the body . . . or to the tissues of the mind—that results in injury or some other disturbance."[41] It is this "some other disturbance" that remains the subject of academic and psychological study, as Erickson relates the experience of the traumatic event like a tale of personal incursion: "Something alien breaks in on you . . . it invades you, takes you over, becomes a dominating feature of your interior landscape."[42] The traumatized body is an invaded body, defeated in a psychic battle which, in this novel, mirrors Toby's physical defeat. Moreover, this almost architectural configuration of trauma—the articulation of self as having an "interior landscape"—is especially pertinent in this case, as Toby's eventual mode of communication is contingent upon a geographic manipulation of objects in space. The interior landscape, invaded and dominated, is recuperated on the exterior landscape of the bowling-green. As I will expand upon in the fourth section of this chapter, spatial dimensions are both metaphorically and literally vital to Toby's traumatic recovery and his adaptation to disability.

Another significant indicator of trauma is the disruption of a sense of time, as a meaningful psychological narrative fundamentally depends upon a logical, causal sequence of events. Thus, the unclear chronological factors of Toby's recovery also exacerbate the traumatic dimensions of his experience. The duration of his convalescence is ambiguous and nonlinear, and it is a process of recovery that seems endless, plagued by the same progressions and digressions of the novel itself. Just as the psychic trauma of a past event can resist resolution due to continued emotional resurgence, Toby's physical recovery is impeded by his inability to recuperate emotionally. Sterne evokes the archaic (but oh-so-Shandean) meaning of the term *digestion* when he implores the reader to "[consider] well the effects which the passions and affections of the mind have upon the digestion . . . why not of a wound as well as of a dinner?"[43] The corporeal wound festers and aches as Toby's unresolved "passions and affections" regarding the traumatic event continue to cause both mental and physical pain. Toby's bodily pain and emotional distress are inextricably linked, and his injury must therefore be read as both traumatic (to the extent to which it resists explication) and disabling (in the sense that it causes psycho-physical impairment).

Linguistically, spatially, and temporally, Toby's internal narrative is fractured— the story of a mind and body in chaos. However, by incorporating the framework of traumatic experience into our reading of Toby's character, we begin to see a greater complexity in Sterne's depiction of human suffering. Sterne's engagement with trauma resists effeminizing the disabled body, and in fact, formulates Toby's idiosyncratic interactions with the world not as escapist, but rather, as empowering.

(I I I)

The problem of Sterne and language is not a new one, and neither is his contentious debt to Lockean modes of thought. Given that the former is often contingently linked to the latter, I begin with Locke. Peter Briggs neatly summarizes the primary questions critics in the last few centuries have posed regarding Sterne and Locke:

> Was Sterne engaged in a fictional translation and exposition of Lockean
> ideas? Or was he subverting Locke, using Locke as a straight man in the
> midst of a Shandean comedy? Or is Sterne better understood simply as
> an artistic opportunist, capitalizing upon the public currency of Lockean
> ideas about the mind's various workings?[44]

I, however, tend to agree with Alexis Tadié's assertion that the key to the Sterne and Locke debate is not "the extent to which Sterne may or may not have borrowed from Locke, but rather the fact that the culture to which he belonged was, by and large Lockean."[45] That is to say, Sterne was familiar with Locke's notions of how people thought and learned through some means or another, a familiarity that influenced his notion of human behavior but did not strictly dictate it. The relevance of Sterne's Lockean debt in this case is the way in which Locke conceived of the human mind's relationship to language. In order for language to function as a means of communication, each man has to hold the same definition of an idea in his mind—words have to be consistent signifiers of a commonly agreed-upon and understood idea: "Words having naturally no signification, the idea which each stands for, must be learned and retained by those, who would exchange thoughts, and hold intelligible discourse with others, in any language."[46]

The Shandean linguistic system, however, is one of disjuncture; meaning is produced not through the dependable linkage of signifier and signified, but rather, through discursive movements that make meaning in contrast and confusion. This aligns language in *Tristram Shandy* more closely with Locke's concept of abstract ideas, ideas that have no absolute signified object or concept. For example, some words—scarp, counterscarp, and glacis—should be concrete terms with definitive, unmistakable meaning. However, as Toby attempts to explain some minor technical differences to Walter between the ravelin and the half-moon, it becomes clear that meaning of this terminology is derived only from context and contrast:

> For when a ravelin, brother, stands before the curtin, it is a ravelin; and when a ravelin stands before a bastion, then a ravelin is not a ravelin;—it is a half-moon;—a half-moon likewise is a half-moon, and no more, so long as it stands before its bastion;—but was it to change place, and get before the curtin,—'twould no longer be a half-moon; a half-moon, in that case, is not a half-moon;—'tis no more than a ravelin.[47]

What should be the most concrete of terms—the names of physical objects, which exist in printed reference books—become some of the most confusing concepts of the novel.[48] The distinction is made, repeatedly, yet slightly differently, multiple times. Toby conveys meaning through repetition and the evocation of physical space, which is precisely how his hobby-horse comes to function. Even more important to the text are the emotional and idiosyncratic abstract terms, which encompass an array of meanings whose nuances can never fully be understood outside of the person uttering them. The titular subject of this paper, a "hobby-horse," bears meaning only in the context of the novel as a whole, not as a concrete linguistic sign. As Briggs puts it, Sterne echoes Locke's "realization that any comprehensive exploration of understanding must include the *expression* of understanding and therefore must explore the capacities and limitations of language."[49]

Sterne's creation of meaning through disjunction is also reflected in the novel's use of communicative modes beyond the written word: from gesture and speech, to symbol and sound, the text's coherence is contingent upon a kind of ordered incoherence. As many critics have pointed out, Sterne's subversion of the boundaries and form of the English language (and on occasion, French, Latin, Spanish, and Greek) reflect his investment in changing modes of communication and expression in the eighteenth century.[50] While his literary compatriots had moved away from oral record and embraced print culture following what theorists have identified as the rise of the canonical novel, Sterne bred orality into his print, corrupted the distinctions between speech and text and body. As Tadié summarizes: "Sterne 'battles' with two paradigms at the same time, displaying an evident nostalgia for orality, as well as a concern for the modes of writing in print culture."[51] The very organicness of *Tristram Shandy*, the fluctuating nature of what constitutes text and novel, explores the possibilities of diverse modes of writing in opposition and apposition[52] to one another. Melvyn New has conducted many excellent studies of the internal texts of the narrative—the borrowings from Rabelais, Cervantes, Burton, et. al., in addition to the fictional texts of Slawkenbergius, the Abbess and Marguerita, the apocryphal *Tristrapoedia* and even Yorick's sermons—which he argues "are all re-stagings of the instinct, the drive to order and comprehend through our language whatever is not yet in our language."[53] By hybridizing his novel through the inclusion of other stories, other texts, Sterne is pursuing that desire for comprehensibility. And it is precisely this drive for pulling that which is outside our language into a meaningful interpretive system that explains the communicative value of Toby's hobby-horse. Objects, too, can be interpolated into the text in an effort to find comprehension. Toby's hobby-horse *is* another one of those alternate texts, as the story of pain he tells on his bowling-green joins the others as gestures at comprehensibility through hybridity.

Thus, although the novel's characters actively seek compensation or restitution through language—from Walter's name-based attempts at salvation, to Toby's own increasing technical expertise—Sterne unfailingly depicts these attempts as futile. Ross King argues that a "procedure of textual compensation for bodily loss testifies to a specific view of the powers and uses of language,"[54] which is ultimately one of unreliable potential. He is moreover correct to assert that in *Tristram Shandy*, "bodily impuissance is not repaired by language but reduplicated in it," as the text proves subject to multiple moments of what King cleverly calls "linguistic invirility."[55] The linkage of sex and language suffuses the entire novel, their destructive relationship never more apparent than in Toby Shandy's case—as I will discuss in the fourth section with regards to his amors with the Widow Wadman.

It is perhaps appropriate now to reposition the relationship between trauma and the failure of language to express that trauma, particularly given that many critics have argued for Toby's effeminacy in part based upon his inability to express himself through language. However, this is to locate the incongruity between disability and language in the body seeking access, rather than the linguistic system itself. This misidentification points to one of the major problems in conceptualizing disability both socially and historically—the tendency to place fault with the tangible body, rather than the discursive structures that confer the epithet of "disability" or the philosophical and social infrastructures that define bodily normativity. Moreover, given that the post-traumatic experience is constructed around a crisis of "[articulating] the story that cannot be fully captured in *thought, memory,* and *speech,*" we note a significant problem with using an inherently unstable language structure to explore unstable experiences.[56] The very nature of trauma as that which resists integration with conventional narrative structures requires the adaptation to new structures, new methods of telling and being.

While the problem of language in *Tristram Shandy* is a predicament for all of its characters, for Toby Shandy, it is a crisis of insufficiency. Through physical pain to trauma and even to desire, language fails Toby in the most intimate of ways. As a disabled man, Toby is subject to multiple linguistic failures in dimensions beyond the comic. I suggest that Sterne provides a unique solution to this failure in the form of his hobby-horse, "An hobby-horse well worth giving a description of."[57]

(I V)

As Walter and his brother await news of the birth of Walter's second son—the narrator Tristram, of course—Walter becomes aware that Toby does not follow his philosophizing ramble on Lockean notions of man and his mind. As Walter finishes yet another set piece (which New tells us is practically verbatim from Locke's *Essay*), Toby exclaims, "You puzzle me to death!"[58] Walter is understandably vexed, as the narrator laments the loss of what could have been a great "discourse upon TIME and ETERNITY . . . a discourse devoutly to be wished for."[59] However, Toby's mind (or attention span) cannot process these thoughts; his head is likened to a "smoak-jack," in which "the funnel [was] unswept, and the ideas whirling round and round in it, all obfuscated and darkened over with fuliginous matter."[60] While this description jests at Walter's philosophizing, Locke, and the bumbling dynamic between the two brothers, it is also a notable description of Toby's self-declared mental state in a period of his life before the bowling-green is up and running. Where Walter likens the human ability to process thoughts to the heat radiating from a candle, Toby declares his own thought process to be more like the wild, unconfined, and smoky heat of a roasting spit which hasn't been cleaned in quite some time. This characterization of his mind as chaotic, formless, and overwhelmed with sensation at the cost of coherence evokes the emotional and psychic symptoms of trauma, and moreover attests to the lingering aftereffects of his infamous wound. The ideas of disarray and filth that the above image generates are more than comic metaphor; they are attributes of a man incapable of relating to his own mind. Now in the Shandy family, sanity is admittedly an unproductive conceit; however, descriptive passages such as this make clear the extent of the mental and emotional damage that accompany Toby's physical damage. Given the disruption of memory and mental coherence that trauma can occasion, this passage cannot be dismissed as merely the source for a unique epithet for an addled older man. Furthermore, the fact that this response is tied to an explicitly Lockean discussion affirms the linkage between Toby's trauma and his untenable relationship with certain kinds of language.

Sterne gives his readers practically no information at all about Toby Shandy before his injury. Aside from a few war stories told intermittently for sentimental value (which themselves usually focus on someone's movement out of the category of able-bodiedness),[61] we know little about Toby as an able-bodied man. Most critics have therefore assumed that Toby's "smoak-jack" mind has been a characteristic constant, that he has always been a little fuzzy around the edges. My contention is that fuzziness or no, the combination of explicit incoherence of thought (as in the cited passage above and several others) and repeatedly articulated frustration with communication in Volumes I and II of the novel can be productively assessed as manifestations of trauma.

Toby's disabling injury is a common enough sort as far as battle-wounds go, although in typically Shandean fashion, it is the rock and not the cannonball that does the wounding: Tristram recounts the injury as "a blow from a stone, broke off by a ball from the parapet of horn-work at the siege of Namur which struck full upon my uncle Toby's groin."[62] He further explains that "unspeakable miseries" which Toby endured for four years altogether were caused by "a succession of exfoliations from the *oss pubis*, and the outward edge of that part of the *coxendix* called the *oss illeum*,—both which bones were dismally crush'd."[63] Despite this seemingly precise description, however, Melvyn New notes that the anatomical chart Sterne likely consulted in *Chambers' Cyclopaedia* "makes clear that the wound site is as close as possible to the groin without a direct hit." [64] This evasion of anatomical specificity through the careful manipulation of terminology obfuscates the part of the body being discussed, and consequently negates the possibility of the reader physically grounding Toby's injury. Thus, Toby's "lameness" is intentionally undefined and un-locatable, rendering him subject to the kind of dislocation from speech that Scarry and Cavell discuss. While Sterne prevents the reader from knowing the precise location of Toby's injury, Toby's traumatic experience prevents him from communicating that location. To evoke Cavell's concept, the reader can neither know nor acknowledge Toby's pain. Without even this superficial referent, the exact nature of Toby's injury remains a much speculated-about mystery: an ambiguity that only points to Sterne's deliberate embodiment of Toby's disability as traumatic and life-altering. Tristram himself elucidates a drastic character shift subsequent to the injury—Toby's development of a "most extream and unparall'd modesty of nature" which "stood eternal sentry on his feelings."[65]

As indicated by Sterne's articulation of modesty as a "sentry on [Toby's] feelings," this modesty is most often manifested as avoidance of confrontation or stressful situations: avoidance he accomplishes not through speech or even silence, but through gesture or wordless vocalization—most commonly, the whistling of Lillabulero and the smoking of his pipe. Toby reverts to the whistling of Lillabulero in difficult emotional situations, such Dr. Slop's post-injury reading of the excommunication text, or his own advances on the Widow's domain.[66] This substitution of non-verbal sound for speech—a signifying vocalization that ultimately becomes readable to his family members—is another unique adaptation to exile from language. The recourse to his "social pipe,"[67] too, becomes a method of avoiding conflict and a way of communicating certain emotions through the manipulation of objects—a companion behavior to his hobby-horse. He may have never been a philosophizing mastermind like his brother or a gifted author like his nephew, but the rupture of his relationship with language is explicitly linked to the disabling injury which occasioned such "modesty."

This rupture and the subsequent failure of language become painfully clear during Toby's convalescence. As he lies recuperating in Shandy Hall, he is frequently asked to recount the traumatic experience to the many household guests, an enterprise with questionable success. While Tristram writes, "The history of a soldier's wound beguiles the pain of it;—my uncle's visitors at least thought so," the very phrasing of that sentiment indicates that these forced retellings, while "infinitely kind" in intention, proved unhelpful and even painful.[68] During the course of these recitations, Toby becomes increasingly agitated: recitation multiplies to repetition, and repetition forces re-experience. This recurrent retelling of Toby's injury thus "[brings] him into some unforeseen perplexities" as he finds that he is unable to recall the details of the event with the exactitude he prefers.[69] Language in *Tristram Shandy* is rapidly proven to be insufficient, and even dangerous, in an attempt to express felt pain. Indeed, if to attempt a retelling of the traumatic experience is to essentially re-experience that event, failed communication is understandably damaging.[70] Toby is caught in a crisis of expression:

> [T]he many perplexities Toby was in, arose out of the almost insurmountable difficulties he found in telling his story intelligibly, and giving such clear ideas of the difference and distinctions between scarp and counterscarp, ---- the glacis and covered way, ---- the half-moon and ravelin, ---- as to make his company fully comprehend where and what he was about.[71]

What becomes clear in this passage is that the concern is not merely with the specificity of details, but with the value of those details to the conveyance of the narrative of the injury, to the explication of the origin of bodily trauma. Military terminology, and the exact names and technical definitions of the objects around him at the moment of injury, provide vital signposts for Toby's self-narrative. Moreover, while the geographic details are, strictly speaking, unnecessary to a summary recounting of the battle, Toby's attempts to situate his memory require the specificity of context and content.[72] Unfortunately for Toby, the intelligibility he seeks seems impossible, as the traumatic memory of his injury remains unintegrated into his narrative memory, and consequently, absent from Sterne's narrative. Without access to a reliable method of communication, Toby's pain remains formless and incomprehensible, and trauma confines his disabled body to that "obfuscated and darkened" state of being.

Sterne here astutely exposes a problem with language in relation to trauma and disability: in some cases, it is not that the right words cannot be found to express the traumatic experience, but that linguistic communication is unsuitable to convey an experience that, as Scarry has long argued, lies at least partially outside the valence of language. Rather than constructing Toby's inability to recapture the traumatic event as memory loss or the result of some personal defect of mental ability or personality, Sterne insists that Toby's problem is "the unsteady uses of words which have ever perplexed the clearest and most exalted understandings."[73] This suggests not merely a problem of usage, but an intrinsic "unsteadiness" of language—the instability of which only further problematizes its relationship with disabled bodies. As we notice, along with James Kim, that "Sterne destabilizes "the equality of words to things," playing with "disproportion[s] between form and substance, writing and matter," [74] we see a pattern through the entire novel that reveals the author's investment in complicating the capacity of language to mean and to bear substantial relationship to that which it purports to describe.[75] As hinted earlier, this mismatch is particularly exclusionary for disabled bodies already outside the discursive matrix of cultural normativity. Linguistic instability only undermines their access to shared systems of meaning.[76]

Toby's appropriation of models and things, then, is a search for meaning outside of language. The individual pieces of his battle recreations become signifying objects upon which to affix the expression of pain; each object becomes a stand-in for that missing referent in the equation of experienced pain. His initial foray in the search for other methods of expression leads him to maps, which Sterne describes in the language of pain relief: "If he could purchase such a thing, and have it pasted down upon a board, as a large map of Namur, with its environs, it might be a means of giving him ease."[77] While this map provides some relief for Toby in the form of guidance towards previously unanswerable questions, including the ability to pinpoint the exact location where his injury was received, this single object itself proves insufficient. Toby then begins to scour books and manuscripts for geographical details about Namur and other battle sites, "carefully collating therewith the histories of their sieges, their demolitions, their improvements, and their new works," a course of research that for a time allows him to "forget himself, his wound, his confinement, [and] his dinner."[78]

Yet this continued engagement with language, a medium that has already failed as a way of communicating Toby's trauma, impedes the healing process. Tristram relates that the "close and painful application to the subject at hand . . . did my uncle *Toby's* wound, upon his groin, no good."[79] While his rapid accumulation of research material temporarily brings Toby "intense application and delight," the second and third year of his convalescence see him acquiring books at an alarming rate, poring through them in a desperate attempt to find the next piece of information. Tristram laments, "No sooner was my uncle Toby satisfied which road the cannon-ball did not go, but he was insensibly led on, and resolved in his mind to enquire and find out which road the ball did go." Reading becomes an endless "labyrinth" of knowledge, a "thorny and bewildered track" that only causes more pain.[80] Reading explodes in the text as a viable possibility, with the passage ending in heated blood, evaporated spirits, and wasted animal strength.[81] It is only the ultimate rejection of language as a vehicle capable of expressing Toby's trauma that allows both physical and mental healing to begin.

> Trim makes the suggestion to bring the imagined spaces and objects of
> the map to physical life: I think . . . that these ravelins, bastions, curtins,

and horn-works make but a poor, contemptible, fiddle faddle piece of work of it here upon paper, compared to what your Honour and I could make of it, were we in the country by ourselves, and had but a rood, or a rood and a half of ground to do what we pleased with.[82]

In this proposition, Toby's traumatized body can physically inhabit that psychic space of memory, without trying—and failing—to tell his story through the inaccessible medium of text. The ability to exist among the physical presence of objects is an important element of these objects' communicative potential for Toby. If, to quote Bessel Van Der Kolk, "only after [a traumatic experience] is placed in a meaningful context can inferences and suppositions about the meaning of the event be made," then for Toby, this large-scale recreation of these battles is that meaningful context. [83] The ability to touch, to feel, to rearrange, and to walk amongst tangible space makes the meaning of Toby's narrative accessible in a way that language cannot.

As part of his creation of a meaningful context, Toby uses those models as the basis for his new form of communication, as a kind of ideogram with physical dimensions. The corporeality of these objects is key, given that his deployment of these objects is dependent upon his physical interaction with them and the way in which body and object function as a unit. Much like the movement of the pipe, which carries with it a series of meanings that convey Toby's emotional state, the positioning and repositioning of the models and objects are the discrete components with which Toby relates the narrative of injury. Thus, the pipe and these objects come to serve a sort of prosthetic function; they substitute or augment parts of Toby's body to facilitate an action or set of actions his own body cannot accomplish. For a disabled man, this substitution of different parts of the body in the speech act can be an effective adjustment to communication in an oral or written culture—for example, "hand" comes to serve the function of "mouth" in Deaf communities. Moreover, the adoption of an intermediary object—a pipe, a trowel, a scale model—is a way of artificially producing the speech act in a situation or set of circumstances under which conventionally corporeal means are impossible, physically or otherwise. While Toby has not lost the physical power of speech, he has lost the connection with the signifying aspect of speech that allows him express that which is most valuable to him. In this way, the models become more than accessories or toys, and the bowling-green more than the "magic universe"[84] of delusion within which Toby shelters from a reality which critics almost unilaterally assume to exist outside of the Shandean universe.[85] As Briggs explains, "reality is not objects, but the play of the mind over objects, and mental amplitude, a variety of attitudes of postures toward those elusive objects, is the fullness of life."[86] The value of these scale models in a meaningful paradigm of human experience is whatever Toby decides it is. The fact that Toby is able to make those objects bear meaning in such a way as to communicate that which cannot be communicated through words is a remarkable recapturing of that "fullness of life" which his injury had so long denied to him.

Jonathan Lamb, in a handy study of the early modern warfare technologies that Sterne employed in the creation of Toby's hobby-horse, makes a suggestion about the significance of warfare that bears particular weight in this argument. If the construction and reconstruction of military structures in warfare creates what Lamb formulates as a "dialectic of ruin and rebuilding,"[87] then the communicative potential of wartime objects that never exist in an unchanging state is crucially different from the communicative value of language, which at least theoretically has an established consistency within major parameters (in the Lockean model, that is). This articulation of warfare and its associated "accoutrements" as necessarily an ongoing cycle of destruction and rebuilding has important ramifications for technology's ability to make meaning for disabled subjects. If an able body is one which largely exists (at least for a time) in a state of contiguous wholeness, then a disabled body is one that is constantly negotiating with its own fractures and gaps. Socially rendered to be persistently aware of its own lack of wholeness, as well as the accompanying pain that these fractures sometimes bring, the disabled body is consistently obliged to "rebuild" from "ruins." Lamb also points to something intrinsic about these artifacts of war which Toby's experience reveals to the reader: "As minds and bodies are spoilt within these defensive works, themselves emblems of ruins remade, so they are to some degree healed and restored by them."[88] Toby's recreation of these objects and his inhabitance of the space among them, in conjunction with his appropriation of their meaning-making potential, begins the healing process.

While Toby's hobby-horse is usually discussed as part of his recuperative process, it also plays a key role in his late-blooming amors, the subject of the narrative cycle with which Sterne ends the novel. As Tristram explains it, Toby's lop-sided affair with the Widow Wadman is "one of the most compleat systems, both of the elementary and practice part of love and love-making, that ever was addressed to the world."[89] As "compleat" as Tristram claims his narration is, however, he evades a definition of love and retreats behind a number of textual digressions.[90] Now, while a love story does not require a foundational definition of its subject, to call attention to the fact that the subject is in some way undefinable (or that the author is for vague reasons unwilling to define it) is to link love to the same paradigm of inexpressibility as Toby's pain and injury. This love affair is moreover especially Shandean: although frequently bawdy in the details, the vignettes of Toby's amors are framed with that blend of sweet earnestness and satire that Sterne reserves for much of his romantic discourse, as uncomfortable as he is with allowing sentiment to exist alone in the text.[91] Consequently, the story of his uncle's love affair becomes articulated as a matter of pathos, more so than romance—as Tristram proposes, "pity be akin to love."[92] While critics have interpreted Sterne's tone and Toby's repeated retreat to the bowling-green during the affair as indicative of sexual impotence or effeminacy, this reading does not sufficiently accommodate the facets of Toby's disability. Rather, Toby's affair with the Widow Wadman re-emphasizes both the emotional importance and the occasional insufficiency of his hobby-horse as a means of communication.

By the time Toby's amors with the Widow commence, he has become reliant upon his hobby-horse and its associated language as means of expressing deep emotion, typically emotions surrounding suffering. However, while his hobby-horse functions successfully as a method of conveying the experience of pain and the interior narrative of injury, it is insufficiently equipped to express other complex private emotions. Toby is perfectly capable of casual conversation and even sentimental speeches, but he is incapable of responding to propositions of romantic love through conventional speech. Now, although love and pain in the Shandean sense have a great deal in common, as Tristram often imbues his vignettes with shades of both, they are not the same thing. That which enables Toby to incorporate and express narratives of pain only confounds his ability to negotiate the experience of love.

Thus, the central problem in this affair is the anticipated barrier of language, which we notice initially as a lack of language. Toby's would-be-lover is, in Tristram's words, the most "concupiscible" woman imaginable.[93] Yet despite the author's purported admiration of her physical qualities, there are no words to describe what his readers will "covet"—there is only a blank page.[94] That blank page upon which Tristram entreats the reader to sketch out his own mistress in order to better picture the Widow stands for that fundamental problem of inexpressibility. By disavowing words in favor of an image—at the moment, a nonexistent one—Sterne models Toby's own discomfort with language. Toby is incapable of expressing desire in words, and so, too, are the readers as we stand in his place. Sterne moreover employs these vocabularies of lack in origin of their relationship: when the Treaty of Utrecht disrupts Toby's re-enactments, thereby suspending his mode of communication, "a vacancy"[95] is created that gives the Widow an opportunity to make her move. The insufficiency of language in this relationship—for Sterne, for Toby, and for the reader—not only obscures emotion, but nearly erases it. The repeated conceits of emptiness and of blankness surrounding Toby's romantic emotions underscore the incompatibility of those emotions with his hobby-horse; just as Toby cannot cogently express love, neither can the text. Unless Toby is able to conduct the affair with the Widow through his hobby-horse, his emotions will remain inexpressible.

Ultimately, it is the Widow who finds a way to use Toby's hobby-horse as the intermediary in their burgeoning relationship. Given that Toby admittedly does not know the right end of a woman from the wrong end, it is only fitting that the she be the active pursuer. Her advances are those of an attacking general, and her attention-seeking forays are in explicitly ballistic terms, as she "endeavor[s] to blow . . . Toby up in the very sentry-box itself."[96] While this use of military idiom places the Widow's actions in parallel with Toby's, it is important to remember that it is Tristram, and not the Widow, who uses that language: which is to say that we should refrain from giving her the credit of fully participating in Toby's communicative scheme, and thereby implying a greater degree of interpersonal connection than exists between these two characters. The Widow is, however, perceptive enough to realize the necessity of engaging with the components of his hobby-horse in such a way as to make her part of his perceptual paradigm. She does so by physically interacting with his objects of communication: her earliest efforts at conversation are initiated by "[taking] hold of the map" of Dunkirk, an action through which "Toby's passions were sure to catch fire"[97] and incite an immediate reaction. Her contact with the map always elicits his simultaneous contact with map; by touching the map, the Widow creates a common referent.

This is problematic, of course, because her presence in and around his sentry-box disrupts the integrity of his physical space—a space where geographical sanctity of a sort is central to its healing function. The importance of preserving the bowling-green in a particular condition—whether pre- or post-siege—has been noted before. His dear companion Trim has occasionally violated the sanctity of Toby's models to the latter's great distress, sometimes by damaging the models, and other times by manipulating them on his own. In addition to her uninvited corporeal presence on the bowling-green and in his sentry-box, the Widow's actions breach Toby's "meaningful context" in other ways. Her physical contact with the map is only a ploy to enable physical contact with his finger, hand, and leg, as she attempts to pull Toby from his scheme of objects-as-communication into her love-making scheme of bodies-as-communication, a mode with which Toby has little to no familiarity.[98] The Widow is not participating in Toby's communicative paradigm in an attempt to understand his narrative or to reach a sort of deeper connection, but to exploit the limits of that model in an effort to achieve her own ends.

During the course of this affair, an additional flaw in the communicative potential of Toby's hobby-horse appears. While the bowling-green itself is an imitative recreation of past and current battles, it seems that Toby cannot continue his productions without some corresponding physical battle occurring elsewhere.[99] In this way, the conceptualization of objects as a type of extra-linguistic communication is more closely tied to the conventional structure of language than previously understood—these objects, signs of something else, still need that symbolized "real" behind them in order to be comprehensible. The peace of Utrecht and subsequent "surfeit of sieges"[100] generate a crisis of articulation, the models falter as vehicles of communication, and Toby retreats into a confused silence: "STILLNESS, with SILENCE at her back . . . drew their gauzy mantle over my uncle Toby's head; ---- and LISTLESSNESS, with her lax fibre and undirected eye, sat quietly down beside him in his arm chair."[101] With his avenue of communication disrupted, Toby is once again beset by apathy, lethargy, and incoherence. The environment he created to accommodate his disability is no longer viable. Briggs gets at part of this gap in Toby's communicative potential when he suggests that the disruption of his hobby-horse "necessitates finding a new fantasy to structure his life [and so] he promptly "falls in love" with Widow Wadman."[102] However, rather than consider Toby's relationship with the Widow as a replacement fantasy or another retreat from an unbearable reality, we should think of their interactions as indicative of the limits of his mode of communication. If Toby is only capable of expressing himself when he can communicate his emotions through objects, then a change in those objects and their communicative potential is understandably disruptive.

One might suggest that the Widow Wadman's arrival in the story signals a sort of conclusion to Toby's recovery or that his eventual proposal of marriage indicates that the models have done their trick and brought Toby fully out of his traumatic lapse—a suggestion with which I heartily disagree. Aside from the fact that Toby's marriage proposal is followed immediately by a reading of the Biblical siege of Jericho[103] (a retreat to his system of emotional support), the Widow's direct inquiry about the state of his sexual organs—"And whereabouts, dear Sir . . . did you receive this sad blow?"—is answered on the map of the siege of Namur.[104] However, as the Widow cannot descry the answer to her question through Toby's hobby-horse, she continues to push the matter linguistically, to Toby's great confusion. As the narrative comes to a close in Volume IV, the obsession with the disabled body only escalates. While Toby's disability comes under increasing scrutiny, the textual peculiarities which replace insufficient language in the novel proliferate: the missing chapters XVIII and XIX; the heavily redacted (or never written) introduction to chapter XX; the sudden shift in typeface, format, and syntax for "The Eighteenth Chapter" and "Chapter the Nineteenth"; the edited conclusion to chapter XXVIII; and an uptick in idiosyncratic en and em dashes. Where Toby's hobby-horse is largely absent, linguistic coherence practically vanishes from the text. Still, there is hope for the future of Toby's bowling-green: as Toby marches off to make his proposal to the Widow, Mrs. Shandy suggests, "I dare say . . . [he and Trim] are making fortifications [on the Widow's lawn]."[105] This is a suggestion to which Walter objects, but which the reader suspects might certainly come to pass at some point in the future.

Furthermore, critical assumption of the "death," as it were, of Toby's hobby-horse neglects two essential truths about the novel. Firstly, *Tristram Shandy* avowedly has no interest in progression without digression, or in ends of any kind (other than that of a woman). This is not a book with a conclusion, or even a gesture at conclusion. The amors of Toby and Widow Wadman are themselves incompletely told, as we never learn the answer to the Widow's burning question regarding her future husband's amatory capacity. In fact, for all of the speculation around sex and childbirth, there is no confirmation that a marriage actually occurs. The narrative of their relationship, as far as Tristram is concerned, exists solely within the process of falling in love—the aftermath of their relationship is ultimately insignificant. Secondly, the journey of healing or recovery in the novel is rarely an upward one, and never a complete one. Tristram slowly dies across all nine volumes, as beauty fades from the world around him and blood flows from his body like ink from a pen. The novel itself is vast enactment of nostalgia, told about a past we know to be long gone; the figures of Uncle Toby and the Widow Wadman, so lovingly rendered, are dust by the time Tristram is putting pen to paper. Toby's movement from the darkness and inexpressibility of trauma to the possibility of communication is just one example of the recursive motion on which the novel thrives.

(V)

An intrinsic fact of disability is that it is a chronic, identity-altering, as well as identity-forming condition. Disability is a state of being that does not revert to an idealized, original able-bodiedness. Toby's injury has left him with a permanent limp and likely a few problems with the pipes: physical differences that cannot be "revised" or "fixed." The narrative beauty of the experience of that injury and the resultant trauma is the creation of his enduring hobby-horse, a series of enactments and objects that remain one of the most striking concepts in *Tristram Shandy*. Sterne is clearly invested in conceptualizing language as incompatible with certain essential human experiences and modes of being, among which are trauma and disability. In the case of Toby Shandy, language is an insufficient means of engaging with his past and present experiences. Only through his hobby-horse is Toby able to create a context in which to express that story that "must be told" and to build a world in which he does not need to be defined against able-bodiedness. It is also in this recognition of the insufficiency of language that contemporary disability studies have the potential to move forward. As Sterne's novel suggests, there are fundamental ways in which conventional modes of communication are inherently incapable of representing or conveying the experience of disability. By locating this failure of representation in the text rather than within the disabled body, critics can move beyond reading disability in literature as an oppositional binary of dis/ability.

Still, Toby's linkage to Shakespeare's motley fool is undeniable. Just as the mottled pages can represent the incoherence and confusion of his traumatic experience, they also stand for the charming eccentricity of his character. Easily flustered, childlike, and possessing an "extream and unparall'd modesty of nature," Toby cannot be said to represent any sort of heroic transcendence of disability.[106] Disability in the sense of impairment is not a novelty in this text, nor does it fall outside the boundaries of normative physicality in a family where all men have some notable physical flaw. To evoke the oft-quoted and rarely inappropriate reminder that "nothing was well hung" in the Shandy family, is it clear that reading Sterne's deployment of extra-linguistic communicative possibilities in Toby's healing process cannot be entirely "straight," so to speak. This revolutionary experiment is ultimately simply that: a masterful experiment that plays with the limits of language and the boundless potential for human communication in alternative modes. Nevertheless, as I hope this review has shown, Toby's character is clearly more than the motley fool, more than the effeminate and beloved figure of Hazlitt's approbation. His legendary hobby-horse transcends play and reenactment to become something greater.

James Kim asserts that Toby's "remasculinizing project proves delectably self-defeating in that it places him on a field of manly valor that is quite literally diminished," but to make such a claim is to misread the ontological importance of that reproduced "field of manly valor."[107] Rather than a pitiable nostalgia for days gone by that allows the emasculated veteran to re-enact his glory days of virility and wholeness (a position that unfortunately all too many critics have taken on Toby's hobby-horse), this "field of manly valor" is a location of healing and bodily recuperation. As Cathy Caruth writes, "The traumatized, we might say, carry an impossible history within them, or they become themselves the symptom of a history that they cannot entirely possess," a history that must be incorporated in a meaningful way for the process of healing to begin.[108] The recreation of these battle scenes, the creation of physical spaces and objects that bear reference to the experience of trauma, prove to be the only means of communicating that traumatic experience for Toby Shandy. In replacing language with this material world, Toby rejects the inexpressible legacy of Philoctetes and reshapes his social context, for a time, to accommodate his disability.

Notes

1. Felicity Nussbaum, *The Limits of the Human: Fictions of Anomaly, Race, and Gender in the Long Eighteenth Century* (Cambridge: Cambridge University Press, 2003), 106.

2. However, a good deal of criticism has essentially relied upon such synecdoche.

3. While Fielding wrote of his nose-less Amelia in 1751, a few decades before the first volume of *Tristram Shandy* appeared in print, Fielding's heroine both hides and (mysteriously) overcomes her disability—it ceases to be an identifying factor in her characterization by the end of the novel. The disabilities of Sterne's characters, on the contrary, do not disappear.

4. Sterne to John Hall-Stevenson, Toulouse, 19 October 1762, in *Letters of Laurence Sterne*, ed. Lewis Perry Curtis (Oxford: Oxford University Press, 1965), 186.

5. *The Complete Works of William Hazlitt in Twenty-One Volumes*, ed. P.P. Howe, vol. 6 (London: J.M. Dent and Sons, Ltd., 1931), 121.

6. One of the more egregious offenders might be Henri Fluchère, who scathingly writes of "Toby's hobby-horse, that beneficent chimera whose total and childlike absurdity shelters him from the hostility of fate and the dangers of ratiocination." Henri Fluchère, *Laurence Sterne: from Tristram to Yorick: an interpretation of Tristram Shandy*, trans. Barbara Bay (New York: Oxford University Press, 1965), 140.

7. Chinmoy Bannerjee, "Tristram Shandy and the Association of Ideas," *Texas Studies in Literature and Language* 15, no. 4 (1974): 706.

8. Laurence Sterne, "*The Life and Opinions of Tristram Shandy, Gentleman,* edited by Melvyn New (London: Penguin Books, 2003), 8.19.511.

9. David M. Turner, *Disability in Eighteenth-Century England: Imagining Physical Impairment.* (New York: Routledge, 2012), 11.

10. "Disability" and "Disabled," in Samuel Johnson, *Dictionary of the English Language*, 3rd ed., vol. 2 (London: W. Strahan, 1765).

11. The term "veteran" in the modern sense (which is primarily applied to a former serviceman) is somewhat anachronistic; in the eighteenth century, the word usually signified what we consider a secondary connotation—a man of long military service or long experience in any field. The *Oxford English Dictionary*, 2nd ed. (Oxford: Oxford University Press, 1989) identifies a 1758 *Idler* essay in which Samuel Johnson uses the term to refer to a military man with lengthy service; at the very least, writers in the second half of the century used the term comparably to our own usage. The definition in Samuel Johnson, *Dictionary* confines the term to the same meaning: "long practiced in war; long experienced."

12. Turner, *Disability in Eighteenth-Century England*, 20. See Sterne, *Tristram Shandy*, 1.25.68 for Sterne's nearly identical phrase.

13. Turner, *Disability in Eighteenth-Century England*, 77.

14. There are of course, notable exceptions: Fielding's Amelia, whose injury is most certainly acquired, is described as deformed. Henry Fielding, *Amelia* (London: A. Millar, 1752) 1:95.

15. This distinction was also tied to a differentiation between injured servicemen and injured laymen in the eyes of the law. As Turner discusses, servicemen were eligible for a national pension until 1679 as compensation for their service to Queen and country. Even after the law lapsed, the social notion of difference persisted (Turner, *Disability in Eighteenth-Century England*, 21).

16. Turner, *Disability in Eighteenth-Century England*, 77.

17. Turner, *Disability in Eighteenth-Century England*, 80.

18. Although, as mentioned previously, it was more common in general parlance to use the phrase "disabled" when referring to servicemen. "Lame" and "crippled" were terms more common in reference to laity and in fiction.

19. Turner, *Disability in Eighteenth-Century England*, 33.

20. Turner, *Disability in Eighteenth-Century England*, 33.

21. See Sterne, *Tristram Shandy*, 2.5.84, 7.26.526, and 9.5.551. Trim, however, who has a bad left leg, is referred to as "lame" twice as many times throughout the novel.

22. See especially Book IV, Baldassare Castiglione, *The Book of the Courtier*, translated by Charles S. Singleton (Garden City, NY: Doubleday, 1959).

23. "Of Deformity," in *The Major Works*, Francis Bacon. (Oxford: Oxford University Press, 2008), 426.

24. Bacon, *Major Works*, 426.

25. Bacon, *Major Works*, 426.

26. Lennard J. Davis, "Dr. Johnson, Amelia, and the Discourse of Disability in the Eighteenth Century," in *Defects: Engendering the Modern Body*, edited by Helen Deutsch and Felicity Nussbaum (Ann Arbor, MI: University of Michigan Press, 2000), 62.

27. Davis, *Defects*, 60.

28. Davis, *Defects*, 62.

29. See, for example, the fainting fit of the old wounded soldier in Henry Mackenzie, *The Man of Feeling* (London: T. Cadell, 1771), 199.

30. A conceit that Sterne plays with by naming the Shandean small nose a birth defect; while certainly a physical peculiarity, a flat nose by no means qualified as a defect in the same way club foot or dwarfism did.

31. Simon Dickie, "Hilarity and Pitilessness in Mid-Eighteenth Century: English Jestbook Humor," *Eighteenth-Century Studies* 37, no. 1 (2003): 1–22.

32. Roger Lund, "Laughing at Cripples: Ridicule, Deformity, and the Argument from Design," *Eighteenth-Century Studies* 39, no. 1 (2005): 91–114.

33. "She was not . . . remarkably handsome; being very short, and rather too corpulent in body, and somewhat red, with the addition of pimples in the face. Her nose was likewise too large, and her eyes too little . . . one of her legs was also a little shorter than the other, which occasioned her a limp as she walked" Henry Fielding, *The History and Adventures of Joseph Andrews* (London: A. Millar, 1742), 1:26.

34. Elaine Scarry, *The Body in Pain* (Oxford: Oxford University Press, 1985), 4–5.

35. Scarry, *The Body in Pain*, 5.

36. Stanley Cavell, *Must We Mean What We Say?* (New York: Charles Scribner's Sons, 1969), 245.

37. Cavell, *Must We Mean What We Say?*, 248.

38. I should also note that I invoke this quote not to draw any parallels between all experiences of war and the Holocaust, but rather, because I believe Laub's words perfectly capture the essence of Toby's dilemma.

39. Dori Laub, "Truth and Testimony: The Process and the Struggle," in *Trauma: Explorations in Memory*, edited by Cathy Caruth (Baltimore: Johns Hopkins University Press, 1995), 63.

40. I do, however, find Melvyn New's argument for a determinacy governing *Tristram Shandy* a convincing one. See "Sterne and the Narrative of Determinateness," *Eighteenth-Century Fiction* 4, no. 4 (1992): 315–29.

41. Kai Erickson, "Notes on Trauma and Community," in *Trauma: Explorations in Memory*, edited by Cathy Caruth (Baltimore: Johns Hopkins University Press, 1995), 183.

42. Erickson, "Notes on Trauma and Community," 183.

43. Sterne, *Tristram Shandy*, 2.1.75.

44. Peter Briggs, "Locke's Essay and the Tentativeness of Tristram Shandy," *Studies in Philology* 82, no. 4 (1985): 493.

45. Alexis Tadié, *Sterne's Whimsical Theatres of Language: Orality, Gesture, Literacy.* (Aldershot, England: Ashgate, 2003), 4.

46. John Locke, *An Essay Concerning Human Understanding 4th ed.*. edited by Peter H. Nidditch. (Oxford: Clarendon Press, 1975), 3.9.5.

47. Sterne, *Tristram Shandy*, 2.12.99.

48. This linguistic confusion, moreover, comes about because the subject of this conversation would be best understood in physical space. Given that Toby is unable to demonstrate that physical space to Walter at the moment, he must make do with such words as he can.

49. Briggs, "Locke's Essay and the Tentativeness of Tristram Shandy," 497.

50. For example, Alexis Tadié in particular writes on this subject.

51. Tadié, *Sterne's Whimsical Theatres of Language*, 9.

52. Cf. Briggs for additional thoughts on Sterne's appositive rhetorical strategies.

53. New, "Sterne and the Narrative of Determinateness," 322. His notes to the Florida edition are his most comprehensive study on the matter, and have been of invaluable assistance to my own work.

54. Ross King, "Tristram Shandy and the Wound of Language," *Studies in Philology* 92, no. 3 (1995): 293.

55. King, "Tristram Shandy and the Wound of Language," 294.

56. Laub, "Truth and Testimony," 63.

57. Sterne, *Tristram Shandy*, 1.24.68.

58. Sterne, *Tristram Shandy*, 2.28.172.

59. Sterne, *Tristram Shandy*, 3.28.172.

60. Sterne, *Tristram Shandy*, 3.29.172–73.

61. Cf the narrative of Le Fevre. Sterne, *Tristram Shandy*, 6.6–10.375–85.

62. Sterne, *Tristram Shandy*, 1.21.60.

63. Sterne, *Tristram Shandy*, 1.25.69.

64. Notes to Laurence Sterne, *Tristram Shandy*, ed. Melvyn New (London: Penguin, 2003), 619.

65. Sterne, *Tristram Shandy*, 1.21.59 and 6.28.411, respectively.

66. Sterne, 3.10.153 and 9.16.564, respectively.

67. Sterne, *Tristram Shandy*, 1.21.56.

68. Sterne, *Tristram Shandy*, 1.25.69.

69. Sterne, *Tristram Shandy*, 1.25.69.

70. Bessel A. Van der Kolk and Onno Van der Hart, "The Intrusive Past: The Flexibility of Memory and The Engraving of Trauma," in *Trauma: Explorations in Memory*, edited by Cathy Caruth (Baltimore: Johns Hopkins University Press, 1995), 177.

71. Sterne, *Tristram Shandy*, 2.1.74.

72. As Cavell explains, "with a sensation [such as pain] . . . the criterion of identity, that is in terms of which various instances count as *one*, is given by a description of it; with other objects—material objects, points?—the criterion may be the identity of location," Cavell, *Must We Mean What We Say?*, 242.

73. Sterne, *Tristram Shandy*, 2.1.78—a claim which he is also making about language in general.

74. James Kim, "'good cursed, bouncing losses': Masculinity, Sentimental Irony, and Exuberance in *Tristram Shandy*," *The Eighteenth Century* 48, no. 1 (2007): 16.

75. Willie Van Peer, in a brief survey of literary paleography, makes an excellent observation about Sterne's disruption of language that informs this instability: "The aim of mutilating linguistic signs as a means of increasing textual reliability . . . is now undermined by bringing it to the textual

surface. . . . The device highlights the instability of textual signs, their embeddedness in human action, in which doubt and uncertainty have by now firmly established themselves. The motive for damaging the sign [in *Tristram Shandy*] has shifted here toward a skeptical function: the central aim of the mutilation is the creation of doubt, geared toward the inadequacy of human knowledge and communication." Willie Van Peer, "Mutilated Signs: Notes toward a Literary Paleography." *Poetics Today* 18, no. 1 (1997): 44.

76. Kim, "good cursed, bounding losses," 16.

77. Sterne, *Tristram Shandy*, 2.1.75.

78. Sterne, *Tristram Shandy*, 2.3.80

79. Sterne, *Tristram Shandy*, 2.3.79.

80. Sterne, *Tristram Shandy*, 2.3.80.

81. Sterne, *Tristram Shandy*, 2.3.81.

82. Sterne, *Tristram Shandy*, 2.5.85

83. Van der Kolk, "The Intrusive Past," 170.

84. Fluchère, *Laurence Sterne*, 140.

85. Recalling the four square miles that constitute the midwife's entire world, I cannot help but suspect that the Shandean universe does not extend far beyond Shandy Hall and the half-acre bowling-green. Sterne, *Tristram Shandy*, 1.7.12.

86. Briggs, "Locke's Essay," 509.

87. Jonathan Lamb, "Sterne, Sebald, and Siege Architecture," *Eighteenth-Century Fiction*, 19, nos. 1–2 (2006): 37.

88. Kim, "good cursed, bouncing losses," 37.

89. Sterne, *Tristram Shandy*, 6.36.420.

90. Sterne, *Tristram Shandy*, 6.37.421–22.

91. I am thinking of the transition between chapters 8 and 9 in volume 9, in which the beautiful sentiment on the transience of life and love, followed by an emotional plea for just one more day, is disrupted by the coarse exclamation, "Now, what the world thinks of that ejaculation ----- I would not give a groat," Sterne, *Tristram Shandy*, 9.8.556.

92. Sterne, *Tristram Shandy*, 6.29.411.

93. Sterne, *Tristram Shandy*, 6.37.422.

94. Sterne, *Tristram Shandy*, 6.37.423.

95. Sterne, *Tristram Shandy*, 7.10.498.

96. Sterne, *Tristram Shandy*, 8.14.502.

97. Sterne, *Tristram Shandy*, 8.14.503.

98. And one which, as Toby's eventual subjugation through the Widow's attacking eye attests, he is particularly vulnerable to.

99. As he explains in his "apologetical oration" in 6.32.414–16.

100. Sterne, *Tristram Shandy*, 6.31.412.

101. Sterne, *Tristram Shandy*, 6.53.419.

102. Briggs, "Locke's Essay," 506.

103. Sterne, *Tristram Shandy*, 9.25.578.

104. Sterne, *Tristram Shandy*, 9.25.580.

105. Sterne, *Tristram Shandy*, 9.11.557.

106. A fact that actually further distances Sterne's depiction of disability from the convention—especially in later sentimental fiction.

107. Kim, "good cursed, bounding losses," 15.

108. Caruth, "Introduction," in *Trauma: Explorations in Memory*, edited by Cathy Caruth (Baltimore: Johns Hopkins University Press, 1995), 5.

6

"ONE CANNOT BE TOO SECURE"

Wrongful Confinement, or, the

Pathologies of the Domestic Economy

Dana Gliserman Kopans

ELIZA HAYWOOD'S *The Distressed Orphan, or Love in a Madhouse* tells the story of Annilia, who is incarcerated in a lunatic asylum by her uncle and guardian because she refuses to marry his son. Horatio "admir'd the Subtilty of his Father in finding out an Expedient which would either oblige [Annilia] to comply with their Desires, or give them, as being next of kin, the Possession of her Estate, her being represented as a Lunatick, and consequently incapable of managing it."[1] As her guardian, Annilia's uncle had control of her property. In order to retain his control when Annilia reached the age of majority, her uncle demands that she either marry his son (giving his son ownership of the estate) or face incarceration in a madhouse, since, as a lunatic, Annilia would not be allowed to control her own property: it would be given to her family to manage for her.[2] Haywood explains that the conditions of Annalia's incarceration "struck so great a Dread into her, that nothing is more strange, than that she did not die with the Fright, or fall into that Disorder of which she was accus'd."[3] In her introduction to *The Distressed Orphan*, Deborah Nestor argues that "the most terrifying aspect of Annilia's situation is not her physical confinement and the state of powerlessness it represents but the danger to her sanity. A similar fear is evident in other literatures representing individuals wrongfully committed to madhouses."[4] While the fear of becoming mad as the result of incarceration in a madhouse was certainly prominent in the literature of wrongful confinement, confinement and the powerlessness of the confined victims are in fact, I would argue, at least as terrifying as the possibility of madness. Confinement threatens not only individual sanity; wrongful confinement signals a danger to the "sanity" of the domestic economy, as Haywood, Daniel Defoe, and others argue—both in the private sphere of the home, and its public, national corollary. Opposed to the safe, sheltered environment of the home, wrongful confinement in the madhouse allows for the victimization of the most vulnerable members of society.

In addition offering madness as a metaphor for a political and legal system which victimizes instead of protecting vulnerable people, and to making the argument that groups of sane people can be—and are—rendered just as powerless as the mad, Haywood's novel is one example of a text which points out the especially problematic status of madness. As Chris Mounsey explains in the introduction to this volume, disability, as a category of analysis, tends to focus at the site of the body. While abilities in their various forms are experienced differently by the individuals who experience them, discussions about them tend to focus on the physical. While Variability, in this volume, requires careful thinking about the body, or, as Mounsey puts it, "thinking through the body,"[5] this conception of it relies on a stable sense of cognitive ability. As Haywood's novel and other writings point out, cognitive ability, and our sense of it, is not always stable. Although the signifiers of disability require work to unpack, the signs of disability are more transparent, and often easier to read. Alexander Pope, to use an example from the introduction, was deformed in a way which was immediately ascertainable to others—except, maybe, to the blind. But mental disability is far more difficult to read: it can be feigned, and it can be imputed to the nondisabled. The anxiety about society's ability to correctly identify the mad intersected, in the eighteenth century, with debates about the therapeutic values and uses of confinement, which was produced alongside the pamphlets and novels in which the madhouse figures.

Whereas scholars interested in the literature representing madness point out the intensity of eighteenth-century interest in madness and the places in which the mad (or those accused of madness) could be confined, historians have largely argued that literature's spectacular treatment of sane people being wrongfully confined was unwarranted by the number of times such cases actually occurred in eighteenth-century Britain.[6] What these different arguments make clear is that the stakes of the issue of wrongful confinement were primarily ideological.[7] The threat that the madhouse represented—a threat both corporeal and economic— was quite real.[8] Legal cases involving allegations of wrongful confinement received dramatic treatment in the popular press.[9] However, as historians have contended, literature overrepresented—at least, in numerical terms—the threat of wrongful confinement. Yet the more accurate, and more limited, history of actual confinement does not account for the cultural anxiety the spectre of wrongful confinement provokes in the eighteenth century. In order to account for both the literary and the literal threat of confinement, we might read the discourse of confinement as one which accounts not only for the situation of those incarcerated within madhouses, but also as one which questions the status of those outside of it. While the mad may have been confined in madhouses, the domestic spaces in which women, children, and others lacking political power lived may, in some ways, have been equally confining and coercive. Discussing the madhouse, then, is a way in which the critiques of Britain's domestic economy may have been carried out, comparing the pathologies of each in relation to the other. As the edifice of the madhouse demonstrates, a well-ordered exterior guarantees nothing about how structures of power function—or fail to function—on the inside.

The system of the domestic economy was threatened both by the mad, who did not contribute and could not be made to conform to rules, and by propertied women, who held a certain independent power. The issue of women's property in the eighteenth century, as Susan Staves has argued, is itself deeply ideological, thoroughly political, and can be understood only in relation to the patriarchal system which enforced the laws surrounding it.[10] While married women's property raised complicated questions both about the nature of marriage and the nature of property, the propertied unmarried woman was, in some senses, even more threatening.[11] The problem with women in control of property was that women who were not under the control of fathers or husbands could seldom be relied upon to correctly transmit the property they controlled. The propertied women functioned as a figure which pointed to a weakness in the patriarchal system: she could act both independently of men (by entering into financial contracts) and contrary to the wishes of her relatives. In holding the property she ought only to have transmitted, the propertied woman complicated the work of the domestic economy.

In those cases in which women held property, unscrupulous relatives could seize both physical and fiscal control of women, as they could in the case of mad people, and neither had easy legal recourse. The cultural production of the home as a safe haven, where vulnerable members of the family were not subject to violence from the world outside, was belied by the discourse of wrongful confinement by greedy relatives, which pointed out the dangers lurking inside of the house. While medical texts—including, for example, Dr William Battie's seminal *A Treatise on Madness*[12]—attempt to establish evidence of confinement's medical efficacy in the treatment of madness, popular literature points to confinement as a travesty of the domestic economy. Arguments against wrongful confinement, however, were not arguments against state authority: on the contrary, polemics against wrongful confinement point out that the state is not intervening enough. With the lack of coherent legal regulations regarding confinement, fears about the breakdown of state authority abroad, on the war-front, echoed fears about the breakdown of paternal authority in the home.[13] The discourse of wrongful confinement points out the consequences of failures of the government, the family, and the medical and legal authorities.

At the beginning of the century, Daniel Defoe connects problems facing familial relationships to problems facing the nation. He expresses a pervasive anxiety about the breakdown of the authority in both the home and in the government. His writings underscore the need for strong male leadership on both fronts. Defoe interrupts *A Review of the State of the English Nation*, dedicated largely to the threat of war, to report the case of a young heiress, declared a lunatic and forcefully confined by her relatives. Defoe hopes that his digression will be "as publickly useful in its Degree, as the other, both to warn the innocent from falling into the Dangers, which Avarice and unnatural Tempers may prepare for them; and a little to caution Persons enclin'd to the same Crimes, that they may avoid the Sin and Shame together."[14] For this didactic purpose, Defoe undertakes "to make a Fact attended with such black and barbarous Circumstances, as publick as possible, in order to expose the Crime."[15] Although Defoe frames the danger to "the innocent" as "avarice and unnatural Tempers," the very "naturalness" of the patriarchal domestic economy—the control that families exercise over women—constitutes the threat. Defoe is not advising women to avoid their families; rather, he is pointing to the dangers women face from the failure of their families to function properly: a failure that Defoe claims is both moral and legal.

Defoe takes the "private" abuses of familial control over women into the public sphere. He demonstrates that women who are disempowered by their families are left vulnerable to the legal and medical systems. The facts of the case on which Defoe reports are, he attests, "plain and open; every thing has been attested in a Court of Justice already; I have Authentick Vouchers to every article, and unquestion'd Authority for the Fact."[16] Defoe publicizes the case as part of an argument to reform the medical profession that he anticipates making to Parliament. This argument begins with Defoe and gains momentum through the first part of the century, resulting in the establishment of a Parliamentary Committee to investigate abuses in madhouses in 1763 and culminating in the passage of the *Act for Regulating Private Madhouses* of 1774.[17]

The letter Defoe publishes purports to contain "a true History of one of the most villainous and most barbarous Actions, that has ever been heard of in a Protestant Country."[18] The young lady's history outlined in the letter, briefly, begins with the death of her father, resulting in her inheritance of a fairly substantial estate. She leaves her family and gives her money to another relation (by marriage) to manage for her, because her mother and two brothers (the elder of whom was the executor of the estate) were unkind to her and she suspects their designs on her portion of the estate. Later uneasy with this arrangement, she asks the relative for either a bond for the money or the money itself, to which the relative replies "*very well, Miss, I'll secure you for that.*"[19] The point here, of course, is precisely that the heiress is not secure at all. Indeed, the reader cannot be certain as to whether the heiress is being offered a legal bond for her money or whether she is being threatened with imprisonment for demanding one. While it is clear that there are problems specific to this family (the loss of the father, the patriarch who had evidently guaranteed order in the family, and the fact that the heiress has control of her own capital, in the absence of a father or husband), the more general problem is that the woman's family and friends, who are supposed to protect her, are the very ones who threaten her.

Shortly after the threat/promise of security, the woman's two brothers and her mother consult an attorney (who is related to the person holding the money) who advises that they petition the Lord Keeper for a Commission of Lunacy against the heiress, giving her relatives control both of her person and her estate. As Defoe describes: "To bring this to pass, great Rewards were given, *as we are inform'd* for Assistants from *Bedlam*, and from a certain infamous Apothecary, but a pretended Doctor for Lunaticks, to get her prov'd a Lunatick, and managed as such."[20] The proceedings, the letter tells us, were suspect, however, in that the attorney suing for the petition on behalf of the family was himself one of the commissioners who granted the petition. In addition, the family of the heiress "made some People, who either did, or *pretended to* belong to her . . . acquaint the said Jury, that she was so *raving Mad*, they could by no means bring her to them."[21] Defoe's concern is not with the mad-doctors but with illegitimate authority: he exposes the pretense of the apothecary and the victim's friends and family in order to point out to his readers that medical practitioners and families acting properly ought to protect their vulnerable charges.

> After hearing testimony, the jury granted the commission without seeing or examining the woman, and the Design being fully ripe, and completed by the rash Verdict of the Jury aforesaid, the rest of the Scene is all Violence and Fury, for these People having provided the proper instruments, come up Stairs to this Gentlewoman into her Chamber . . . seize upon her in a most barbarous manner; hand-cuff her Hands behind

her with Irons; bound her Legs together with Cords, and attempted to
thrust a Hankerchief or Cloth into her Mouth; and in this cruel manner
carried her away by Force, put her into a Coach, and hurried her to one
of our private *Bedlams*.[22]

The failings of the family are thus magnified by social institutions which rely
upon the same power structure that promises women protection but denies
them a voice: the jury pronounces the absent woman mad on the basis of hearsay
evidence. Just as the legal system fails to protect her, the woman is left vulnerable by a medical system which has not established standards in the diagnosis
or treatment of madness, leaving her to the "care" of an unscrupulous and economically interested party.

The letter continues to outline her mistreatment at the hands of the apothecary who owned this "private Bedlam," an account the writers of the letter merci-
fully condense:

It may suffice to tell you for the present, they kept her bound Hand
and Foot in her Bed, such a one as it was, and ty'd to the Bed Post for
several Days, reduc'd to strange Extremity, beat and pinch'd by her cruel
and barbarous Wretches called Nurses, and forc'd nauseous Draughts
down her Throat, *which they call'd Physick*; and which she, being ap-
prehensive they design'd her Destruction, and might poison her, *refus'd*;
but they forc'd her Mouth open with Iron Instruments, and pour'd into
her, what they though fit, wounding her very much with their Violences
and Inhumanities.[23]

Defoe suggests that the very notions of family, protection, and privacy can fail
particularly for women, who largely rely on financial guardianship. When women
do own property, Defoe contends, their very promise of economic power marks
them as targets. Fortunately for the unfortunate woman of Defoe's story, some
neighbours discover her situation and, overcoming the resistance of her family,
petition the Lord Keeper to examine her. When he finds her, he revokes the Commission of Lunacy against her.

Defoe implies that the danger abroad—that is, the war—is no more significant than the dangers at home, as this case represents. By interrupting his
discussion of war with this particular story of wrongful confinement, Defoe demonstrates that the military protection of the home front is useless without the Parliamentary protection of the defenseless at home. Women—both unmarried and
married—and mad patients are especially vulnerable, Defoe explains, because their

persons and their money are left to the management of their families. When these families fail to protect them, or when, indeed, the families themselves constitute the threat, the legal and medical systems offer little recourse.[24]

A Review of the State of the English Nation surveys the public debate over the legal and medical treatment of lunatics, and the abuses in which the legal and medical communities may collude by incarcerating people, not for therapeutic but for economic purposes. Defoe makes this argument even more explicitly in his 1728 *Augusta triumphans; or, the way to make London the most flourishing city in the universe*, wherein he is led to

> exclaim against the vile Practice now so much in vogue among the better Sort, as they are called, but the worst sort in fact, namely, the sending their Wives to Mad-Houses at every Whim or Dislike, that they may be more secure and undisturb'd in their Debaucheries: Which wicked Custom is got to such a Head, that the number of private Mad-Houses in and about London, are considerably increased within these few Years. This is the Height of Barbarity and Injustice in a Christian Country, it is a clandestine Inquisition, nay worse. How many Ladies and Gentlewomen are hurried away to these Houses . . . How many, I say, of Beauty, Virtue, and Fortune, are suddenly torn from their dear innocent Babes, from the Arms of an unworthy Man, who they love (perhaps too well) and who in Return for that Love, nay probably an ample Fortune, and a lovely Off-spring besides; grows weary of the pure Streams of chaste Love, and thirsting after the Puddles of lawless Lust, buries his vertuous Wife alive, that he may have the greater Freedom with his Mistress? If they are not mad when they go into these cursed Houses, they are soon made so by the barbarous Usage they there suffer.[25]

As Defoe argues, Parliament and the legal system, which have not regulated "the Trade in Lunacy," allow the abuse of wives at the hands of their husbands.[26] Defoe explains that a system which leaves wives vulnerable to abuse ought not to underpin the domestic economy of a functional, civilized nation. While husbands are supposed to protect their wives from the dangers of the world outside of the home, some bad ones are moving them to the madhouse, a pathological version of the home in which women are treated with violence and barbarity. For Defoe, the proliferation of the madhouse stands for everything foreign and monstrous in the domestic sphere.

In order to deal with public fears of a "clandestine Inquisition," Parliament met on February 22, 1763, to hear the *Report from the Committee of the House of Commons on the State of the Private Mad-houses of the Kingdom.* The *Report* enumerated the disturbing details of several cases of wrongful confinement, and included the testimony of Mr. King, keeper of Mr. Turlington's madhouse in Chelsea. King, formerly employed in the wool trade, confessed that "out of the whole number of persons whom he had confined, he had never admitted one . . . lunatic during the six years he had been entrusted with the superintendency of the house."[27] The committee also interviewed Drs. Battie and Monro as the leading experts in the medical care of the mad.[28] Battie testified that "the private madhouses require some better regulations . . . [because] the admission of persons brought as lunatics is too loose and too much at large, depending upon persons not competent judges."[29] The committee asked Battie "if he ever had met with persons of sane mind in confinement for lunacy," and he replied that "it frequently happened," relating "the case of a woman perfectly in her senses, brought as a lunatic by her husband to a house under the doctor's direction, whose husband, upon Dr. Battie's insisting he should take home his wife, and expressing his surprise at his conduct, justified himself by frankly saying, he understood the house to be a sort of Bridewell, or place of correction."[30] The testimony recorded by the committee and reported to Parliament provides evidence that the process for incarcerating people was much too lax. In the case against Turlington's madhouse, Monro concurs with Battie's opinion, testifying "that he does not doubt but several persons have been improperly confined, upon the pretense of lunacy."[31] The committee, satisfied of the rampant abuses of (and in) madhouses, resolved "that the present State of the Private Madhouses in this kingdom requires the interposition of the legislature."[32] While Parliament, with the aid of the medical establishment, wanted to solidify their powers over the incarceration of their subjects, the proposed legislative initiatives did not undermine the powers of the family over the rights of women. Rather, Parliament proposed to secure women by protecting them from the "unnatural" families who would illegally incarcerate them.

At the same time that Parliament attempts to address the very public anxieties regarding abuses in the madhouse, pamphlet literature written by those claiming to have been wrongfully confined argues that the law in fact facilitates such abuse. Polemics against the confinement of the mad center on the abuse of patients in madhouses, and also on the legal system which permits or facilitates such confinement. Besides the many narratives of former lunatics grateful for their cures,[33] accounts from the formerly incarcerated "sane" are published throughout the century.[34] These "mad writings"[35] have similar aims: proving their writers sane and accusing those who contributed to their wrongful incarceration of a kind of lunacy, and, therefore, similar rhetoric.

While women are especially vulnerable to abuse, in 1774, Samuel Bruckshaw published two pamphlets exposing the vulnerability of men: *The Case, Petition and Address of Samuel Bruckshaw, who Suffered a Most Severe Imprisonment for Very Nearly the Whole Year*[36] and *One More Proof of the Iniquitous Abuse of Private Madhouses.*[37] In *One More Proof*, Bruckshaw claims that by "AN ILLEGAL EXERTION OF AUTHORITY" he was caught in "the arbitrary Fangs of Despotic Violence."[38] Bruckshaw's account, startling in its minute and legal detail, outlines his confinement in Wilson's, a private madhouse in Lancashire, for the best part of a year. He writes it, he claims, in the interests of "the cause of GENERAL LIBERTY,"[39] in that "the oppression which crushes me today, may fall on my neighbour to-morrow, nor can any one assure himself He shall be able to escape."[40] The "melancholy narrative"[41] documents the conspiracy against, persecution, and confinement of Bruckshaw by neighbours who resented his purchase of a piece of land in Stamford.[42] Apparently, after the purchase (which was fraught with legal and financial intricacies, detailed exhaustively) Bruckshaw "found every engine at work to destroy [his] credit;"[43]—strategies which apparently worked—and his trustees sold his possessions out from under him. He writes: "Mature reflection upon the iniquitous manner in which I was thus deprived of everything that was dear to me, in the very flower of my life, brought on an anguish disorder, and which held me several months so low, that I never expected to recover."[44] He never admits to having been mad, and he does eventually recover from his "anguish disorder" and tries to re-establish himself in business. The Stamford issue, however, resurfaces, and Bruckshaw makes some enemies (not through any fault of his own, he contends) in trying to get what he feels is his due. The cruel and oppressive people with whom Bruckshaw has business purposely "irritate" him and cause him to be arrested. Bruckshaw is at pains to note that the arrest, having occurred in the absence of any juridical procedure, was entirely illegal. Bruckshaw vividly describes his assault and robbery by his captors, and explains that they "seized me, threw me upon the bed, *clapped irons on my hands and legs*, and dragged me into a chaise."[45] Matters only get worse for Bruckshaw when he arrives at Wilson's madhouse:

> When Wilson shewed me to bed, he carried me up into a dark and
> dirty garret, there stripped me, and carried my cloaths out of the room,
> which I saw no more, for upwards of a month, but lay chained to this
> bad bed, all that time; this appears to be their breaking in garret; under

the ridgetree is a box for the harbour of pigeons, which they disturb in
the night time, to affright their prisoner when he should rest. For this
purpose some of Wilson's family are up all night long, sometimes they
throw pails of water down under the window, now and then brushing
across, with a few small rods, or rubbing with a stone or brick upon the
wall, sometimes put a light up to the window, and every now and then
make a disagreeable noise, to awake you in a fright . . . to keep these
inquisition-like transactions a secret from the world, Wilson's wife does
the office of a barber. [46]

Bruckshaw continues his confinement in another garret of the Wilson's, this one
cold and smoky, and continues to be physically restrained, beaten, and threatened. Bruckshaw's description of the miseries of confinement is echoed in the
contemporary fictionalized depictions of the deplorable conditions of the confined
mad, but his purposes are very different than those of the novels of sensibility.
Bruckshaw warns his readers of the dangers of the dysfunctional legal and medical
systems: he wants to elicit action and not merely sympathy. Hence, considering
the detail with which he describes the legal and financial transactions in which he
is (unwillingly) involved, the description of his suffering in confinement occupies
very little of the pamphlet. In fact, the relation of all of the circumstances surrounding his confinement takes up less than half of the pamphlet, the remainder
of which is dedicated to the legal tribulations which ensue. He is not vindicated,
but, in Bruckshaw's perception, because of the corruption and incompetence of
the judges and his lawyers, he is placed in further financial difficulties by having to
pay the costs both of his own lawyers and those of the defense. While novels like
Haywood's imagine the miseries of confinement, Bruckshaw describes the horrors
of a system which enables British civil liberties and political justice to be perverted
in the service of a continued persecution of an innocent victim.

While the extent of Bruckshaw's narrative and the descriptions of himself as
the perfectly innocent victim of a (almost, it appears, universal) conspiracy against
him do little to convince a modern reader of his sanity,[47] Bruckshaw's treatise, with
its extensive description of the terrors of illegal confinement, is intended to hor-
rify the reader, making him anxious for his own liberty. Bruckshaw explains that

if by that general detestation which must follow this narrative, other
Magistrates are withheld from such shameful and flagrant oppression;
or, being hardy enough to commit such acts, should not be able to escape condign punishment by Chicanery or Venality, this unhappy man

will at least enjoy the melancholy satisfaction of not having wholly suffered in vain.[48]

The Case, Petition and Address of Samuel Bruckshaw and *One More Proof of the Iniquitous Abuse of Private Madhouses* were both published in the same year that Parliament passed the *Act to Regulate Private Madhouses.* As history would have it, however, the abuses of private madhouses continued, denying Bruckshaw even the "melancholy satisfaction" he was seeking. Bruckshaw's pamphlets argued for a stronger state intervention in the institutions which facilitated wrongful confinement. The problem with the *Act to Regulate Private Madhouses* was that Parliament's intervention, as it turned out, was not forceful enough.

Two decades after the publication of Bruckshaw's account, William Belcher's story of incarceration emphasizes the continuing abuses of wrongful confinement. Belcher's account is not only similar to that of Bruckshaw, it is also reminiscent of the letter published by Defoe at the beginning of the century. In his treatise, Belcher positions himself as a hero of sensibility abused by the legal and medical systems which enabled his incarceration. At the end of the century, in 1796, Belcher, "A [self-proclaimed] Victim to the Trade of Lunacy"[49] published his *Address to Humanity*, in which he contends that the legal and medical systems which had allowed him to be confined as a lunatic for years when he had been sane are not only criminal, they are mad. Far from being productive of a cure, Belcher argues, the conditions of the asylum were almost sufficient to drive a sane person mad—the same argument, made fictively, by Haywood. *Belcher's Address to Humanity: Containing, a Letter to Dr. Thomas Monro; a Receipt to Make a Lunatic, and Seize his Estate, and a Sketch of a True Smiling Hyena* was written, the author explains, in the hopes that those in power would come to recognize the difficulties of the sane person incarcerated as a lunatic. The first part of the pamphlet addresses Dr. Monro, who, finding Belcher sane, in effect rescues him "from legal death, and the most insupportable situation possible to a man of feeling, that of imputed . . . insanity.[50] The conditions of his confinement, as he tells it, were brutal:

> I was driven to the verge of desperation and real lunacy, through want of sleep, occasioned (I speak as if on oath) chiefly by the thinness of the partitions of the apartments, whereby I was disturbed by night with snoring and coughing, and by day with ranting and raving; so that I know not what I would not have given for an hour's peace, and am now astonished that I survived at all.[51]

He was abused, he explains, by both the medical and the legal establishments:

> when as perfectly in my senses as I trust I am at present, I have been
> bound and tortured in a strait waistcoat, fettered, crammed with physic
> with a bullock's horn, and knocked down, and at length declared a lu-
> natic by a Jury that never saw me; and, what would make a man tear his
> flesh from his bones, all through affected kindness.[52]

According to Belcher's reading, the "affected kindness" of the medical system,
which pretends to care for people in need of such care, is, in fact, "mad:" instead
of protecting individuals, legal and medical authorities are, largely unwittingly,
enabling their victimization. Belcher is not arguing, as many other writers of this
period do, for improved conditions in madhouses.[53] Rather, he references the
literary horrors of the asylum to prepare the reader for the literal horror of the
situation—the "legal death" as he terms it earlier—the powerlessness of the victim
against imputations of lunacy.

The horror Belcher expresses is the potential for the legal and medical mis-
uses of power, and the inability of the sane person committed as a lunatic to escape
from their clutches. Once a person has been found legally insane, despite the lack
of medical evidence or, indeed, evidence to the contrary, everything that person
does is taken as further evidence of insanity:

> Another dreadful aggravation is, that every degree of resentment against
> the authors of their ruin, is considered as a presumption of remaining
> insanity in the sufferer, who has hardly any chance of restoration without
> their consent, though he adduces thousands of proofs that the whole
> was a scene of iniquity thus countenanced and encouraged. And so dead
> is society to these notorious breaches of it, that hardly an instance has
> occurred of legal redress obtained, even for the loss of property, the least
> part (though mine has amounted to thousands of pounds) of the incal-
> culable and inexpressible injury.[54]

The injuries sufferers sustain, however, are precisely calculable and expressible.
Economic victimization

> commences with depriving the sufferer of his property, the means of
> redress; a system controlled by no provisional guard in the nature of a
> Grand Jury; but a person, body, and often mind, is at the mercy of in-
> terested or offended relations, who thus have it in their power to inflict,

without the charge of any crime, a punishment in comparison of which, transportation for life, or death itself, would be mercy.[55]

Belcher warns that English society must be afraid of the gross misappropriation of power against which those pronounced lunatics have no recourse. The pamphlet literature about wrongful confinement presents a case—albeit, an often hysterical one—about the problems of a system in which any individual may be, somewhat arbitrarily, incarcerated. This threat of wrongful confinement certainly operates at the personal level: the pamphlets indicate that anyone who is disliked or envied by his neighbors, may, regardless of his mental state, be locked up and abused. However, the larger problem to which the pamphlets point is that the institutions which ought to control the trade in lunacy have a vested interest in incarceration. As Defoe had argued earlier in the century, pamphlet literature also makes the case for the strong and impartial control of madhouses by the state.

The actual legislation which resulted from the committee report took eleven years to pass. The legal community dealt reluctantly with the issue of the incarceration of the mad: legislation regulating private madhouses was resisted through much of the eighteenth century. Arguments were made that introducing legislation regulating private madhouses would establish them in law and thus might actually legitimate abuse. Perhaps more accurately, it was feared that instances of madness in private families would become a matter of public record.[56] Public pressure, however, forced the issue of legislation, and in 1774, Parliament passed the *Act for Regulating Private Madhouses*, which required medical certification before a person could be confined. The act did little, however, to regulate private madhouses, in that no grounds were established by which a license could be refused or revoked; the licensing committee seemed to have no authority to do either in any case; and inspections, when they were conducted, which was infrequently, were not a surprise. The legislation is nonetheless important precisely because it points to a pervasive concern surrounding wrongful confinement, a concern significant enough to require a legislative response. The preamble to the *Act* indicates the degree to which the fear of wrongful confinement had become general:

> Whereas many great and dangerous abuses frequently arise from the present state of houses kept for the reception of lunatics, for want of regulations with respect to the keeping such houses, the admission of patients into them, and the visitation by proper persons of the said houses and patients: And whereas the law, as it now stands, is insufficient for preventing or discovering such abuses.[57]

The *Act* was thus enacted in an attempt to respond to the hysteria engendered by a significant social problem, a problem in part attributable to the lack of laws designed to combat the abuses taking place in madhouses. As the preamble makes clear, regardless of the actual statistics, the abuses in madhouses were generally regarded as being rampant. The *Act for Regulating Private Madhouses* recognizes the dangers of failing to police the private sphere: the law thus assumes power over, and responsibility for, the vulnerable incarcerated individuals.

In order to respond to the hysteria regarding wrongful confinement, perpetuated in part by print culture, the mad-doctors—including Battie, physician to St. Luke's Hospital for Lunaticks and former teacher of Horace Walpole—professed faith in the therapeutic benefits of "rightful" confinement.[58] Arguments for the right, therapeutic kind of confinement functioned as a counter-discourse to the threat of wrongful confinement. The mad-doctors used the rhetoric of professionalism to reassure an uneasy public that, while it had not always been the case, the appropriate authorities would now monitor and control the incarceration of the mad.

Mad patients and women thus faced a medical profession intent upon establishing authoritative control over them. The new medical sub-specialty focused on the care and treatment of the mad had profound implications economically as well as socially, and confinement of the mad was certainly profitable for mad-doctors in ways that being the physician in a public madhouse was not. The ownership of madhouses by mad-doctors also supported the self-conception of mad-doctors as patriarchs, naturalizing their control over their patients. Mad-doctors establish control over their discipline by configuring madness as the patient's rejection of his or (more likely) her appropriate social role. Treatment was therefore a process of the mad patient's redomestication, and the madhouse was conceived as the training ground for this process. Mad-doctors thus attempted to assert themselves as the logical madhouse proprietors and gain a monopoly on the trade in madness. However, the lack of legal regulations until the last quarter of the century meant that the ownership of madhouses was not the exclusive province of the mad-doctors. For this reason, amongst others, not every doctor supported the confinement of the mad.[59] The efficacy of confinement as a method of treatment is debated in medical circles, but ultimately, confinement served both the economic interests of the mad-doctors and the social interests of Britain.

As a medical professional acutely aware of the economic consequences of confinement, the English physician William Pargeter maintained a cautionary tone in his writings about confinement. In 1792, Pargeter published his *Observa-*

tions on maniacal disorders, which is notable for the history of psychiatry as one of the first texts to provide case histories documenting the success of moral management in cases of madness. *Observations on maniacal disorders* is also interesting due to its cultural, rather than economic, concern with confinement, as Pargeter writes specifically about the private madhouses without having a vested interest in them. Pargeter was among the physicians who called for moral management, or the "government of maniacs"[60] claiming that humane treatment by a qualified physician will cure the lunatic: mechanical restraints, physical abuse, forcing medications, and "stupefying liquor" only exacerbate the patient's problems.

Although he pities the lunatic who requires confinement, Pargeter certainly does not condemn confinement altogether. "The conduct of public hospitals or institutions, for the reception of lunatics, needs no remark" Pargeter remarks; "the excellence in the management of them, is its own encomium."[61] He also discusses private madhouses, distinguishing sharply between those managed by physicians and clergymen, and those which are run by "exceedingly illiterate" men who have no medical knowledge and are "in other respects extremely ignorant"[62]—in short, entirely unqualified for an occupation better left to the experts. Pargeter contends that physicians who manage madhouses do not participate in the wrongful confinement of the sane for the sake of economic motives:

> In such hands [which is to say, those of medical men or the clergy] we may place an implicit confidence; and a perfect assurance, that in such an abode, dwells nothing offensive or obnoxious to humanity—here, no greedy heir, no interested relations will be permitted to compute a time for the patient's fate to afford them an opportunity to pillage and plunder. But such dwellings are the seats of honour—courtesy—kindness—gentleness—mercy; and *whatsoever things are honest and of good report.*[63]

Although the evidence does not always bear Pargeter out—madhouses owned by physicians were occasionally managed by less scrupulous underlings—he implies that the medical practitioners who own private madhouses do so for reasons other than purely economic interest. Pargeter contends that other madhouse-keepers have neither medical nor humanitarian interests at heart, and "it cannot be supposed that any very great advantages in favour of the patient, can be hoped for, or obtained; when compassion, as well as integrity, in those houses, is oftentimes to be suspected: this truth is as notorious as it is lamentable."[64] Pargeter warns of the possibility, even probability, of abuse in private madhouses run outside the medical establishment, and argues that the possibility of wrongful confinement will be safeguarded against by placing the responsibility for confinement in the hands of the medical profession. Pargeter argues that control over the mad ought to be more firmly in the hands of the medical professionals, who, he believes, exercise a disinterested use of their power, acting in place of and opposed to the "interested relations" and the ignorant madhouse keepers who collude to victimize the powerless. Like Defoe, Pargeter argues that the madhouse, run by unscrupulous men, victimizes powerless people—the mad in need of treatment and wrongfully confined women—who are most in need of protection. Pargeter stresses that appropriate owners of madhouses are honourable, courteous, kind, gentle, and merciful—the same affect that characterizes the good patriarch upon whom the domestic economy depends.

In his treatise, which is substantially medical and often fairly technical, Pargeter cites the popular press, using newspaper articles documenting the abuses in private madhouses as evidence. From September 1791, he reproduces the following:

> Notwithstanding the recent regulations, [by which is meant the *Act for Regulating Private Madhouses* of 1774] there are many private madhouses in the neighbourhood of the metropolis, which demand a very serious enquiry. The masters of these receptacles of misery, on the days that they expect their visitors, get their sane patients out of the way; or, if that cannot be done, give them large doses of stupefying liquor, or narcotic draughts, that drown their faculties, and render them incapable of giving a coherent answer. A very strict eye should be kept on these *gaolers of the mind*; for if they do not find a patient mad, their oppressive tyranny soon makes him so.[65]

The article Pargeter reproduces from the following December makes the economic motivation for wrongful confinement more clear:

> Private mad-houses are become so general at present, and their prostitution of justice so openly carried on, that any man may have his wife, his father, or his brother confined for life, at a certain stipulated price! The wretched victims are concealed from the inspecting doctors, unless it can be contrived, that they shall be stupefied with certain drugs, or made mad with strong liquors, against the hour of visiting![66]

Much the same argument is made by the article appearing in January 1792, which states that "Some of these [private madhouses], which were originally a refuge for the *insane* only, are now *pension-houses* for those whose relations wish to be the

guardians of their fortunes, overseers of their estates, and receivers of their rents."[67]
Clearly, the complaints Pargeter outlines—of the ease with which the sane may be
confined as mad for the economic purposes of their relatives, the abusive treatment
which is allowed to occur, and how this abuse may in fact drive the formerly sane
patients mad—were not novel in the 1790s: they were precisely the same complaints articulated by Defoe at the beginning of the century. Pargeter, having read
"sufficient and convincing proofs that such villainy exists"[68] blames unscrupulous
family members and unprofessional madhouse keepers for the problem of wrongful confinement. While he concedes that confinement is an unfortunate necessity
for the mad, he argues that the management of madhouses must be trusted only
to those with the proper medical authority.

After providing a medical explanation of the problem of mania and its cultural corollary of wrongful confinement, Pargeter provides a legal analysis. He explains that, while the *Act for Regulating Private Madhouses* had clearly intended to
rectify their problems, evidence proves that private madhouses continued to produce the economic and physical abuses the *Act* purportedly barred. Thus, Pargeter
concludes that the *Act* itself is insufficient, and he proposes to work to amend it
(provided, he modestly maintains, someone better qualified for the task does not).
Just as Pargeter has no economic stake in private madhouses, he makes clear that
his motivation for proposing an amendment to the *Act* is similarly disinterested.

In his *Observations*, Pargeter demonstrates that he understands not only the
medical, but also the legal issues involved in the treatment of the insane. He is
familiar with ways in which cultural anxiety surrounding the issue of confinement
was in circulation:

> The idea of a mad-house is apt to excite, in the breasts of most people,
> the strongest emotions of horror and alarm; upon a supposition, not
> altogether ill-founded, that when once a patient is doomed to take up his
> abode in those places, he will not only be exposed to very great cruelty;
> but it is a great chance, whether he recovers or not, if he ever more sees
> the outside of the walls.[69]

As Pargeter makes clear, the very idea of the madhouse is alarming to the general
public. At stake for Pargeter was the necessity for the medical community to negotiate the threat of wrongful confinement: by professionalizing confinement, the
medical authorities could exercise the same power currently held by families and
unscrupulous madhouse keepers. By ensuring a medical monopoly on the management of madhouses, the medical system could reassure the public that their

exercise of power would be in the service of protecting and treating their patients. The discourse of wrongful confinement proves useful as a foil to legitimate "rightful" confinement by a medical professional.

The medical establishment parlays a cultural anxiety about confinement into an economic opportunity. In providing evidence of confinement's therapeutic value to the insane and maintaining the necessity for their own control over the trade in lunacy, mad-doctors reassure the public that the madhouse protects society's weakest members. Both the medical and legal establishments recognize that they are implicated in the literature of wrongful confinement, in both the specific stories published in periodical literature and the more general threat presented in the novels. Although the confinement of the sane may not have happened on the scale proportionate to the interest in its accounts, the literature criticizes those who are supposed to protect the vulnerable members of society but who, in fact, contribute to their victimization. Of course, the most vulnerable are the mad patients themselves, who lose control over their own persons and property when they lose their senses. The madhouse, however, threatens those wrongfully confined as well, not only with the loss of sanity, but also with the loss of legal rights. The most precarious rights were those of women in possession of property. While these women are assailed by the families supposed to guarantee their rights, the unscrupulous madhouse keepers and families also threaten men, stripping them of both their property and their ability to participate in the patriarchal system. While the protagonists of many of the actual and fictional accounts of wrongful confinement are women, the men who publish their own accounts of wrongful confinement indicate that the legal position of a person perceived to be a lunatic is no different from that of an actual lunatic or a woman: he becomes legally, medically, politically, and socially powerless. In a culture which had become deeply suspicious of the threats to the liberty of British people, the legal and medical systems solidify their control over the madhouse in order to maintain a rhetoric of social control—the control and protection of the weak by those invested with the authority upon which the domestic economy rested.

Notes

1. Eliza Haywood, *The Distressed Orphan, or Love in a Mad-house* (1726; repr, New York: Published for the William Andrews Clark Memorial Library and the UCLA Center for Seventeenth- and Eighteenth-Century Studies by AMS, 1993), 35.

2. Susan Staves, *Married Women's Separate Property in England, 1660–1833* (Cambridge: Harvard University Press, 1990), 1–5 and 178–95, demonstrates the success of Restoration legal efforts to

recognizing the contractual status of married women's property. For much of the eighteenth century, however, these efforts were countered by a reassertion of the common-law principle that a husband and wife were one person (the husband) and thus could not hold property separately. It was not until the end of the nineteenth century that English marriage law came to recognize the property rights of women.

3. Haywood, *The Distressed Orphan*, 41.

4. Deborah Nestor, introduction to Haywood, *The Distressed Orphan*, vii.

5. See Chris Mounsey, introduction to this volume.

6. Michel Foucault *Madness and Civilization*, trans. Richard Howard, (New York: Vintage Books, 1988), 38–64, theorizes the eighteenth century as the period of the "Great Confinement" of the mad (1660–1800) while pointing out that madness was more on display than ever: although there was an attempt to lock up the mad, discourses and representations of madness proliferated. Roy Porter, *Mind-Forg'd Manacles: A History of Madness in England from the Restoration to the Regency* (London: Athlone Press, 1987), argues that the fears of confinement, both wrongful and "legitimate" are overstated in the eighteenth century, and that a large-scale confinement of the mad was not accomplished until the nineteenth century. See also Andrew Scull, *Museums of Madness: The Social Organization of Insanity in Nineteenth-Century England* (New York: St Martin's Press, 1979); Andrew Scull, Charlotte MacKenzie and Nicholas Hervey *Masters of Bedlam: The Transforming of the Mad-Doctoring Trade* (Princeton: Princeton University Press, 1996); Jonathan Andrews and Andrew Scull, *Undertaker of the Mind: John Monro and Mad-Doctoring in Eighteenth-Century England* (Berkeley: University of California Press, 2001).

7. William Parry-Jones argues that "It is not unnatural that the possibility of the violation of an individual's liberty, by incarceration in a madhouse, should have aroused public concern, but surviving evidence in support of the view that sane persons were detained in this way is not, in fact, substantial." *The Trade in Lunacy: a study of private madhouses in England in the eighteenth and nineteenth centuries* (London: Routledge and Keegan Paul, 1971), 222.

8. See Parry-Jones, *The Trade in Lunacy*, 232.

9. For example Daniel Defoe, *A Review of the State of the English Nation* 3, no. 70 (1706): 277; Daniel Defoe, *Augusta triumphans or, The way to make London the most flourishing city in the univers: first, by establishing an university . . . concluding with an effectual method to prevent street robberies, and a letter to Coll. Robinson on account of the orphan's tax* (London: J. Roberts, 1728); Alexander Cruden, "The London-Citizen exceedingly injured or a British inquisition display'd, in an account of the unparallel'd case of a citizen of London, bookseller to the late Queen, who was in a most unjust and arbitrary Manner sent on the 23d of March last, 1738, by one Robert Wightman, a mere Stranger, to a private madhouse Containing, I. An Account of the said Citizen's barbarous Treatment in Wright's Private Madhouse on Bethnal-Green for nine Weeks and six Days, and of his rational and patient Behaviour, whilst Chained, Handcuffed, Strait-Wastecoated and Imprisoned in the said Madhouse: Where he probably would have been continued, or died under his Confinement, if he had not most Providentially made his Escape: In which he was taken up by the Constable and Watchmen, being suspected to be a Felon, but was unchain'd and set at liberty by Sir John Barnard the then Lord Mayor. II. As also an Account of the illegal Steps, false Calumnies, wicked Contrivances, bold and desperate Designs of the said Wightman, in order to escape Justice for his

Crimes, with some Account of his engaging Dr. Monro and others as his Accomplices. The Whole humbly addressed to the Legislature, as plainly shewing the absolute Necessity of regulating Private Madhouses in a more effectual manner than at present," in *Voices of Madness: Four Pamphlets, 1683-1796*, ed. Allan Ingram, (Gloucestershire: Sutton Publishing, 1997); and William Belcher, "Address to Humanity: Containing, a Letter to Dr. Thomas Monro: A Receipt to Make a Lunatic, and Seize his Estate; and a Sketch of a True Smiling Hyena," in *Voices of Madness: Four Pamphlets, 1683-1796*, ed. Allan Ingram, (Gloucestershire: Sutton Publishing, 1997).

10. Staves, *Married Women's Separate Property*, 4–6.

11. As Staves argues, "In the property regimes of patriarchy, descent and inheritance are reckoned in the male line; women function as procreators and as transmitters of inheritance from male to male." *Married Women's Separate Property in England*, 4.

12. William Battie, *A Treatise on Madness* (London: J. Whiston and B. White, 1758).

13. Michael McKeon, "Historicizing Patriarchy: The Emergence of Gender Difference in England, 1660-1760," *Eighteenth-Century Studies* 28, no. 3 (1995): 295–322, especially pages 296–300.

14. Daniel Defoe, *A Review of the State of the English Nation* 3, no. 70 (1706): 277.

15. Defoe, *Review*, 3.70.277.

16. Defoe, *Review*, 3.70.277.

17. 14 Geo. III, c. 49. See also, Richard Alfred Hunter and Ida Macalpine. *Three Hundred Years of Psychiatry, 1535-1860: A History Presented in Selected English Texts* (Oxford: Oxford University Press, 1963), 265–7.

18. Defoe, *Review*, 3.70.278.

19. Defoe, *Review*, 3.70.278.

20. Defoe, *Review*, 3.70.279.

21. Defoe, *Review*, 3.70.279.

22. Defoe, *Review*, 3.70.279.

23. Defoe, *Review*, 3.70.279. Max Byrd points out the erotics of this passage in "The Madhouse, the Whorehouse, and the Convent," *Partisan Review* 44, no.2 (1977): 268–78. He does not, however, mention the letter Defoe publishes from the girl's relatives in response, in which they maintain that the girl was probably a lunatic, evinced by her tendencies for "wearing Rags, and in Nakedness and Nastyness, exposing her self in the Streets, and a thousand Extravagancies of the like Nature."

24. See Elizabeth Foyster, "At the limits of liberty: married women and confinement in eighteenth-century England," *Continuity and Change* 17 (2002): 39–62. See, especially, pages 45–49.

25. Defoe, *Augusta Triumphans*, 30–31.

26. William Parry-Jones explains that "Trade in Lunacy . . . [is] . . . A phrase seen, not infrequently, in eighteenth- and nineteenth-century literature." *The Trade in lunacy: a study of private madhouses*, 6.

27. William Cobbett, *The Parliamentary History of England, from the Earliest Period to the year 1803*, vol. 15, *1753–1765*. (London: T. C. Tansard, 1813), 1288.

28. William Battie was the physician to St Luke's Hospital for Lunatics from 1750–1764. John Monro was the second of four generations of Monros to hold the office of physician to Bethlem Hospi-

tal: his tenure was from 1751-1791. He was author of *Remarks on Dr Battie's treatise on madness* (1758), and the owner, from 1759, of Brooke House, a private asylum in Hackney.

29. Cobbett, *Parliamentary History*, 1289.

30. Cobbett, *Parliamentary History*, 1289.

31. Cobbett, *Parliamentary History*, 1290.

32. Cobbett, *Parliamentary History*, 1290.

33. Hannah Allen, "A Narrative of God's Gracious Dealings With that Choice Christian Mrs. Hannah Allen, (Afterwards Married to Mr. Hatt,) Reciting the great Advantages the Devil made of her deep Melancholy, and the Triumphant Victories, Rich and Sovereign Graces, God gave her over all his Stratagems and Devices," in *Voices of Madness: Four Pamphlets, 1683-1796*, ed. Allan Ingram, (Gloucestershire: Sutton Publishing, 1997).

34. A particularly striking early example is Cruden, "The London-Citizen Exceedingly Injured: or a British Inquisition Display'd."

35. Porter, *Mind-Forg'd Manacles*, 263.

36. Samuel Bruckshaw, "The Case, Petition and Address of Samuel Bruckshaw, who Suffered a Most Severe Imprisonment for Very Nearly the Whole Year," 1774 in *Voices of Madness: Four Pamphlets, 1683–1796*, ed. Allan Ingram, (Gloucestershire: Sutton Publishing, 1997).

37. Samuel Bruckshaw, "One More Proof of the Iniquitous Abuse of Private Madhouses," in *Voices of Madness: Four Pamphlets, 1683–1796*, ed. Allan Ingram. (Gloucestershire: Sutton Publishing, 1997).

38. Bruckshaw, "One More Proof," 77.

39. Bruckshaw, "One More Proof," 77.

40. Bruckshaw, "One More Proof," 78.

41. Bruckshaw, "One More Proof," 78.

42. The only surviving documents of the case, however, are those written by Bruckshaw himself.

43. Bruckshaw, "One More Proof," 83.

44. Bruckshaw, "One More Proof," 83.

45. Bruckshaw, "One More Proof," 93.

46. Bruckshaw, "One More Proof," 95.

47. The modern reader of Bruckshaw's account might conclude that if he is not mad, he is at least anxious, paranoid, depressed, and not a little megalomaniacal.

48. Bruckshaw, "One More Proof," 80.

49. Belcher, "Address to Humanity," 1.

50. Belcher, "Address to Humanity," 1.

51. Belcher, "Address to Humanity," 4.

52. Belcher, "Address to Humanity," 5.

53. For the most pointed example, see William Battie's *A Treatise on Madness*. For others, see the anonymous *Proposals for Redressing Some Grievances Which Greatly Affect the Whole Nation*. (London,

Johnson, 1740), and "A Case Humbly Offered to the Consideration of Parliament" in *Gentleman's Magazine,* 33 (1762): 25–6.

54. Belcher, "Address to Humanity," 5–6.

55. Belcher, "Address to Humanity," 6–7.

56. Jonathan Andrews and Andrew Scull, *Customers and Patrons of the Mad Trade: The Management of Lunacy in* Eighteenth-*Century London,* (Berkeley: University of California Press, 2003), 176–177.

57. 14 Geo. III, c. 49

58. As Andrews and Scull argue "In reality . . . worries about false confinement were an extremely sensitive issue in this period, and concerns of this sort clearly profoundly affected Monro's and other mad-doctors' practices." *Undertaker of the Mind,* 177.

59. See Andrew Harper, *A Treatise on the real cause and cure of insanity; in which the nature and distinctions of this disease are fully explained, and the treatment established on new* principles. (London: Stalker and Walter, 1789) and Erasmus Darwin, *Zoonomia; or, The laws of organic life.* (London: J. Johnson, 1794–1796).

60. William Pargeter, *Observations on maniacal disorders.* (Reading: Smart and Cowslade, 1792), vi.

61. Pargeter, *Observations,*vi.

62. Pargeter, *Observations,* 49.

63. Pargeter, *Observations,* 123.

64. Pargeter, *Observations,* 124.

65. Pargeter, *Observations,* 125.

66. Pargeter, *Observations,* 125.

67. Quoted in Pargeter, *Observations,* 126.

68. Quoted in Pargeter, *Observations,* 127.

69. Quoted in Pargeter, *Observations,* 127.

Part Three

EXPERIENTIAL

7

"ON THAT ROCK I LAY"

Images of Disability Found in Religious Verse

Jamie Kinsley

SUSANNA HARRISON'S "Longing for Public Worship" serves as an example of how religious poetry provides voice for the silence of disability. Through personal interaction with the divine in the space of her religious poetry we gain insight into the everyday life of an individual who not only struggled with debilitating illness, but also craved physical inclusion. Harrison used the form of the hymn as the vehicle for her poems about pain and suffering. What we know of her life—her popularity as a hymnist as well as the support she received from her fellow parishioners—read together with "Longing for Public Worship" provides a clear voice for the experience of disability in the eighteenth century.

What we know of Harrison's life comes largely from the preface to *Songs in the Night* (1780). When her father died, he left a large family unprovided for. Harrison, at the age of sixteen, went into service as a necessity for economic survival. She had to leave her station in 1772 " when Disorders seized her."[1] In fact, her poems suggest she suffered several debilitating conditions. While the title page states that *Songs in the Night* is written "by a Young Woman under deep Afflictions," her poems hold evidence of trouble breathing, bedridden periods, and physical aches and pains.

Many of her hymns describe the lack of strength that accompanies illness. Hymn LXXXVI focuses on the weakness of her body as she struggles for life while preparing for death,

> My Life declines, my Strength is gone,
> Disease and Pains prevail;
> Death threatens to arrest me soon,
> My Heart and Flesh doth fail.[2]

Although many of Harrison's hymns about physical pain present an image of longing for death, this particular hymn calls the idea of leaving the body behind an "awful Thought!" Harrison draws our attention to the daunting task of facing everyday with immobilizing pain. We feel her weakness, yet the speaker in the hymn uses death only as the final reward from the divine. As the poem continues, her longing for life exists as a desire for greater preparedness before being "Renew'd and justified by Grace."[3] In the *Book of James*, found in the New Testament, the concept of being justified relies on having a right relationship with God. For the apostle Paul, justification in faith speaks not only to the forgiveness of sins through the sacrifice of Jesus Christ, but, perhaps more importantly for Harrison's hymns, to the saving from God's wrath and thus to an ensured afterlife. Although many eighteenth-century hymns focus on the grace found in heaven, Harrison's desire for a life after death presents itself as a release from her current pains. In this we receive insight into the experience of Harrison's debilitating pain and feelings of confinement that accompany this pain.

When Harrison mentions confinement, the word occurs in a place trapped amongst images of low spirits and troubled thoughts, unable to appear at the surface of the poem. Hymn LV is an excellent example of this technique,

> Break thro' the Darkness of my Mind,
>   And drive the Powers of Hell away;
> I cannot bear to be confin'd,
>   My Spirit longs for brighter Day.[4]

The darkness of her mind and the spirit longing for a brighter day create bookends for this stanza. However, even within the center of the stanza, a statement such as "Powers of Hell" cloud her comment that she "cannot bear to be confin'd." Confinement presents the speaker with a situation she cannot endure. Images of Hell overpower ideas of confinement; thereby creating the sense that confinement is as endurable for the speaker as she imagines Hell would be. This image paints a picture of isolation equal in hopelessness to an eternity in darkness. Silence imposes upon the speaker in the poem as she reveals the situation of the body—confined, alone, and isolated.

That nearly half of the poems in *Songs in the Night* contain images of pain, confinement, or illness is testament to Harrison's preoccupation with her physical suffering. Specific instances of Harrison's concern with her body riddle the collection; yet, her direct apprehension about struggling with nature exists in only one hymn. Hymn XCII speaks to the destruction wreaked on her body by dust.

Whether this dust comes from nature's pollen or winds from the east is uncertain.[5] That this hymn narrates how physicians were called in to help her suggests the danger of this dust. The hymn calls for divine relief from her peril through stanzas that expose the very real fear of being interminably ill,

> XCII
> But where is now my humble Trust
>   In God's Almighty Voice?
> Why do I think of yellow Dust,
>   Which often Health destroys?
>
> How vain are all the Drugs and Skill
>   Of great Physicians here!
> If God denies a Blessing still,
>   I languish in their Care.[6]

Although Harrison finds comfort in the idea of God in control of her health, her trust in the divine represents the situation of disability in the eighteenth century. Individuals relied on medical professionals to heal their ailments and prolong their lives; yet, the remedies did not always work and many people felt trust was better placed in hope in divine intervention rather than in medicine. The physicians in Harrison's hymns function only to create a greater separation between her and the community with which she wishes to fully participate. In this way, she is further isolated. Her pleas to the divine are presented as a means by which to draw her closer to the community she feels separated from. Harrison's questioning of the divine appears only tacitly as she asks where her trust in "God's Almighty Voice" has gone, but this question reveals the deep distress experienced when medicine no longer works and she must fight against nature for physical relief.

At this time the hymn was a form charged with many influences flowing into one another. Religious poetry, meditational and devotional poetry, personal lyrics, and congregational singing would have impacted Harrison's writing. These genres flowed into one another in the eighteenth century. They informed one another and therefore informed the way poets used genre to their own ends.

Religious poetry moved from highly personal to increasingly public as the eighteenth century progressed. The elite religious poetry of the seventeenth century, the poetry of John Milton and George Herbert for instance, began to be replaced by less formal poetry. Isaac Watts' publication of Elizabeth Singer Rowe's *Devout Exercises of the Heart* (1738) create a pattern for the formulaic progression of religious writing from personal, to coterie, and then to published collections.

Rowe did not publish these essays in her life time, but she published much religious poetry from a very young age and in prominent places, both in her own books of poetry and in prestigious collections done by others. Rowe's *Devout Exercises* was so popular that in the 1780s there were seven editions and in the 1790s an amazing thirty-two editions. Her popularity meant that Harrison would have been aware of Rowe's writing as well as the coterie nature of it. Watts' preface contains effusions on Rowe's piety and talent. Within these moments of praise are insights into the movement of Rowe's writing from personal to published. He asserts her popularity throughout the preface in moments such as "The admirable Author of these Devotional Papers has been in high esteem amoung [sic] the Ingenious and the Polite," and "excellent Woman who has bless'd and adorn'd our Nation."[7] By praising Rowe through assertions of her fame, Watts lays a foundation for acceptance of her writing that assumes a national following. In raising Rowe above all others, Watts allows for perceptions of her to begin with respect before moving into a reading of her work.

Rowe's audience approached her writing with respect, but their responses, like Watts's response, contained a relationship with the content of *Devout Exercises*. In the preface, Watts raises Rowe's writing to the status of divine instruction. He says of those who read her *Devout Exercises of the Heart* that "when they have shut out the World, and are reading in their Retirements, let them try how far they can speak this Language, and assume these Sentiments as their own."[8] Watts asserts that if readers follow the divine affection and zeal laid out in Rowe's work, they will learn lessons that will bring them closer to divine love. Throughout the preface Watts suggests that Rowe's personal darkness provides an opportunity for others to benefit. He builds this argument by revealing that her friends and close acquaintances benefitted from her writing long before the collection ever reached his hands.

The coterie nature of Rowe's writing provided a widely useful formula for other religious poets to follow. When speaking of the admiration others will possess for Rowe once they read her work, Watts says, "those who were favour'd with her chief Intimacy will most readily believe it."[9] In establishing a precedent for Rowe's reception, Watts not only gestures toward the quality of her writing, but also to the devotional instruction it provides to communities of believers. Further, in attempting to assert the originality of these supremely talented writings, Watts uses her circle of friends to date some of these essays as originating from "her Younger days."[10] We begin to gain a vision of an intimate group gathered to exercise their devotional meditations together, with Rowe's writing guiding them in these exercises. Rowe's enduring popularity in the eighteenth century, combined with the tremendously positive reception of her devout poetry, created a pattern for others to follow with their private religious meditations.

Harrison's poetry participates in this formulaic pattern. Her hymns are first and foremost intensely personal expressions of pain and suffering. Some of these hymns, however, contain evidence that she shared her works with others. That her hymns belonged as coterie before they found their way into publication illustrates the importance of community not only for Harrison as a writer, but also for Harrison as a body in pain. If others gather intimately to share her poetry in a devotional way, then her poetry becomes a shared experience. Harrison's experience with the divine becomes an example for others to participate in as they exercise their devotional meditations together. When she writes of her friends, she does so as if apologizing to them. In Hymn LXXXiX, she gestures toward her community by saying,

> Let Friends no more my Suff'rings mourn,
> Nor view my Relicks with Concern;
> O cease to drop the pitying Tear,
> I'm got beyond the Reach of Fear.

> Thro' Tribulation sharp and long,
> I'm brought to join the sinless Throng;
> Glory to God for every Woe,
> For every Pain I felt below.[11]

The speaker in these stanzas imagines herself leaving her earthly body to join a community of believers in the afterlife. She sets the stage for this removal from her present sufferings by quieting her friends' grief. The image we receive of the body in pain is one where life in the present produces more concern from friends than life after death. She requests that her friends not mourn her by hanging on to those material things she leaves behind but recognize that she is "beyond the Reach of Fear." These lines reveal the experience of disability in the eighteenth century through the response from community. The speaker addresses the "Friends" of this hymn with the knowledge that they are acquainted with her sufferings enough to understand the joy found in her imagining of a release from pain.

As a Congregationalist, Harrison would have associated worship with a community joined together by the Holy Spirit. This belief system places emphasis on the community aspect of worship. In this system, community is made up of individuals. The connection between individuals within a worshiping community such as Harrison would have belonged allows her hymns to infuse the audience with a real sense of her sufferings. The image of friendship in her hymns provides a vehicle by which Harrison can connect the physical experience of her body to members of her community through a shared spiritual experience—that of reading the hymn together. Hymn XCIX uses the image of friendship in order to empha-size the extent of the speaker's suffering. It begins,

> To Thee, my God, I make my moan,
>   Lend Thou a gracious Ear;
> Let every Sigh, let every Groan,
>   Before thy Throne appear.
>
> For Friends my Sorrows swell too high,
>   My Woes they cannot bear;
> Helpless and destitute I lie,
>   Expos'd to every Snare.[12]

Within this hymn we gain insight into the role of friends for the experience of dis-ability in the eighteenth century. Here, we receive an image of friendship that exists outside the moment of the hymn. Friends for whom "Sorrows swell too high" appear as a community that stands by the poet and experiences her distress with sympathy.

The coterie nature of Harrison's poems is important to recognize. In mov-ing through coterie on the journey from personal to published, religious poetry such as Rowe's and Harrison's develops through a community experiencing an individual's deepest emotions. Sharing religious poetry in small groups in this way allows for others to learn from the experiences of the poet, to gain insight into their most intense pains and joys, and to connect with the divine through communal meditations. The experience of deeply personal feelings belongs to the community, but the respect given to the poet provides Harrison the space to freely express her emotions.

Since religious poetry allows the poet the freedom of honest expression, we receive some of the most profound expressions of personal pain within forms such as the hymn. The hymn as a form changes throughout the eighteenth century. The narrowing definition of hymn in the late eighteenth-century began to move toward a form marked by congregational singing, this shift in form also signaled a greater regard for hymns as spiritually educational.[13] Often directed at a com-munity, the hymn is created from the perspective of an individual. It is worthwhile to note that Harrison's hymns utilize both the traditional restriction of the hymn as intended for a community to rehearse and the first-person singular pronoun found in more personal hymns.[14] Harrison alters the traditional form of hymns by crafting poetry that laments an individual's situation. However, this shift in form retains the collective audience. This melding of the individual voice with a communal experience draws attention to the desire for the community to identify with the pains of the individual body. This identification of the communal body with the individual body allows for representations of the disabled body to rise to a place of importance.

Poems describing disability were not uncommon in the eighteenth century. Within eighteenth-century religious poetry, however, we often receive the most profound expressions of pain. For instance, Mary Chandler uses the majority of her stanzas in *On My Recovery* (1736) to express the pain and debilitation she experienced,

> When sinking to the silent Grave,
> My Spirits dy'd away;
> Thy quick'ning Word new Vigour gave,
> Thy Voice commands my Stay.
>
> In my Distress to Thee I cry'd,
> When tossing in my Bed;
> Thou sent'st thy Mercy to my Aid,
> And eas'd my aking [sic] Head.
>
> Thou bidd'st the vital Current flow
> In a less rapid Tide;
> My dancing Pulse beat calm and low,
> And fev'rish Heats subside:
>
> Thou lend'st to my Physician Skill,
> Right Med'cines to apply;
> And my Disease obey'd thy Will,
> The painful Symptoms die.[15]

Here we receive a view of physicians as able to heal only because of divine will. The speaker bestows thanks upon the divine, but does so through an emotionally charged expression of the disease that nearly took her life. She, like Harrison, expresses the spirits as affected by physical pain. She also demonstrates medical knowledge regarding her disease as she details her fever, headache, and rapid heartbeat. Chandler's poem reveals a voice for disability not unlike Harrison's. She remains isolated and in pain throughout the memories presented in *On My*

Recovery. By addressing her desire for relief to the divine, she allows herself the space to express depth of feeling about her experience with a body in pain.

Experiences of pain find expression in religious poetry with a depth of feeling because of the way the divine connects to these works. That poems such as Chandler's, Harrison's, and Anne Bannerman's *Ode III—To Pain* (1800)[16] utilize religious poetry as a forum for expressing to the divine their experiences with pain reveals the place of religious poetry as important in seeking interpretation for disability. Anne Bannerman's *To Pain*, like many of Harrison's hymns, expresses with intense emotion the overwhelming experience of pain.[17] Bannerman's poem puts into words what seems inexpressible, and in this we receive an illustration of pain that moves beyond the physical:

I.
Hail! fiercest herald of a power,
    Whose harsh controul each nerve obeys!
I call thee, at this fearful hour;
    To thee my feeble voice I raise.
Say, does compassion never glow
Within thy soul, and bid thee know
    The pangs, with which thou fir'st the breast?
Or dost thou never, never mourn,
To plant so deep the hidden thorn,
    Forbidding aid, and blasting rest?

II.
Think'st thou my wavering fickle mind
    Requires so much, to break her chain?
Alas! what earthly joys can bind
    The wretch, who sees thy figure, Pain!
For ever fleet before his eyes;
For him, no glories gild the skies;
    No beauties shine in nature's bound,
In vain with verdure glows the spring,
If, from within, thy gnawing sting
    Bid only demons scowl around.

III.
Too sure, I feel, in every vein,
    With thee soft Pity ne'er can dwell.

Shall pleasure never smile again
 Or health thro' ev'ry channel swell?
Yes! tho' thy hand hath crush'd the rose
Before its prime, another blows,
 Whose blooms thy breath can ne'er destroy;
Say, can thy keen cruel chains
Corrode, where bliss seraphic reigns,
 Where all is peace, and all is joy.

IV.
Then, wherefore sighs my fearful heart,
 And trembles thus my tottering frame?
Alas! I feel thy deadly dart,
 More potent far than fancy's frame?
I bend, grim tyrant! at thy throne;
But spare, ah! spare that sullen frown,
 Relax the horrors of thy brow!
O! lead me, with a softer hand,
And lo! I come at thy command,
 And, unrepining, follow through.[18]

Bannerman combines physical pain with emotional and spiritual pain in order to come close to her experience with the body. In doing this we receive a picture of physical pain as inextricably intertwined with the emotional and spiritual pain it causes. Moreover, her expression of pain illustrates its all-encompassing nature in affecting the body. Every nerve, every vein, every channel is taken over by pain, causing the speaker to cry out for a softer hand. Even an image of the body unable to follow the command of the divine until her pain alleviates finds its way into this remarkable poem. She alludes to a youth consumed by pain as a way to express the never-ceasing agony her body experiences. Such depth of feeling reveals the experience of disability in the eighteenth century not only for Bannerman, but also for others whose bodies were familiar with chronic pain.

For many of the hymns in Harrison's *Songs in the Night*, life's experiences involve pain, weakness, and isolation. In these poems we gain insight into the weight an individual such as Harrison carried from day to day. The burden that accompanies Harrison's distress affects her spirit, causing many of these hymns to call for relief in the form of a wish for death. In Hymn CV, Harrison calls herself *chastened* from day to day and says, "From Year to Year I groan."[19] Sadness overwhelms the tone of this poem as we receive further images of the everyday experience of her debilitating illness,

> Chasten'd I am from Day to Day,
>   From Year to Year I groan,
> When will my Troubles cease, or stay?
>   When will my Griefs be gone?
>
> Such Pain and Sickness wastes my Strength,
>   Such Weakness bows me down;
> My Spirit dreads the tedious Length,
>   As Morn or Night comes on.
>
> Anxious I wish with sad Concern
>   To end these gloomy Days;
> When will my Lord again return,
>   And fill my Mouth with Praise?[20]

Here we see the pain and sickness that consumes her strength. The image of her anxiously living through the days and nights waiting with sad concern for physical relief haunts the collection as a whole. Rather than images of youth as fleeting or patient waiting for the afterlife, this hymn presents a portrait of the length of days as tedious. In this we receive a depth of emotional expression. Harrison presents a pain that overwhelms even praise for the divine. She sees the only release as one found in death; yet, we also feel the consuming sorrow that accompanies a view of death as the only escape.

The image of morning *or* night suggests a blending of time, which adds to the feeling of tedious length. Rather than praising the divine for the time she has, the speaker laments the blending of time into one long period of suffering. It matters not whether the sun or the moon moves over the speaker's head, she wants life to end so that,

> My suffering Time will soon be o'er,
>   Soon shall my Soul away;
> Then shall I sigh, and sin no more,
>   But sing thro' endless Day.[21]

Ending the hymn with this final stanza emphasizes that no hope exists for the speaker in her current situation. The psalmists often use the word "chastened" to mean the test individuals must endure in order to come closer to the divine.

Within the *Psalms* this use of the word chastened also often refers to a community experiencing distress together. Further, the word "distressed" in the *Psalms* means caught in a tight place; in this, Harrison creates a link between herself and the psalmists through her feelings of entrapment. In the New Testament, Paul writes to the Corinthians about persevering through their opposition together, as a community. If they do this, they will be rich with rejoicing. Being chastened together brings comfort to the community of believers. In using the word chasten, Harrison places herself in this orthodox tradition. In doing so, she presents her deeply personal feelings about pain within an allusion to the original community of believers who suffered through trials together.

Using the form of religious poetry allows for allusions such as these. Within Harrison's hymns we receive a picture not only of everyday life, but also of personal interaction with the divine in that everyday existence. For instance, Hymn LXXXVII begins with the epigraph, "*Job vii.16, I lothe it, I would not live always.*" Harrison then plays with this allusion to create her own vision of a life freed from pain and isolation:

> 1 When will my sweet Release be sign'd,
>   To quit this House of Clay?
> When shall my Spirit, unconfin'd,
>   To Glory wing her way?
>
> 2 O how I lothe [sic] this mortal Life,
>   I hate this slavish Fear;
> I long to end this tedious strife
>   With Sin and Sorrow here.[22]

Here, she longs for a release from her body. The suggestion that her body confines her spirit allows us insight into her everyday life. In beginning this hymn with *Job vii.16* Harrison establishes a narrative of her situation that expresses a wish for freedom from her confinement. Fear enslaves her and the sin and sorrow of the world causes tedious strife. In *Job vii* the suffering Job uses a parody of *Psalm viii* in order to point out irony in creating humankind as superior to all other creation, yet placing on Job misfortune upon misfortune. Further, in reminding the divine that life is all too brief, Job—and thus Harrison in utilizing this verse—requests divine intervention. This request gives us access into the experience of disability in the eighteenth century. It is important to see that the voice for disability in this hymn does not lament her disability, but, rather, the societal lacking that allows her to continue confined, isolated, and without the community her hymns long for.

Longing for Public Worship

As a hymn expressing the personal experience of an individual separated from "the Courts of the Lord," Harrison's hymn, "Longing for Public Worship," cloaks discussion of the body in religious language. The speaker addresses her plea to the divine being, yet couches it carefully, as if she is tacitly expressing her pain to God. Although the poet could use the final stanza to turn her lament into a request for patience in her present state, Harrison's final stanza is a request for place—not an apology for lament. The final stanza does express a wish for her soul to wait the will of the divine,

> O bring Thyself thy Graces near,
>   And teach my Soul to wait thy Will;
> Then shall I serve and praise Thee here,
>   And own Thee just and righteous still.[23]

However, this insinuates a questioning of divine will. There is an *if/then* statement in this final turn of the hymn. She wishes for closeness to the divine, a similar reward as received in public worship, in order to see the divine as still "just and righteous" and thus deserving of her service and praise. Although the hymn retains a sense that she will meanwhile worship in her place of isolation, this is not viewed as a fair substitution for public worship. The speaker longs for public worship, but is unable to physically attend. This hymn allows us insight into the pain of the chronically ill body—not in terms of what the ill body must undergo physically, but in terms of the painful separation created when a body belongs as a part of a community, but cannot join that whole.

In connecting Harrison's personal relationship with the divine, the community in turn experiences a degree of Harrison's life. In creating a public connection with a personal experience, Harrison's "Longing for Public Worship" gives insight into the pain and prohibitions placed on the individual body. The dominant focus of the hymn remains the body absent from the place longed for. Once the dominant focus is present, the speaker moves into what she imagines as the reward for receiving what she longs for. She proclaims:

> I'd praise thee for the meanest place,
>   To stand as Waiter at thy Gate;
> Could I but there behold thy Face,
>   I'd think the Favor truly great.[24]

The speaker asserts that even the lowliest of positions in this place of mixed worship would be a "favor truly great." She uses words such as "I'd" and "could" to portray a sense of what she would do if only her longing found reprieve in an answer to her desires. Importantly, however, she breaks the repetition of "I'd" and "could" to insert "To stand" as the beginning of the third line in this stanza. This anomaly draws our attention to its importance. What she would praise the divine for is "to stand as Waiter at thy Gate." The importance of being able to stand at the gates with all the other worshippers is emphasized by the contrast between the plaintive figure in the first stanza and the joyful standing requested in the third stanza. To join in with others in worship is all that the body desires. The pain of confinement comes from the separation of the individual body from the other bodies in her community. What is so visibly longed for is to join those other bodies, but her inability to do so does not restrict her ability to imagine this longing fulfilled.

Importantly, this is the first presentation of the understanding that the longing for public worship and all its rewards is a longing for something before experienced. The image shifts in the middle of the poem from longing to remembering that which the speaker has participated in previously, and that which she desires to participate in again. Here, in stanza four, we receive the filling of all the senses:

I long to tread that happy Ground,
  Where oft my Soul has richly fed;
To hear the Gospel's joyful Sound,
  To taste substantial, living Bread.[25]

She has experienced treading "that happy Ground," has heard "the Gospel's joyful Sound," and has tasted "the substantial, living Bread." In this we receive the elements of public worship. Public worship for the speaker consists of going to a specific place, of hearing the Gospel spoken or sung, and of partaking in communion. The body is ever-present in this hymn. The senses of sight, sound, taste, and touch appear throughout as the speaker illustrates the world she longs for. Emphasis is placed on the physical as the three middle stanzas exemplify an almost climatic moment of sensory joy.

The happiness that results from experiencing all these sensations is a result of the relief that comes with participating in public worship. Immediately following a stanza that focuses on the spiritual rewards of the physical experience of public worship, the hymn reads

> There have I often left my Fears,
>   When I have gone o'erwhelmed with Grief;
> There have I left my Wants and Cares,
>   And in returning, sung Relief.[26]

Here, following the description of the physical experience of public worship is a glimpse of what life consisted of before public worship. The image of place remains at the forefront of this stanza, as we are not to forget that "there" is where she left her fears, wants, and cares. She explains going with overwhelming grief and returning with sung relief. This juxtaposition, of what life is without public worship, and what life is after public worship draws us back to the image of her isolated and confined. If, without public worship, life consists of overwhelming grief, fears, wants, and cares, then the longing speaker must be experiencing this misery in her present situation.

The painful separation of the body from its community is made ever more painful through contrasts between the body as whole with others and the body as weak in isolation. Although the fourth stanza explores the sensory pleasure of public worship, images of confinement and tones of loss riddle the poem. At the start of each stanza we receive a note of desperation, a desperation that comes with a mind restlessly longing for even the meanest place to commune with others. These first lines underscore the isolation of the speaker; even in stanzas expressing joy at the remembrance of public worship, we are not to forget the pain that immobilizes her as she writes. Her present situation is further highlighted by the contrast between singing relief in the last line of the fifth stanza and "In sad Complaints I spend my voice" in the last line of the sixth stanza. The speaker's isolation away from public worship, away, importantly, from the waiting throng mixing in humble worship of the second stanza, is the lament. This lament brings the body once again in the focus. The body desires a joining in with other bodies; a joyful voice is one that can join other voices, while the voice of isolation is mournful. These stanzas present a parallel to standing at God's gate. Physical participation in this community—the ability to simply be in the space where worship takes place—would provide happiness for the speaker, a removal of fears, and a bringing nearer of the divine.

It is important to note that the repetition of "there have I left" that occurs directly before the sixth stanza shifts us abruptly into the isolation the speaker feels in being left at home alone and isolated Sabbath after Sabbath. This immediate proximity reveals the fears, wants, and cares that the speaker feels in her confined situation. Further, we gain the sense that these burdens would find relief if only participation in public worship were made available to the speaker. The body that is not participating is one that only expresses voice as a physical response to the situation, while the participating, remembered body is full of physical sensations. The remembered body joins, mixes, stands, waits, beholds, treads, feeds, hears, and tastes. However, it is important to emphasize that the obtainment of these sensations comes not from the act of mixing, standing, treading, and so on, but from the participation in worship with other bodies. Her present situation is highlighted by the contrast between singing relief in the last line of the fifth stanza and "In sad Complaints I spend my voice" in the last line of the sixth stanza. The speaker's isolation away from public worship, away, importantly, from the waiting throng mixing in humble worship of the second stanza, is the lament.

Longing Relieved

As the conversation continues, the speaker shifts from an expression of her current situation to an expression of what would heal her current distress. Addressing the divine again, the speaker expresses her longing for the Courts of the Lord,

> 'Tis for thy Courts, O Lord, I long;
>   When shall I in thy House appear?
> When shall I join the waiting Throng,
>   And mix in humble Worship there?[27]

Here, she presents her connection to the divine through a place where they would meet. She further names this place as "thy House." Here, she desires an appearance with others. The repetition of the word "When" not only adds to the longing she feels, but also assumes that this arrival will take place. The repetition of "I" in conjunction with "when" focuses the audience on her presence in the Courts of the Lord. However, the anticipation of her presence is combined with the use of the verbs "join" and "mix." These combinations raise the longing to one in which the individual will find contentment not only in the Courts of the Lord, but also in uniting with other individuals who appear in this place. The "waiting Throng" that participates in "humble Worship" now becomes the dominant focus alongside the individual "I" that is the speaker.

This melding of the individual experience into a communal response connects to the form of "Longing for Public Worship" as a hymn. Further, in connecting to the form in this way, the content speaks to more than a plea for healing from her god. Harrison's deft intertwining of the personal and the communal requests an alleviation of her removal from public worship that holds her fellow worshipers responsible as well. "Going to the Lord's Supper, after long Confinement," a hymn that follows "Longing for Public Worship" in *Songs in the Night*, integrates communal response with a personal sense of identification. Harrison writes of participating in this event:

> My Thoughts from trifling Objects turn,
> > Give me the Conquest over Pride;
> O may I look on Him, and mourn!
> > For Him *I* pierc'd and crucified.[28]

She later ends the poem with

> Enter, my Soul, his Gates with Praise,
> > And thankfully adore his Name,
> Whose Mercy lengthens out thy Days,
> > Whose Love to thee is still the same.[29]

This individual response to a communal experience harkens back to "Longing for Public Worship." The themes of spiritual dependence on the physical act of movement—of going to a place—carry through both these poems. This similarity directs our attention to the power of other bodies on Harrison's spiritual life. Although she speaks of her own experience in being absent from public worship, and then in going to the Lord's Supper, her happiness in these moments is wrapped up in the collective experience of these acts. What remains at stake is not a spiritual or physical healing, but a return of the individual body to the collective body.

In "Longing for Public Worship" Harrison gestures toward herself as a missing member of this body. Many of the hymns she wrote when she could not attend services came to be used for public worship, but even more telling is evidence in the preface to *Songs in the Night* that members of Harrison's religious community would come to her in her home to hear her latest hymns read. In imagining the respect Harrison's hymns garnered, together with the shift in understanding of the hymn as a poetic form, we begin to see the influence of her voice. Her plaintive confinement carries through to other voices, each of which join together to express her experience. This further emphasizes the distress the individual body feels over being separated from the bodies it wishes to join. If the other bodies do not join their voices to Harrison's hymn of longing, then they do not receive the spiritual education she has to offer.

The everyday distress of the separation of the individual body from its community is visible in "Longing for Public Worship." The desire for worship is not a spiritual grasping for understanding of the divine, but physical yearning for inclusion with other worshipers. Careful not to end her poem in complaint, she ends it with a determination to worship at home with all the strength of conviction worshiping with others might provide. However, the plaintive questions concerning when the speaker's body will be present in worship do not speak to an afterlife—they demand a presence in the present. They ask for a reason why the body cannot be present at the place of worship. The image of restlessness drives the poem from the first line, and although she calls the *mind* restless, it is connected to images of the pensive, confined, lonely body. Directly after "relief," and the stanza imagining the emotional reward that comes from public worship, however, the speaker begins the next stanza with "But now I'm left at Home to mourn." This is a more active representation of the disabled body, left behind by the community she wishes to join, left outside of the space she feels she rightfully belongs.

The desire for community becomes the center of this work when we acknowledge the presence of the body in order for this experiential education to occur. The speaker separates herself from "the Saints" in "the Courts" who rejoice and participate with one another as she longs to do. The body becomes heavily present with words such as "lie," "sigh," "stand," "tread," in the first two stanzas, and "strength," "weakness," "heal," "pain" in the last two. The juxtaposition of these words signals not only the presence of the body, but also the anguish associated with the inability to mix in worship. She spends her voice in "sad complaints," then immediately desires for her strength to be renewed. Rather than presenting visuals of a divine that sustains the speaker's mind, or ending her poem with apologies for her sad complaints, she requests of the divine to remove her weakness and heal her pain. She desires this so that she may be a part of the worship community—lifting her voice, not alone in the confines of her home, but in a place with other worshipers. If other voices raised in unison experience the hymn with the speaker, then the lament of the hymn is answered.

A Voice for the Disabled

Harrison's hymns offer a voice for disability that would otherwise be lost. The editor of her collection provides a voice for the social ostracism that Simi Linton discusses in "Reassigning Meaning."[30] Expecting to die, Harrison gave her manuscripts to the Congregational minister John Condor, who edited the poems and published them for her as *Songs in the Night* (1780). Condor uses the space of the preface as an appeal to readers through a description of Harrison's hardships. He intertwines her writing with her "bodily affliction" thereby securing a perception of Harrison's poetry that cannot escape the body.

Focus on Harrison's hardships move from physical to economic as Condor expounds on her life. He writes first of her father dying and leaving a large family unprovided for, then of Harrison, at the age of sixteen, going into service, and finally of her leaving her station in 1772 "when Disorders seized her, which ever since have baffled the Power of Medicine and the Skill of Physicians."[31] Information about Harrison's condition stops with words such as *disorders* and *pain*. The addition of confounded physicians to this narrative places her disability into a realm outside of the mortal world. In doing this, Condor begins to secure a vision of Harrison as connected to the divine. In connecting her to the divine in this way, he removes Harrison's disability from her physical body. This, in turn, weakens a connection between Harrison's poetry and her illness. The preface presents Harrison's body as connected to the divine through revelations that would otherwise have been unavailable to her. That her body exists outside of the power of medicine and the skill of physicians empowers it for the purposes of the preface. However, in doing this, Condor separates Harrison from her body, delegitimizing the body as anything other than a vehicle for divine instruction.

If the preface's purpose is to position Harrison as a source of divine revelation, then her body becomes other than physical. A vision of the body as connected to the divine through illness grows as the preface continues. Condor's discussion of her illness moves immediately into a description of "God, who is rich in Mercy, was pleased, in Love to her Soul, at the beginning of the Affliction" manifesting himself to her in order to instruct her.[32] The disabled body is now forgotten as anything other than a chosen vessel for divine interaction. As a vessel, the disabled body creates poetry in order to present revelations given to her by the divine. This separation of the physical body from the writing body creates a gap where a clear representation of the disabled body might otherwise be. The understanding of her body remains one that attaches words such as suffering and affliction, while also perceiving of the disabled body as the only means by which to receive instruction from the divine to share with others who suffer.[33]

Condor uses Harrison's divinely disabled body as a means by which to draw in readers. However, this use of the body determines a distinct line between discussion of a physical body as a real living, breathing body and a spiritual body that does not bleed, sweat, convulse, or break.[34] Lennard J. Davis discusses the mid-eighteenth century as a period in which the signifiers for disability begin shifting from perceived vice to perceived virtue.[35] Harrison certainly writes at a moment in history when the disabled body was read as a virtuous body; however, she is an excellent example of the slippage of signifiers attached to disability in the later part of the eighteenth century. While her disability allows for others to "read" her as virtuous, once read as such her disability becomes seen only as the vehicle for moral instruction. This act moves the experience of disability away from clear representation. However, Harrison's poetry functions as clear representations of the experience of disability and the accompanying isolation, even though the preface does not. Although the preface participates in socially categorizing in ways that "threaten to solidify into cultural norms that demarcate the limits of the human," readings of Harrison's poetry as representations of her experiences with debilitating illness allows us insight into the experience of eighteenth-century disability.[36]

Harrison's editor takes her experience and narrows it into the definitions that marginalize disabled men and women. The editor of *Songs in the Night* stands as an early example of the type of rhetoric that places disability at the periphery. Disability Studies works to place disability at the center, thereby exposing the silences created through such rhetoric. Although Harrison's poetry itself reveals the experience of disability in the eighteenth century, the rhetoric of the preface silences her poetry by assigning her body meaning. Rather than treating "the social processes and policies that constrict disabled people's lives," society often keeps disability a personal matter and attempts to treat the condition and the person with the condition.[37] Harrison becomes categorized not by what her poems present about her body, but by what the preface has to say about her body. Condor's use of her disabled body is simpleminded, while her poetry expresses the complex feelings she experiences. However, it is his pattern that becomes the formula for representing disability, while her voice is silenced. It is our job to find new ways of reading in order to reveal not only the way the voice of disability in the eighteenth century is silenced, but also what that voice has to say.

Notes

1. Susanna Harrison, *Songs in the Night, by a young woman under deep affliction* (London: R. Hawes, 1780). This selection comes from the preface, written by the editor, John Condor.

2. Harrison, *Songs in the Night*, 83.

3. Harrison, *Songs in the Night*, 84.

4. Harrison, *Songs in the Night*, 57.

5. The image of "yellow dust" was sometimes used to denote eastern winds in the late eighteenth century.

6. Harrison, *Songs in the Night*, 94.

7. Elizabeth Singer Rowe, *Devout Exercises of the Heart in Meditation and Soliloquy, Prayer and Praise. By the late Pious and Ingenious Mrs. Rowe. Review'd and Published at her Request, by I. Watts, D.D.* (London: R. Hett, 1738), xi.

8. Rowe, *Devout Exercises of the Heart*, xxiv.

9. Rowe, *Devout Exercises of the Heart*, xi.

10. Rowe, *Devout Exercises of the Heart*, xx.

11. Harrison, *Songs in the Night*, 90.

12. Harrison, *Songs in the Night*, 102.

13. See Donald Davie, *The Eighteenth-Century Hymn in England* (Cambridge: Cambridge University Press, 1993): 16–20. However, it must be recognized that congregational singing may not have been a common practice for all Congregationalist in the eighteenth century. Harrison could have written her hymns without congregational singing in mind. Indeed, some Congregationalists did not embrace the singing of hymns as a congregation until the nineteenth century. Cf. Geoffrey Wainwright and Karen Westerfield Tucker, *The Oxford History of Christian Worship* (Oxford: Oxford University Press, 2005).

14. For an instructive reading of the hymn as a richly varied form, see Paula R. Backscheider, *Eighteenth-Century Women Poets and Their Poetry: Inventing Agency, Inventing Genre* (Baltimore: Johns Hopkins Press, 2005), 123–74.

15. Chandler's poetry refers occasionally to her crooked spine. Mary Chandler, "On My Recovery," in *British Women Poets of the Long Eighteenth Century: An Anthology*, eds. Paula R. Backscheider and Catherine E. Ingrassia (Baltimore: Johns Hopkins University Press, 2009), 526.

16. Anne Bannerman, *Poems* (Edinburgh: Mundell, 1800), 66.

17. Bannerman also experienced physical pain and deformity. Sydney Smith, an acquaintance of Bannerman's, and a founder of *Edinburgh Review* called her a "crooked poetess." Quoted in Backscheider, *Inventing Agency*, unpag.

18. Bannerman, *Poems*, 66–68.

19. Harrison, *Songs in the Night*, 104.

20. Harrison, *Songs in the Night*, 105.

21. Harrison, *Songs in the Night*, 105.

22. Harrison, *Songs in the Night*, 88.

23. Harrison, *Songs in the Night*, 81. "They also serve who only stand and wait" is the last line from Milton's *On His Blindness*. That she references another poet who experienced disability acknowledges a community of poets with disability.

24. Harrison, *Songs in the Night*, 80.

25. Harrison, *Songs in the Night*, 80.

26. Harrison, *Songs in the Night*, 80.

27. Harrison, *Songs in the Night*, 80.

28. Harrison, *Songs in the Night*, 81.

29. Harrison, *Songs in the Night*, 82.

30. Simi Linton, *Claiming Disability: Knowledge and Identity* (New York: New York University Press, 1998) 161.

31. Condor, "Preface" in *Songs in the Night*, iii.

32. Condor, "Preface" in *Songs in the Night*, iv.

33. According to Linton, "'The loss of community, the anxiety, and the self-doubt that inevitably accompany this ambiguous social position and the ambivalent personal state are the enormous cost of declaring disability unacceptable," Linton, "Reassigning Meaning," 230. The editor categorizes Harrison's body as "afflicted" in order to align her with others who might benefit from her instruction, but this creates a community that is socially outside the "norm." What the editor says about Harrison, then, becomes an early example of the type of work that alienates disabled men and women from society.

34. Julia Kristeva and Jeanine Herman write a beautiful dissection of the disabled body in society, the terms used to seek interpretation, and unique ways each individual experiences disability. See "Liberty, Equality, Fraternity, and . . . Vulnerability" *WSQ: Women's Studies Quarterly* 38:1/2 (Spring/Summer 2010): 251–268.

35. Lennard J. Davis, "Dr. Johnson, Amelia, and the Discourse of Disability" in *"Defects": Engendering the Modern Body*, edited by Helen Deutsch and Felicity Nussbaum (Ann Arbor: University of Michigan Press, 2000), 54–74.

36. Deutsch and Nussbaum, *"Defects": Engendering the Modern Body*, 23.

37. Linton, "Reassigning Meaning," 232–233.

8

ATTRACTIVE DEFORMITY

Enabling the "Shocking Monster"

from Sarah Scott's *Agreeable Ugliness*

Jason S. Farr

I
N AN EIGHTEENTH-CENTURY CONTEXT, "deformity" refers either to forms of physical abnormality, or to "moral disfigurement." The *Oxford English Dictionary* defines the former of these two usages as "the quality or condition of being marred or disfigured in appearance; disfigurement; unsightliness, ugliness" and "abnormal formation of the body or of some bodily member."[1] According to these definitions, "deformity" encompasses unattractiveness and what we think of today as physical disability. In his 1754 tract *Deformity: An Essay,* William Hay addresses the topic of "Bodily Deformity," which he notes "is visible to every Eye."[2] Thus, for Hay, deformity denotes visible bodily impairment. Elsewhere, in *Crito; or, a Dialogue on Beauty* (1752), Joseph Spence discusses deformity as that which stands in opposition to beauty, but he also argues that vice is "the most odious of all Deformities."[3] Spence's rendering of "deformity" exhibits the overlap between physical ugliness and sin, implying that the latter exacerbates the former. These archival examples suggest that, in a Georgian context, the cultural and social rifts between those who are physically known as the "common standard" and those who deviate from the norm in their physical appearance or bodily ability are vast. Further, these uses of "deformity" offer insight into how the physically disabled are viewed as unsightly and deviant in the eighteenth century.[4] This discourse of deformity, however, undergoes important transformations. As Lennard Davis argues, for example, the mid- to late eighteenth century is a period in which deformity begins to be viewed less as an occasion for public spectacle and more as a kind of god-given tribulation which individuals can overcome in order to become more virtuous.[5]

The shift that Davis has identified can be traced in part by examining the role of sensibility in shaping English consciousness. One of the important figures within this cultural paradigm is Edmund Burke, whose *Philosophical Enquiry into the Origin of Our Ideas of the Sublime and Beautiful* (1757) considers the relationship between sympathy and human suffering, and in doing so illuminates eighteenth-century thought regarding an Englishman or woman's ability to relate to the "other." For Burke, sympathy enables us to "enter into the concerns of others; that we are moved as they are moved, and are never suffered to be indifferent spectators of almost any thing which men can do or suffer."[6] Burke adds that sympathy is a kind of "substitution, by which we are put into the place of another man, and affected in good measure as he is affected."[7] He later argues that because of the delight we take in observing "the real misfortunes and pains of others" we are unable to shun "scenes of misery; and the pain we feel, prompts us to relieve ourselves in relieving those who suffer."[8] Sympathy, in Burke's view, closes the gap between "self" and "other." His philosophy illustrates how individuals of varying physical and mental abilities might elicit sympathy and, consequently, assistance from able-bodied individuals. In light of Burke's highly-influential writings, it is perhaps no coincidence that schools for the deaf and blind are first established in England during the late eighteenth century.[9]

The writings of William Hay and Sarah Scott, however, go beyond merely procuring sympathy for the disabled: they attempt to reconfigure cultural perceptions about the body by extolling deformity as a most desirable physical condition. Exceptionally small, hunchbacked, sight-impaired, and lame, Hay challenges longstanding assumptions about disfigurement in his landmark work *Deformity: An Essay* (1753). Hay's writing is groundbreaking due to his explicitly-stated intention to "write of deformity with beauty."[10] His essay, which is part memoir, part cultural critique, and part medical testimony, presents deformity as an opportunity for personal, intellectual, and moral growth.[11] Throughout the piece, Hay contends with deeply-embedded cultural presuppositions that deformity is at best laughable, and at worst, an indication of god's displeasure. At a couple of junctures in the essay, Hay accepts the notion that people are naturally repelled by physical difference, but I would argue that these parts of his essay have been given undue emphasis by scholars.[12] More often than not, I argue, Hay interrogates, questions and critiques cultural assumptions about deformity, and in the process recasts it as a personally transformative experience. In particular, Hay disputes the work of the scientific luminary Sir Francis Bacon, who had argued in the early seventeenth century that people with deformities are "void of natural affection" due to the fact that those who "induce contempt, hath also a perpetual spur in himself, to rescue and deliver himself from scorn."[13] Hay responds by claiming that far from being a hindrance or a cause of unnatural behavior, deformity in fact facilitates a strengthening of character, intellect, and health: "On the whole I conclude, that Deformity is a Protection to a Man's Health and Person; which (strange as it may appear) are better defended by Feebleness than Strength."[14] Hay argues that if one is incapacitated by physical limitations, that individual is likely to be more temperate, to cultivate a refined love of reading and study, and to not overexert oneself in exercise. In countering the common wisdom of the time, Hay expresses gratitude for his extraordinary body as it enables a healthier lifestyle and mindset than 'ordinary' individuals. Moreover, Hay is, to my knowledge, the first English thinker to explicitly codify deformity as encompassing a set variety of physical conditions, including sensory impairment, mobility impairment, and physical disfigurement.[15] Hay thus provides an early framework of what we think of today as physical disability. For his day, Hay's essay is a unique and brave challenge to entrenched scientific thought and common assumptions about the Variable human body.

Like Hay, Sarah Scott understood well what it meant to be different, and would likely have sympathized with many of Hay's arguments. A novelist and reformer who was at least peripherally involved with the Bluestocking Circle, Scott often deals with the topic of deformity in her novels, such as *Millenium Hall* (1762) and *Sir George Ellison* (1766). Perhaps Scott's pockmarked face, a consequence of a case of smallpox she contracted during her teenage years, is what inspired her to write about deformity and to consider the physically disabled as being in need of her protection. Whatever the cause, Scott's second novel, *Agreeable Ugliness, or, the triumph of the graces. Exemplified in real life and fortunes of a young lady of some distinction* (1754), deals extensively with the themes of beauty and plainness in the context of a young woman's coming of age. Moreover, it portrays ugliness as a desirable, virtue-enhancing characteristic for women. Though this novel is a translation from a French novel, Pierre Antione de la Place's *La laideur aimable, et les dangers de la beauté*, it is significant that Scott chose to translate it. Like the novel's protagonist and narrator (who deliberately omits her first name), Scott was obligated to navigate a society in which women were often admired for, or judged by, their beauty or perceived lack thereof. Scott's novel, in turn, assumes that being disagreeable of visage compels a lady to be agreeable in every other way, and it advocates the fulfillment of women's desire through its celebration of corporeal difference. Along with the work of William Hay, *Agreeable Ugliness* offers a mid-eighteenth-century cultural register of physical difference-as-means to empowerment and agency. Though Scott's novel is a conventional novel of sensibility in a number of ways, it is also, I argue, innovative for its portrayal of physical otherness and for the way that it challenges gendered social codes about the body that are readily apparent in eighteenth-century ugly clubs. *Agreeable Ugliness* portrays the inner-subjectivity of a "shocking monster" who uses her various talents, intellect, and charm to captivate suitors and superiors. More significantly, the novel's heroine employs her deformed body as a measured defense against patriarchal authority. Her subtle refusal of the law of the father becomes the catalyst for the eventual fulfillment of her emotional and sexual desire.

Ugly Clubbing in the Eighteenth Century

Ugly clubs provide some insight into the ways that deformity was commonly perceived and embodied in the eighteenth century. The values and principles behind the establishment of this gentlemen's club reveal a general bias toward, and mockery of, individuals who were considered unusual because of their physical aspect. The first two published accounts of ugly clubs' existence are from the year 1711.[16] The most significant of these sources, Richard Steele's *Spectator No. 17*, goes into detail about the emergence of ugly clubs, where groups of gentlemen would gather to inure themselves to their "obliquity of aspect." [17] Steele reveals that these gatherings were intended to foster a sense of humor among anomalous gentlemen so that they might better assimilate themselves into the heart and goodwill of their better looking peers and neighbors. In this entry, Steele manages to demonstrate some sympathy for people with physical abnormalities. He argues, in particular, that since we have no control over our physical attributes, it does no good to worry about how we appear in public: "We ought to be contented with our Countenance and Shape, so far, as never to give our selves an uneasie Reflection on that Subject." He states that when folks appear either "Defective or Uncomely," it is "an honest and laudable Fortitude to dare to be Ugly; at least to keep our selves from being abashed with a Consciousness of Imperfections which we cannot help, and in which there is no Guilt."[18] Steele admits his discontentedness with his own face, which, he complains, "is not quite so long as it is broad," and yet his injunction for people to take comfort in how they have been born extends only so far when he suggests that a deformed man should learn how "to jest upon Himself" so that those "Women and Children who were at first frighted at him, will afterwards be as much pleased with him."[19] Steele condemns ridiculing the ugly, but leaves it to the ugly to deride themselves. This proposed solution would supposedly allow "ordinary" individuals to feel more comfortable while in the vicinity of deformity.

Steele concludes his entry by quoting at length a letter from one Alexander Carbuncle, who mentions the existence of an ugly club that has arisen in response to other gentlemen's clubs such as the Punning Club, the Witty Club, and the Handsome Club.[20] Carbuncle accounts for a group of ugly gentlemen who meet together under the rules and guidelines set forth by "The Act of Deformity," which stipulates, among other things, that only those who have a "visible Quearity in his Aspect, or peculiar Cast of Countenance" may join, and that those with big noses or other atypical physical characteristics will likewise be granted membership. The guidelines further stipulate that if there are "two or more Competitors for the same Vacancy . . . he that has the thickest Skin to have the Preference." The admitted members meet regularly to break bread and drink to the health of their ugly female counterparts such as Mrs. Touchwood, who has had the misfortune of losing her front teeth, and Mrs. Vizard, whose face has been scarred by the smallpox. These same gentlemen praise Aesop, who in an eighteenth-century context is often cited for his insightful fables and exoticized for being disfigured, ugly, and of African descent.[21] This particular detail suggests that ugly club members are socially situated along a similar continuum to that of racialized foreigners. *Spectator No. 17* had an enormous impact on the way physical beauty was constituted and embodied in the eighteenth century. With the success and availability of the *Spectator*, it is no wonder that many years later, at the tail end of the century, a play titled *The Ugly Club* (1798) would dramatize many of the ideas and principles that Steele had previously espoused.

Discovered in a private collection and subsequently archived in the Liverpool Library in 1901, *The Ugly Club Manuscript* (1743–1754) details the existence of a Liverpool-based ugly club, lending historical credence to eighteenth-century ugly clubs through its meticulous accounting ledger, meeting minutes, and names and physical characterizations of individual members. This manuscript further substantiates the impact that Steele had on the reading public. It contains a set of rules, which are much more extensive than the few included in Steele's entry, as well as an accounting ledger that details the club's expenditures over an eleven-year period. The first rule stipulates that to be admitted, one must be a bachelor and a "man of honor," or of certain ways and means to be able to afford the membership expenses.[22] The fact that the club is for genteel men suggests that in terms of gender and class, this club is in line with other clubs of the era. However, the subsequent rules reveal the ugly club's extraordinary contours. In addition to being a gentleman, for example, one must have "something odd, remarkable, droll or out of the way in his face, as in the length, breath, narrowness, or in his complexion, the cast of his eyes, or make of his mouth, lips, chin, &c., of which the majority of the society are to judge, and the president to have the casting voice."[23] The physical abnormality of the figure in question is a must, and it is up to already admitted club members to determine whether the candidate fits the bill. In particular, characteristics such as "a large mouth, thin jaws, blubber lips, little goggyling, or squinting eyes" are deemed desirable attributes for membership.[24] Physical difference, however, is not enough for one to be admitted; the candidate in question must also have "a facetious disposition" as well as a "temper, humour, character and face" commensurate with the club's self-deprecatory outlook.[25] The club met every Monday evening at a local coffee house, and rules regarding one's bachelorhood were strict. If a club member were to marry, he would have to forfeit his place in the club and donate money to its continued subsistence. The rules reveal that though this club was meant to be facetious, its members took their participation seriously. They formed a tight-knit fraternity of eligible bachelors in the mid-eighteenth century.

Perhaps the most compelling aspect of this historical record is its brief physical characterizations of the club members, all of whom are described in satirical terms as a means of justifying their membership in the group. These passages often indicate that beauty is codified according to an English sense of selfhood which is constituted by religious and racial difference. Some of the members, for example, are given anti-Semitic depictions, such as John Brancker, whose "Jewish sallow phiz," "prominent uneven nose" and "little hollow pig eyes" compliment his "rotten irregular set of teeth resembling an old broken saw."[26] The club also boasts of certain foreign-born gentlemen, too, and these individuals are racialized in no uncertain terms. William Tunball of Tortola, for example, is a merchant who has a "mohagony complexion, carved face, negro teeth" and "monkey chin" but is also considered to have "a fine grin" and is in "every way an excellent member."[27] John Kennion, Esquire, meanwhile, hails from Kingston and is described as having "a Jewish face and negro grin" which make him "well qualify'd for a Member."[28] These and other demeaning depictions make clear that, at this historical moment, English beauty is codified in accordance with a sense of Anglican, British identity that defines itself in opposition to stereotypes of people from colonial locales and of dissenting religions.[29] The fact that Tunball is a Creole, in this case a white man of West Indies origin, dictates the caricatured depiction of each of his facial features. Kennion is likewise portrayed in outrageously exaggerated terms that are contingent on racial and religious difference. This free and indiscriminate mixing of derogatory images calls attention to the immense social importance placed on being recognizably English and Anglican in appearance. In addition to reflecting these "English" values, the manuscript reinforces heterosexuality through homosocial exchange: the Ugly Club members rely on each other to understand their place within the social order so that they may eventually marry women who occupy likewise liminal positions. Women and men with deformities, this logic states, should be paired up. Until said unions occur, ugly bachelors should fraternize with one another, creating bonds that reinforce binaries such as English/foreigner, Anglican/dissenter, and beautiful/ugly.[30]

Hay and Scott disrupt these binaries by suggesting that deformity is an important component of Englishness. For his part, Hay gives a public voice to disfigured men who have been marginalized by the spectacle of ugly clubs. He argues that ugly clubs are problematic due to the fact that a gathering of ugly or physically disabled people "draws the Eyes of the World too much upon them, and theirs too much from the World." According to Hay, attracting attention, or paying undue heed to the views of society in general, is bound to cause trouble for a deformed man or woman. He further stipulates that social pressure will increase when deformed persons appear together in public since "it doubles the Ridicule, because of the Similitude."[31] Hay is adamantly opposed to the ugly club in a way that subverts Steele's argument about self-deprecation, even if he shows some self-loathing in his inability to imagine himself in public with another physically disabled person. His argument that mocking oneself is not the way to garner self-respect or acceptance defies conventional wisdom surrounding deformity. Kathleen James-Cavan rightly argues that Hay "insists throughout on the social virtues of the marked, deformed body, thereby resisting the devaluation of the second term that plagues the binary distinction of ability and disability" (11). Hay's challenge to the ugly club is another example of how he subverts established modes of thinking that were promoted by both the literary establishment, represented by Steele, and scientific thought, epitomized by Bacon.

The Curse of Beauty

Like Hay's *Deformity: An Essay*, Scott's *Agreeable Ugliness*[32] imparts the message that deformity is in fact desirable. Though this novel confronts the question of female, not male, ugliness, its representation of the righteous deeds and right-mindedness of its plain narrator provides an experiential framework for physical anomaly which counters that of the ugly club. For one thing, the heroine is the center of the novel's moral consciousness, while a beautiful woman, the narrator's fatuous sister, becomes anathema to everyone around her. As the narrator comes of age, she becomes the quintessence of womanhood and domesticity, standing in direct contrast to the ugly club members who are marginalized for their foreignness.[33] *Agreeable Ugliness* domesticates ugliness, converting it into a standard condition of Western European (female) selfhood.[34] Secondly, the *Ugly Club Manuscript* codifies the belief that men and women with deformities should marry each other, while *Agreeable Ugliness* pairs the ugly heroine off with handsome husbands. These contrasts aside, the novel's biggest challenge to established modes of corporeal normalcy consists of the narrator's coming of age, in which she successfully learns to traverse the social obstacles of being born into a genteel family in "native Ugliness."[35] As the novel reveals, the heroine's appearance becomes highly attractive to the handsome, well-situated men around her, while her fair sister proves to be toxic to the men who fall for her good looks.

Throughout *Agreeable Ugliness*, the narrator is fortunate to be a "shocking monster" in her mother's eyes, while her older sister, the Fair Villiers, is cursed to be the most beautiful woman in the novel. The Fair Villiers is vain, superficial, and selfish, while the narrator exhibits all of the traits and conduct that a heroine of a novel of sensibility typically possesses. The narrator reveals the reason behind her advanced moral and intellectual superiority: "As I had continually been told I was a Monster, I really believed it; and had employed my utmost Endeavors to cultivate some natural Talents, and acquire such Accomplishments, as might make me endured in Society."[36] Like Hay, Scott is interested in how physical anomaly facilitates social acceptance, wellbeing, and happiness. If a woman is told she is ugly, there will be an inclination to "cultivate" social graces, moral uprightness, and intellect, while attractive women, such as the Fair Villiers, are never compelled to develop these qualities because they effortlessly please society with their good looks.[37] Without the struggle, the novel suggests, there is no incentive to develop moral and intellectual depth. As Robert W. Jones argues, "for Scott ugliness had an almost moral quality as the sign of virtuous femininity."[38] Jones makes an important point here, but beyond this, Scott's representation of physical abnormality—like Hay's essay—contends with Bacon's assumption that deformed persons have unnatural desires. If the narrator reveals anything in her tale, it is that she is the embodiment of female virtue. Her obedience to her two fathers (her biological father, Mr. de Villiers, and her godfather and aristocratic benefactor, the old Count St. Furcy) throughout much of the novel make her anything but unnatural.

The narrator's ugliness allows her to reap the social benefits of a masculine, genteel education. This has everything to do with the narrator's emotional intimacy with her father, while her sister's closeness with their conceited and vain mother brings about her ruin. As the beginning of the narrative makes clear, the sibling rivalry reflects a parental rift in which the narrator's father and mother are at odds over just about everything, including how to raise their daughters. Mr. de Villiers takes charge of the narrator's moral instruction, while Madame de Villiers coddles and enables the elder sister's unseemly behavior. As Caroline Gonda argues, this sort of intimate father-daughter relationship is characteristic of other novels from the Age of Sensibility, including Sarah Fielding's *The Adventures of David Simple* (1744), Henry Fielding's *Tom Jones* (1749), and Scott's own *The History of Sir George Ellison* (1766). In the case of *Agreeable Ugliness*, the narrator benefits from her father's tutelage, which allows her to develop into a captivating young woman.[39] If the narrator is not physically attractive at the beginning of the novel, she makes up for this with her talents and disposition. Despite her "shocking" appearance, the heroine is eventually seen as an ideal wife and attractive woman by many men, including the middle-aged, wealthy gentleman, Mr. Dorigny, whom she marries at her father's behest; the young Count de St. Furcy, her true love whom she marries at the end of the novel; an artist who is commissioned to paint the narrator's portrait; and even the old Count St. Furcy, who for a time has designs on her himself. Throughout the course of the novel, men's responsiveness to the narrator is indicative of the many ways that the narrator is morally and intellectually superior to (and thus, more attractive than) her sister.

Scott's privileging of deformity over beauty may be countenanced by examining the absolute havoc wreaked by the Fair Villiers everywhere she goes. A significant amount of blame is to be placed squarely upon the shoulders of the girls' mother, the Madame de Villiers, whose mercenary drive to procure a favorable marriage for the Fair Villiers instigates a series of dramatic episodes among her daughter's suitors. When the Fair Villiers is received as a guest at Beaumont, the seat of the de Villiers' aristocratic benefactors, she is censured for her "Imperiousness of Manner" and her "Coquetry and Art."[40] Her "double Intrigue" with two young aristocratic suitors provokes a narrowly avoided duel between them, and she is subsequently sent home.[41] Later on in the novel, when the Fair Villiers and her mother spend a season in Paris, similar coquettish games lead to a violent, public scene in which one of the daughter's suitors almost kidnaps her from a masquerade. The incident ends with the death of Dorigny, the narrator's first husband, who saves the Fair Villiers from her tormentor, but not from her loss of reputation. Again, the

Fair Villiers and her mother are forced to leave——this time from Paris. Late in the novel, the Fair Villiers and her mother cause yet another dispute between an elderly gentleman and his nephew, each of whom seeks to undermine the other in his vying for her hand in marriage. In each of these instances, the Fair Villiers causes tension among her suitors, dividing them in tumultuous ways.[42]

Unlike her older sister, whose beauty and cunning set men against each other, the narrator unifies her suitors due to her temperament and righteousness. After her sister is dismissed from Beaumont, the narrator is invited there as a guest and wastes no time in ingratiating herself to her aristocratic hosts and their friends. The heroine's charm, virtue, and submissiveness inspire the old Count St. Furcy to arrange a marriage between her and Mr. Dorigny. The narrator is not thrilled with the arrangement, but she submits to old St. Furcy's will. Shortly after the count introduces the narrator to Dorigny, she performs for a company of genteel and aristocratic guests by singing a duet with the young Count de St. Furcy, the man she secretly adores. Her voice is so moving and beautiful that Dorigny and the young Count de St. Furcy are overwhelmed with sensibility. Between fits of sobbing Dorigny says, "One must weep, one must adore any one who sings with so much Expression." Young St. Furcy agrees with this assessment: "Oh my dear Sir . . . let me embrace you, how exactly my Opinion agrees with yours!" [43] These two men's esteem and love for one another continues even after Dorigny secures the narrator's hand in marriage. Instead of causing division, jealousy, and violence between her suitors as her sister does among hers, the narrator's virtue and talent bring her male suitors together in a tear-filled embrace, a remarkable eighteenth-century literary example of male suitors expressing affection toward each other in the presence of their shared object of affection.

The narrator also claims a physical advantage over her sister. In Spence's *Crito*, Sir Harry Beaumont uses a frame narrative to attempt to define and codify female beauty. In particular, the narrator, Crito, remarks that a woman's eyes must reflect her inner virtue. This resonates in *Agreeable Ugliness*, in which the heroine's sister has "dark blue, large, and finely formed" eyes that are "without Fire or Expression . . . fine Eyes without Meaning," while the narrator's eyes are "a little too much sunk" and "tolerably large," but are also "of very uncommon Vivacity, and seemed to indicate . . . sense."[44] This "uncommon vivacity" is crucial to Sir Harry Beaumont's formulation of beauty because eyes are the "Seat of the Soul."[45] A virtuous and beautiful face, reflected primarily through a woman's eyes, should convey the inner virtue of that woman. This is why, as Crito opines, "Kind Passions add to Beauty; and all the cruel and unkind ones, add to Deformity."[46]

Crito's view of "expression" justifies the attractiveness of Scott's heroine to all of the men in the novel, and explains why the Fair Villiers is not "fair": her eyes reveal her vacuous inner life and immorality. In this way, the Fair Villiers becomes the novel's true symbol of deformity, while the ugly heroine comes to embody both inner and outer beauty. One's attractiveness, the novel reveals, is not merely skin deep, but the discerning man will be able to decipher this in the eyes and expression of his prospective mate. The narrator's outward appearance is, in this sense, attractive, even if she regularly reminds the reader of her ugliness.

Agreeable Bodies, Agreeable Desires

Agreeable Ugliness is a somewhat conventional novel for its time. Its depiction of the high stakes of a young woman's conduct, the potential pitfalls inherent in courtship, and the values of bourgeois sentimentality align it with other popular novels from the mid-eighteenth century. Moreover, the novel's various plot developments might seem at first glance to do little to challenge marital norms or prevalent, adverse discourses of deformity. After a close reading of some passages from *Agreeable Ugliness, Millenium Hall,* and *The History of Sir George Ellison,* Robert W. Jones claims that, in Scott's fiction, "Ugliness is . . . a more attractive quality than beauty—more attractive because, curiously, it is more regular and more obedient." "As such," he concludes, "Scott's representation of ugliness cannot be read as a redemptive or liberating ideal."[47] Jones suggests that Scott's use of ugliness is "no counterdiscourse" because it is too "implicated in the morality that causes feminine beauty to be repudiated."[48] Caroline Gonda has also argued that *Agreeable Ugliness* promotes a daughter's obedience to her father.[49] I would point out, however, that though the narrator is submissive to her two fathers throughout much of the narrative, she plays her cards in just the right way to marry her true love, the young St. Furcy, even if her fathers do not initially approve of their union. Ultimately, the heroine resists her fathers by insisting that the consequences of her submission to their will would be the death of her own "shocking" body, as well as that of her lover. The traditional elements of the narrative, which Jones and Gonda are right to point out, mask the narrator's ultimate, corporeal resistance to patriarchal mandate and the denouement's endorsement of female desire. *Agreeable Ugliness* thus celebrates a deformed woman's ability to indulge that desire by selecting a partner for herself. Some of the events leading up to this conclusion likewise suggest that this novel is not entirely about a young woman's submission to the law of the father.

While *Agreeable Ugliness*'s social commentary is not exactly a "counterdiscourse," as Jones argues, Scott's endorsement of female agency in this and her other novels is forward-thinking in a Georgian context. Scott's novels regularly portray women's agency as a critique of patriarchal standards, and this is evident in parts of *Agreeable Ugliness*. For example, when Mr. de Villiers approaches his daughter about the possibility of an arranged marriage with Dorigny, the heroine tells her father that she is content with her current companionship with the Mademoiselle de Beaumont, whom she loves "sincerely":

> What Husband could render me more happy than I am with her? In short, Sir, can the most amiable Women long preserve the Esteem of their Husbands? As for Love, I am formed neither to give it, nor to render it lasting; and how, without Love, can a Husband have for me those Attentions, which, when mutual, alone continue the Happiness of married Life?[50]

At this point in the novel, the narrator shows her resolve to opt out of the arranged marriage with Mr. Dorigny by continuing her present relationship with her benefactress.[51] In the process of showing favor for homosocial companionship, the narrator simultaneously critiques marriage by questioning her capacity to love a man. She further substantiates this critique by observing that happiness between a man and a woman is not "lasting" due to the short-lived passion of a husband for his wife. Marriage without love is not the stuff of happiness, the narrator implies, and in any case, she feels that she is not "formed . . . to give it." The remainder of the narrative emphasizes the importance of choice in marriage, but as Scott's most well-known novel, *Millenium Hall*, and this passage indicate, choice also entails having the option to be partnered with someone of the same sex. In *Agreeable Ugliness*, the narrator's desire for female companionship is short-lived, but on the other hand, she does not meekly acquiesce to the father figures in her life, as this passage indicates.

The novel's opening pages likewise call into question the status quo. In her introductory remarks, the narrator sets up a contrast between the social values of beauty and deformity so that she can then undermine these ideas in her subsequent account. In the opening line of the novel, she writes, "A Handsome Woman is, by her Beauty, placed in a more distinguished, and more conspicuous Light in the World, than a Dutchess is at Court."[52] She then compares "a Lady of the first Fashion" who is "watched, sought and followed" to her own humble upbringing. The narrator reveals that she "was born ugly" and has been raised at a modest

estate far from the reaches of Paris and courtly life. In considering the stark difference between her own situation and that of the hypothetical lady, she wonders,
"May we not reasonably conclude from this, that in order to interest Mankind
in general, and to excite the Envy of every Particular of our own Sex, in short,
that to deserve to be known, it is necessary we should be distinguished either by
Beauty or a Title" (3). She denounces the attention paid to attractive women by
lamenting the marginalizing effect this has on women like her: "Mediocrity keeps
a worthy Mind in a State of Depression, and an ugly Face reduces a Woman into
a kind of Non-existence."[53] With this commentary, the narrator sets herself up as
an outsider in terms of her appearance, geographical location, and social station.
The "non-existence" that she laments is exactly the point that she is to defy in the
narrative which follows. By tracing the thoughts of the outsider-narrator in this
way, *Agreeable Ugliness* grants subjectivity to women who have been overlooked
by a society that is too moved by surface beauty and status. Thus, in bringing the
peripheral to the center, *Agreeable Ugliness* employs a normalizing strategy which
illuminates the novel's imbrication of bourgeois values, gender, and deformity.[54]

In its movement from the first arranged marriage, to the happier, concluding companionate marriage, *Agreeable Ugliness*'s plot beautifully illustrates Ruth
Perry's argument that the eighteenth century registers a shift from an emphasis
on the strictures of alliance marriage to that of companionate marriage.[55] The
narrator's first marriage to Mr. Dorigny, though not roundly condemned, is still
a disappointment to the narrator, who yearns for the young St. Furcy. She views
her arranged marriage to Dorigny as a kind of consolation: "Oh, Dorigny, how
much shall I be indebted to thee, if thy Hand saves me from the Precipice, on
whose Brink I am now placed."[56] The "precipice" in this passage is an allusion to
her ardent, unfulfilled desire to be with the young St. Furcy, and his likely rejection of her due to her "plainness." It is fitting that the metaphor she uses involves
the threat of bodily danger as her body is supposed to have been the seat of all
of her torment. She laments, "I could not drive the Idea of the young Count de
St. Furcy from my thoughts . . . I looked on him as excelling every one I had
ever seen . . . in Person, Understanding, and Disposition . . . I called to mind the
Plainness of my Person . . . I appropriated to myself all the Mortifications which
generally attend it."[57] As this passage conveys, the narrator's resolution to marry
Dorigny is at once an obedient gesture to her fathers' commands and a conscious
move to circumvent the heartache that would result from the young St. Furcy's
refusal of her. The narrator's submission to her fathers is in part a consequence
of her own self-preservation.

The arranged marriage between the narrator and Dorigny is far from a complete disaster. From this perspective, one might surmise that *Agreeable Ugliness* does not launch a full-fledged attack on a marital system in which a young woman's desires are disregarded in favor of her father's monetary and social interests. After all, the narrator learns to love Dorigny in her own way. After Dorigny is stabbed and killed by the Fair Villier's attacker, the narrator reminisces on their relationship in the following terms: "I own I married Mr. Dorigny with Indifference; but Honor . . . should have rendered him dear to me; and he could not but become more so by his Attentions, his Regard for me, his Indulgence, and the sincere Esteem he had for me, I will venture to add, by the Proofs of his Love."[58] Words such as "honor," "regard," and "esteem" all connote the narrator's tepid response to her first husband, and yet she becomes convinced of his love and is treated with respect and kindness. Respect notwithstanding, if we compare the narrator's rapport with Dorigny to that of her eventual husband, the young St. Furcy, we may observe that the novel is endorsing companionate marriage, and thus, a good deal more agency for women. Both Jones and Gonda omit this narrative detail in their respective readings of *Agreeable Ugliness*, but I argue that this is important to consider in the context of the novel's stance on female desire. It is not that the novel stipulates that this desire does not matter, nor that it should be repressed entirely; it suggests, on the other hand, that a young woman must exercise a great deal of caution and subtlety in her expression and realization of said desire.

Agreeable Ugliness's conclusion portrays the difficulty of this tightrope walk, but it also suggests that young women may successfully navigate their way to more egalitarian, loving relationships than those inherent in arranged marriages. In considering the fact that the narrator is by novel's end widowed, her newfound agency, precariously situated as it is, makes a bit more sense. In order for the narrator to win the hand of young St. Furcy, she must first defy the wishes of her two fathers without being too forward. Her subtle defiance may be attributed in part to her widowhood, which allows for a certain amount of autonomy that would otherwise not be available to her as a young, unmarried woman. Indeed, wealthy widows (such as the narrator, who has presumably inherited Dorigny's wealth) had a good deal of independence at the time that *Agreeable Ugliness* was published. Amy Froide uses the terms "ever-married" and "never-married" to distinguish between eighteenth-century women who had married and were left widowed, and "singlewomen" who did not marry, and she uses this distinction to argue that "widows had a public and independent place within the patriarchal society" that unmarried, or "never-married" women did not have.[59] Froide goes on to show that a widow could head her own household "with another woman, and the majority chose to do so."[60] *Millenium Hall*'s central relationship is a great example of this point: after having survived her horrendous husband, Mrs. Morgan sets up a house with her long-term romantic friend, Ms. Mancel, at the estate she has inherited. This scenario would not have been thought strange, according to Froide's analysis. She argues that eighteenth-century widows were seen as having "earned [the] right to live outside a male-controlled household. And if more prosperous, widows could opt to establish their own households, where they could gather around them whichever children, servants, relatives, and friends they could accommodate."[61] The widow, having survived her husband, has an out from compulsory patriarchal mandates, and even compulsory heterosexuality, as *Millenium Hall* makes clear.

In the case of *Agreeable Ugliness*, the narrator's increased autonomy in widowhood means that she is capable of entertaining and pursuing (in her restrained way) a marriage with the young St. Furcy. She does this by separating the will and desire of her body, as well as the physical well-being of the young St. Furcy, from the designs of her two fathers. When Mr. de Villiers approaches his daughter about a marriage to an eligible bachelor, Richecour, the narrator responds by articulating the dire physical consequences of her repressed desire:

> I ask no Favor for myself, but do not suffer me to give Death to the Man who saved my Life, to the most worthy Man in the World, in short, to the Man I love. Alas, if I cannot excite your Compassion, if you will not relieve my Anxiety, consider that in destroying *St. Furcy* you at the same time destroy me; I would die sooner than disobey or even displease you; but my Obedience would kill me.[62]

Here, the narrator makes a bold declaration for the love that she feels for young St. Furcy, and she implies that an arranged marriage with Richecour will happen quite literally over their dead bodies. While the narrator does not completely disobey her father, she conveys that her own desire is at odds with that of her father's. Her body's desire, she also suggests, is not entirely her own. A few pages later, the heroine makes a strong claim for her lover, whom she addresses in a letter, "I will never marry Richecour . . . For you only I live. You alone I live, or ever can love."[63] The narrator's invocation of the life of her "shocking" body underscores the novel's movement from the beginning of the novel, in which the narrator's deformity is an unresolved social problem, to its climax and resolution, in which that same body has become the narrator's means of resisting patriarchal authority. Her body is no longer a deficiency, but a strength (even in its purported mortality) to be invoked as a line of defense against tyranny. In this way, the narrator insists that the greatest authority figure in her life is not her father, but her own self.

Moreover, the narrator's resistance also imparts the message that fulfillment of women's desire is necessary for the wellbeing of both women and men. The final plot complication consists of the old count St. Furcy's intention to make the heroine his bride (as a high ranking aristocrat, he would have it in his power to do so). In her confrontation with the old count, the heroine invokes the fragile physical and emotional state of his son, who languishes on account of his unfulfilled love for the heroine:

> It is the Affection you owe your Son, and that which I had for him, which have determined me. If he cannot lose all Hopes of me without Grief, it must still be less than he would suffer at being deprived of your Love . . . but since the depriving him of all Hope is necessary to your Tranquility, I readily consent to rob him of it for ever. There is my Hand, Sir.[64]

The narrator's acceptance of the old count's hand in this scene can hardly be viewed as an obedient gesture. More to the point, she goes beyond speaking of her own body to make a bold declaration for the salutary happiness and physical wellbeing of the old count's son. In fact, throughout the novel, the young count St. Furcy is incapacitated on account of his heightened sensibility. The narrator speaks of his compromised body as a way of directing the old count to his filial responsibilities. The young St. Furcy's inability to act on his overwhelming desire contrasts sharply with the heroine's own agency, which is amplified by her concerted effort to reject the old count without outright rejecting him.

The heroine is rewarded for her resolve, and for her subtle defiance of tyrannical authority. After the narrator speaks of the young count's fragile state, the old count reveals that he has merely been testing her: "Oh, Madam . . . what fortitude appears in you! I am neither worthy of such Virtue, nor of so great a Felicity as you offer me. Could you think that at my Age I would exact such a Sacrifice from you? No, I only wanted to try you thoroughly. Oh! you are my Daughter, and deserve to be so."[65] Finally, the old count grants his soon-to-be daughter-in-law her desire by consenting to her marriage with his son. The narrator thus employs her body, once deemed unsightly and plain, and the body of her lover as forms of resistance to patriarchal authority and as means to the fulfillment of her desire. Her response to the old count allows her to pass what seems a cruel test, and the threat of incest which has been apparent throughout the novel is eradicated.[66] For her successful balancing of desire and paternal obedience, the narrator is rewarded with "happiness," "reward," and "delight," leaving the reader with the distinct impression that love is essential for marriage, and that a woman should be capable of taking an active part in the courtship process. Given the details of this ending, *Agreeable Ugliness* contests certain patriarchal and corporeal codes by imagining that the deformed, female body may be a locus of sexual desire and agency.

Conclusion: The Privilege of Deformity

Agreeable Ugliness emphasizes the heroine's intellect, virtue, and talent, which combine to make her a highly attractive woman to the men who meet her. And yet these attributes also enable her to recognize and fulfill her sexual and emotional desires. Her marriages to Dorigny and St. Furcy overturn Steele's assumption that men and women with deformities belong together. Since Dorigny and St. Furcy are handsome, socially distinctive, and wealthy, Scott suggests that people of differing social stations and physical embodiments may be joined in marriage so long as there is an egalitarian love between them. Scott's novel does not merely invoke sympathy for those with deformities: it reveals that physical difference may make women more virtuous, intelligent, and attractive than beautiful women. In a similar fashion, Hay rejects common notions about what deformity does to an individual. Deformity does not, as Hay claims, turn one against nature: it allows one to cultivate health and a keen intellect. Scott and Hay propose that far from being undesirable, deformity allows for the development of an acute sensibility, which in a mid-eighteenth-century context is one of most important characteristics that a genteel woman or man could possess.

Edmund Burke's take on the subjectiveness of beauty is, to an extent, consonant with what Scott and Hay propose. He claims, "I call beauty a social quality; for where women and men . . . inspire us with sentiments of tenderness and affection towards their persons; we like to have them near us, and we enter willingly into a kind of relation with them, unless we have strong reasons to the contrary."[67] Burke does not attempt to codify attraction, though he suggests that beauty is subjective and undefinable. Sentiments of "tenderness and affection" in the eighteenth century are not necessarily dependent upon a beautiful face, as Burke allows for here, and as we have seen in Hay's and Scott's writings. Attraction and its consequence, affection, are most likely to be garnered by one with a kind disposition, a refined moral framework, and a sharp intellect. Moreover, if we look to Hay and Scott, we find that, in this historical and literary context, people with deformities are the most capable of developing these attributes. While Steele urges his readership "to dare to be ugly," Scott insists that the ugly can and should dare to be attractive by using their mental acuity, virtue, and bodies—strengthened by deformity—to marry the man or woman whom they truly desire.[68] Hay likewise sees his deformity as something which has enriched his life in ways that able-bodied people could not personally understand. Thus, these writers imagine empowerment, and not sympathy, as the true objective for the likes of shocking monsters and lame, hunchbacked men. Since we can safely assume that deformity was such a common embodied experience in the Georgian period, we might imagine many eighteenth-century readers of *Agreeable Ugliness* and *Deformity: An Essay* identifying with these texts' central figures while feeling the privilege of their own deformities; or, for those ordinary readers, questioning for perhaps the first time their supposed superiority to the beautiful faces of deformity.

Notes

1. "deformity, n." *Oxford English Dictionary*. 2nd ed. (Oxford: Oxford University Press, 1989).

2. William Hay, *Deformity: An Essay* (London: George Faulkner, 1754), 5.

3. Spence, Joseph, *Crito: or, A Dialogue on Beauty* (London: R. Dodsley, 1752), 59. The work was published pseudonymously "By Sir HARRY BEAUMONT."

4. Felicity Nussbaum uses the term "anomaly" to signify "a variety of irregularities or deviations from that which is presumed to be the natural order of things." Anomaly, in Nussbaum's estimation, can encompass everything from a variety of disabilities—including deafness, blindness, and lameness—to "physical and mental oddities (for example, dark skin, pock-marked complexion, eunuchism, giantism)" and can also include ailments that occur naturally or by accident. For her explanation of "anomaly," see Felicity Nussbaum, *The Limits of the Human: Fictions of Anomaly, Race and Gender in the Long Eighteenth Century* (Cambridge: Cambridge University Press, 2003), 1.

5. See Lennard J. Davis, "Dr. Johnson, Amelia, and the Discourse of Disability in the Eighteenth Century," in *Defects: Engendering the Modern Body*, eds Helen Deutsch and Felicity Nussbaum (Ann Arbor: University of Michigan Press, 2000), 54–74; and his book length work *Enforcing Normalcy: Disability, Deafness, and the Body* (New York: Verso Press, 1995).

6. Edmund Burke, *A philosophical enquiry into the origin of our ideas of the sublime and beautiful* (London: printed by R. and J. Dodsley, 1757), 21.

7. Burke, *A philosophical enquiry*, 21.

8. Burke, *A philosophical enquiry*, 23, 25.

9. For more on sensibility, see G.J. Barker-Benfield, *The Culture of Sensibility: Sex and Society in Eighteenth-Century Britain* (Chicago: University of Chicago Press, 1992).

10. Hay, *Deformity: An Essay*, 13.

11. Kathleen James-Cavan, introduction to *Deformity: An Essay* by William Hay (Victoria, University of British Columbia Press, 2004), 10.

12. Hay, *Deformity: An Essay*, 36, quotes Montaigne, who argues that "Deformity of Limbs" is more striking to observers than "ill features" or "ugliness" because it is the more "uncommon" kind of physical anomaly. Hay concludes, "As [Deformity of Limbs] is more uncommon, it is more remarkable: and that perhaps is the true reason, why it is more ridiculed." This and a few similar passages have inspired Lennard Davis to argue that Hay reinforces stereotypes about people with disabilities. Roger Lund has concluded that Hay assumes ridicule of the physically disabled as inevitable. See Lennard J. Davis, "Dr. Johnson, Amelia, and the Discourse of Disability in the Eighteenth Century," and Roger Lund, "Laughing at Cripples: Ridicule Deformity, and the Argument from Design," *Eighteenth-Century Studies* 39, no.1 (2005): 95.

13. Francis Bacon's short essay, "Of Deformity" can be found in various collections. See, for example, Francis Bacon, *Essays moral, economical, and political* (London: T. Bensley, 1798) 201–203.

14. Hay, *Deformity; An Essay*, 27–28.

15. Hay, *Deformity: An Essay*, 34–35, argues that "it is not easy to say why one species of deformity should be more ridiculous than another, or why the mob should be more merry with a crooked man than one that is deaf, lame, squinting, or purblind." Thus, for Hay, these different kinds of disabilities fall under the umbrella term "deformity."

16. Daniel Defoe, *The secret history of the October Club: from its original to this time. By a member* (London, 1711), 37–38, mentions the ugly club in passing.

17. Richard Steele. "On Personal Defects; Proposals for an Ugly Club" from *Selections from the Tatler, Spectator, and Guardian* (Oxford: Clarendon Press, 1885), 172.

18. Steele, "On Personal Defects," 172–173.

19. Steele, "On Personal Defects," 172–173.

20. Alexander Carbuncle's last name is a tongue-in-cheek allusion to deformity.

21. See Jane Elizabeth Lewis, *The English Fable: Aesop and Literary Culture, 1651-1740* (Cambridge: Cambridge University Press, 1996). Several incarnations of Aesop appear with the emergence of print culture in England. These renditions of Aesop's life usually precede the fables themselves, and depict Aesop as having a speech impediment, a "swarthy" complexion, and a misshapen body. See for example *Aesop Unveil'd: or, the Beauties of Deformity* (London, 1731) or Samuel Croxall's *The Fables of Aesop, With a Life of the Author*, (London, 1793).

22. The Ugly Club, MS UGL 367, Liverpool Central Library, Liverpool, UK.

23. The Ugly Club, 1.

24. The Ugly Club, 1.

25. The Ugly Club, 1.

26. The Ugly Club, 14.

27. The Ugly Club, 18.

28. The Ugly Club, 20.

29. Roxann Wheeler, *The Complexion of Race: Categories of Difference in Eighteenth-Century British Culture* (Pennsylvania: University of Pennsylvania Press, 2000) 15, 21, argues that in the eighteenth

century, religion and climate play integral roles in constituting English constructions of subjectivity and appearance. She claims, "Religion, in fact, was arguably the most important category of difference for Britons' understanding of themselves at various time during the [eighteenth] century" and "The linchpin to understanding most eighteenth-century pronouncements about the body's appearance is climate." Wheeler's arguments are largely supported by the content of the Ugly Club Manuscript, wherein parts of the body, especially the face, are exoticized and caricatured in the descriptions of individuals who are associated with foreign climes.

30. I am indebted to Chris Mounsey for his insight into the ways that *Agreeable Ugliness* disrupts these kinds of binaries.

31. Hay, *Deformity: An Essay*, 14.

32. All references are to Sarah Scott, *Agreeable Ugliness: or, the Triumph of the Graces. Exemplified in real life and fortunes of a young lady of some distinction* (London: R. and J. Dodsley, 1754).

33. *Agreeable Ugliness* is originally a French novel and therefore takes place in a French setting, but due to the novel's translation and English readership, Englishness and Frenchness may be viewed as representative of a broader Western European perspective.

34. Nancy Armstrong, *Desire and Domestic Fiction* (Oxford: Oxford University Press, 1987), 8, has famously argues that "the modern individual was first and foremost a woman." The fiction of women writers such as Sarah Scott had much to do with Armstrong's gendered vision of eighteenth-century selfhood.

35. Scott, *Agreeable Ugliness*, 13.

36. Scott, *Agreeable Ugliness*, 57.

37. Scott, *Agreeable Ugliness*, 13.

38. Robert W. Jones "Obedient Faces: The Virtue of Deformity in Sarah Scott's Fiction." In *Defects: Engendering the Modern Body*, edited by Helen Deutsch and Felicity Nussbaum (Ann Arbor: University of Michigan Press, 2000) 284.

39. Caroline Gonda "Sarah Scott and 'The Sweet Excess of Paternal Love.'" *Studies in English Literature, 1500-1900* 32, no.3 (1992): 511–35.

40. Scott, *Agreeable Ugliness*, 23.

41. Scott, *Agreeable Ugliness*, 30.

42. The narrative reinforces the misogyny of the era in its contempt for the mother's ability to educate her daughter.

43. Scott, *Agreeable Ugliness*, 66.

44. Scott, *Agreeable Ugliness*, 19–20.

45. Spence, *Crito*, 20.

46. Spence, *Crito*, 22.

47. Jones, "Obedient Faces," 298.

48. Jones, "Obedient Faces," 298.

49. Gonda, "Sarah Scott and 'The Sweet Excess of Paternal Love," 531.

50. Scott, *Agreeable Ugliness*, 62.

51. Companionship between young women of inferior rank and older, well-situated women is a fairly standard arrangement in eighteenth-century novels. See, for example, Maria Edgeworth's *Belinda* (for its depiction of Belinda and Lady Delacour's friendship) or Frances Burney's *Camilla* (for its portrayal of Camilla and Mrs. Arlbery's companionship).

52. Scott, *Agreeable Ugliness*, 1.

53. Scott, *Agreeable Ugliness*, 3.

54. Along with other novels of its time, *Agreeable Ugliness* documents the inculcation of middle-class morality over aristocratic mandate. Samuel Richardson's *Pamela: Or, Virtue Rewarded* (London: C. Rivington, 1740) portrays the struggles of its eponymous heroine, a servant girl, who resists the predatory advances of her libertine master, Mr. B. Pamela manages to maintain her virtue, and her writing converts Mr. B to her virtuous, domestic values. As Nancy Armstrong argues, if a servant girl can resist Mr. B's authority, so can any individual in the "modern form of exchange with the state." Armstrong, *Desire and Domestic Fiction*, 118.

55. Ruth Perry, *Novel Relations: The Transformation of Kinship in English Literature and Culture, 1748-1818* (Cambridge: Cambridge University Press, 2004).

56. Scott, *Agreeable Ugliness*, 74.

57. Scott, *Agreeable Ugliness*, 73.

58. Scott, *Agreeable Ugliness*, 158.

59. Amy Froide, *Never Married: Singlewomen in Early Modern England* (Oxford: Oxford University Press, 2005) 17.

60. Froide, 18.

61. Froide, 18–19.

62. Scott, *Agreeable Ugliness*, 225.

63. Scott, *Agreeable Ugliness*, 229.

64. Scott, *Agreeable Ugliness*, 251–52.

65. Scott, *Agreeable Ugliness*, 252.

66. "The threat of incest, which has been present, though unvoiced, in the exclusive intensity of the father-daughter relationship, finally emerges in another form: a proposal from the man who calls her 'our dear Daughter,' and loves her 'as my own Child.'" Gonda, "Sarah Scott and 'The Sweet Excess of Paternal Love,'" 516.

67. Burke, *A philosophical enquiry into the origin of our ideas of the sublime and beautiful*, 18–19.

68. Steele, "On Personal Defects; Proposals for an Ugly Club," 172.

9

READING "THE BLIND POETESS OF LICHFIELD"

The Consolatory Odes of Priscilla Poynton

Jess Domanico

P RISCILLA POYNTON (ca. 1740–1801) is a figure of eighteenth-century women's poetry who offers researchers and critics new territory. Poynton is evidence that the recovery act of women's pre-nineteenth-century texts is still in progress. At this moment in scholarship, however, Poynton is still overlooked as a blind poet who did not produce a significant amount of work, whose conversations with fellow writers of her age were of minimal importance, and who did not have much to contribute to the body of literature generated by women writers during the eighteenth century. A thorough discussion of Poynton must rely heavily on her poetry, as it is one of the only artifacts available at this point in time. Contemporaneous reviews are nonexistent, and no full-length scholarship examines Poynton exclusively, her life or her texts.

Best known for her identity as a blind poet, Poynton has been mentioned more and more frequently in current eighteenth-century studies scholarship in relation to disability studies. These mentions in the scholarship span no more than a sentence in length and do not expound upon her work in any way.[1] Arguably, the underlying assumption here is that Poynton has little scholarly worth because her blindness prevented her from perfecting her craft and establishing herself as more than a regional poet. This assumption has prevailed since 1770, when she published her first poems. There is no doubt that her blindness is important, but what is needed is a clear reason for continuing to discuss her and her poetry in this particular context. To provide a reason, the best method is to examine closely Poynton's treatment of her poetry and discover what her blindness, specifically, contributed to her work.

Poynton reads her own life via her poetry, which is also her method of interpreting the world. Included in that reading is her understanding of her own disability—her blindness—and how she utilizes that blindness as an author. The "silence," Poynton's absence from scholarship, does not originate from her—she wrote what and when she was able. Poynton's silence is a result of readers' failure to review or document her writing, and the pattern repeated throughout the nineteenth, twentieth, and twenty-first centuries. Now, in the act of recovering her work, readers curious about Poynton come across a serious obstacle: a silence of source material, both primary and secondary. What worthwhile reading still exists or is known about Poynton comes from Poynton herself. Although it may not appear to be so, this is an advantage. It allows Poynton's work to be read isolated and as her own, instead of through the eyes, so to speak, of contemporary critics of the eighteenth century and of today.

As the introduction to this volume suggests, Poynton deconstructs the able-bodied and disabled binary and becomes an example of Variability. Poynton's poetry, when situated within current scholarship of the quickly emerging feminist disability studies, demonstrates that her blindness is actually enabling—i.e., it enables her to read her own life as she envisions it. Through a synthesis of life writing theory and feminist disability studies, this essay will demonstrate Poynton's ability to manipulate her blindness and overcome the obstacles she faces as a writer by examining what are, arguably, her two most significant poems—one a revision of the other. Thus, her narrative is one of overcoming by way of poetic reflection.

Poynton's understanding of gender as she reads is also important to understanding the significance of her poetry. According to Judith Fetterly, "Women can read women's texts because they live women's lives; men can not [sic] read women's texts because they don't lead women's lives."[2] If reading commonly "functions to reinforce the identity and perspective which the male teacher/reader brings to the text,"[3] and Poynton's contemporary readers could not recognize or relate to the experiences she portrayed in her poetry, then her work would inevitably be lost, according to that mentality. We are lucky, if this is the explanation for Poynton's silence, to have access to her two known volumes of poetry. But what is more important here is the ways in which Poynton reads herself. Her poems are frequently labeled as "extempore," suggesting that she composed most of her material in response to an immediate occasion or in reply to an acquaintance. Because of the nature of her poems, many of them were probably composed in her head. We can only assume, based on the information from her editors, that she possessed a transcriber who documented her extempore recitations to audiences. The presence of an amanuensis is a significant aspect of Poynton's work that would otherwise have not existed if she had the ability to write on her own and remain legible enough for her transcriber to read her handwriting. The editor of Poynton's second volume, Joseph Weston, complains of the difficulties he had procuring Poynton an amanuensis because her handwriting was indecipherable and thus nearly impossible to transcribe. This is merely speculative, but Poynton probably could not afford to keep a full-time amanuensis; she most likely reserved him or her for poetry recitations. This would make it extremely difficult to stay in touch with her long-distance friends, acquaintances, and relatives, especially if she did not have enough vision to write letters, diary entries, or other modes of life writing on her own. She nevertheless labels herself as a writer, though she is frequently unable to physically compose—or, when she does, others have difficulty reading what she writes. She hopes that her readers "bid P.P. to write again!" even if they find it presumptuous and her "writing then, perhaps, might laughter raise."[4] Poynton's poetry, therefore, is where we encounter Poynton reading herself—and subsequently defining herself—as a woman writer, because it is the only avenue she has available to do so.

A brief overview of Poynton's canon of poetry might suggest that she does not, in fact, read her own narrative through the act of composition, but instead simply replies to friends and acquaintances or responds to their wish for her to recite her work. Of the sixty-nine poems in *Poems on Several Occasions*, thirty-six of them are addressed to a specific audience, whether it is one single reader or a group of readers from a specific area of Staffordshire. Thirty-one of the total poems are labeled as "extempore," which implies that they were composed in front of a listening public who provided the occasion—or the subject matter—for them. Despite this very obvious audience, however, Poynton's work is a strong example of self-presentation. Much of life writing, after all, examines the diaries and letters of women writers as its objects of interpretation. Poynton's work, though versified, is similar; when she addresses poems to members of her friends or family, they act similar to letters, and when she chronicles her tours across Staffordshire and describes her reception there, those poems act much like travel writing or a travel diary.

Because material on Poynton is difficult to locate, there is only a small amount of full-length scholarship dedicated to her and her poetry.[5] However, that does not suggest Poynton's contribution to poetry is insignificant. Knowledge of her might be limited, but her poetry is easily accessible and her example is an important avenue of scholarship in eighteenth-century women's writing because it allows us to examine a woman poet reflecting upon her own circumstance via the methodologies of disability studies, an increasingly popular field, and life writing, which feminist advocates have often chosen in favor of biography or autobiography because of its genre permeability and fluidity. The concept of Variability is an important development for life writing as well—both approaches highlight distinct features of the writing of an individual like Poynton without categorizing her poetry as representational of blind eighteenth-century writers or blind writers in general.

Marlene Kadar defines life writing as "a way of seeing literary and other texts that neither objectifies nor subjectifies the nature of a particular cultural truth."[6] Life writing,[7] a term commonly used in the eighteenth century in place of the terms autobiography and biography,[8] allowed more fluidity between genres— including poetry. *The Annual Register* for the year 1771, one year after Poynton published *Poems on Several Occasions*, writes, "Of all the fantastic amusements in which modern genius indulges itself, the most whimsical is Life-writing" and "This species of writing is so replete with opportunities of gratifying the little vanities, and indulging the caprices of the human breast, that vain and capricious men are seldom able to resist it. Hence it is that our age is the repository of Live, Opinions, Memoirs, and Anecdotes."[9]

Life writing challenges strict genre boundaries and situates multiple genres into its discourse. "Thus life writing, put simply," Kadar defines, "is a less exclusive genre of personal kinds of writing, that includes both biography and autobiography, but also the less 'objective' or 'personal,' genres such as letters and diaries."[10] What makes life writing appealing to feminist scholars is this fluidity, this inclusiveness that incorporates forms of writing into its theory. Poynton, for her own part, fits into this genre not by virtue of her poetry, but by virtue of the content of her poetry.

The recent focus of life writing, according to Kadar, is often on "proliferation, authorization, and recuperation of autobiographical writing" by women.[11] Because there is very little biographical information available, we must turn to Poynton herself to gain a sense of who she was and what she accomplished as a writer. Although she never wrote her own autobiography, she did include significant amounts of information about her life in her poetry, especially in the first volume published in 1770. Poynton fits Kadar's definition of life writing because she rarely writes about other people (real or imagined), nor does she pretend that she is separate from the text she's writing.[12] Although poetry is not often considered a genre of life writing, Poynton's poetry is an apt fit because

Poynton, during her recitations of extempore poetry, could not separate herself from the verses; she simultaneously composed and recited her own work. Furthermore, life writing is a suitable designation for Poynton's poetry because, despite the fact that we learn the most about her life through her poetry, calling it "autobiographical" or "biographical" is too constricting and doesn't allow for Poynton's extemporaneous process of invention.

The concept of life writing, when juxtaposed with poetry, "concentrates attention on poetry writing as process and practice, a contextualizing, horizontal look at writing that shifts away from canon, a vertical construct."[13] Poynton's two volumes of poetry easily lend themselves to this model, especially because of their common trope of reflection and the "processes of the self,"[14] which allow both readers—the blind poet and her audience—to examine how Poynton reads the text of her own life. This is best exemplified by what I call the two consolatory poems, which I will discuss in depth later. In the first poem, Poynton introduces her situation and her initial hope for the future. In the second, she revises the language of the original poem to skew her recollection and further develop her poetic self-reflection.

This type of life writing operates under Susan Sniader Lanser's assumption that every writer who publishes her work, or makes it available publicly in some form, "wants it to be authoritative for her readers . . . within the sphere and for the receiving community that the work carves out."[15] Lanser, developing a narratology of mid-eighteenth-century women writers of the novel, uses terms in her analysis that are indirectly related to Poynton's poetry. Lanser describes distinctions between private voice and public voice as well as distinctions between "narrative situations that do and those that do not permit narrative self-reference," or the "act of narration itself."[16] What's unique in Poynton's example is that her poetry is not always specifically narratological, or in the recognized form of narrative—but, upon closer inspection, Poynton publicly narrates her own experience as a dual-method of allowing her audience a glimpse of her world while simultaneously reading and responding to her own experiences as a blind woman poet. Poynton, therefore, has what Lanser calls "authorial voice," or instances in a narrative that are both public and refer to the "self" of the text.[17] The reason Poynton's poetry can be considered authorial, according to Lanser's definition, is because it is intended for a viable public audience. The audience members during Poynton's recitations and the names inscribed on the pages of Poynton's subscription list are "narratees" (defined by Lanser as a reading audience); they witness Poynton reading her own narrative.

We know Poynton recited her work before specific audiences because of the poetry she publishes in *Poems on Several Occasions*. Several of her poems suggest that she was favorably received in the towns and cities she traveled to, such as Lichfield, Birmingham, Coventry, Warwick, and Chester. Poynton risked a great deal by reciting her poetry extemporaneously and in front of an audience. In doing so, she surrendered the safety net of published text by eradicating the potential generic nature of words on a page.

"A female personal narrator," Lanser explains, "risks the reader's resistance if the act of telling, the story she tells, or the self she constructs through telling it transgresses the limits of the acceptably feminine."[18] It is important to note just how vulnerable Poynton and her poetry were—in addition to being a female poet, she was blind, and her poetry often referred to her inability to see her surroundings, read, or perform daily tasks without assistance.

Being blind minimizes Poynton's desirability as a woman because it is considered a defect or deformity of the body, but in exchange it allows her to write without any awareness of social obstacles, save the fact that she cannot write without an amanuensis or transcriber. In place of desire, audiences perhaps attended Poynton's readings because of her anomalous nature as a blind poet. This was true of the readers of Thomas Blacklock (1721–1791), a contemporary poet of Poynton's who went blind sixth months after his birth. Blacklock's poetry helped audiences believe that the blind author possessed what Edmund Burke called "a great facility in the employment of poetic language, which depends on its power on the exploitation of associations and not only on its capacity to make pictures."[19] William Paulson explains that in France, the new interest in blind authors as curiosities sparked a change in "the way the blind enter speculative and imaginative discourse; new possibilities for defining and conceptualizing blindness appeared alongside other myths and stories, [whence] the blind became the objects of psychological speculation." [20] To this end, Paulson refers to Denis Diderot's *Lettre sur les aveugles,* his *Letter on Blindness*,[21] which discusses the difficulty the blind have in attaching "visual concepts to the words that signify them,"[22] calling this obstacle the "poverty of denomination."[23] According to the French, those without vision "must rely on abstraction and figures, on the systematic, self-referential properties of language, the production of meaning out of contextual and formal relations rather than by denomination or reference."[24] Poynton, as this article demonstrates, relies heavily on revising language to craft the poetic narrative of her experience as a blind poet. To do so, she takes one particular poem and modifies it, consequently altering the meaning, three times.[25] Paulson's point is nevertheless clear in this framework: Poynton creates meaning in her revisions of her words in context with her life, not in relation to the things she cannot see.

Thus, it is not possible to study Poynton without awareness of her blindness. At the age of twelve she became blind, "occasioned by a violent head-ach."[26] It is difficult, however, to practice disability studies when examining eighteenth-century literature and culture because the term, and the approach, is anachronistic. The eighteenth century's understanding of disability—and blindness, specifically—was shifting as the century continued. In the beginning of the century, much effort was made to investigate and examine subjects with defects or deformities (the terms used in place of "disabled" or "disability"),[27] but toward the nineteenth century, humans with deformities were "increasingly believed to be the province of enthusiastic and superstitious vulgar folk" and the study of physical difference "diverged from a more enlightened curiosity that spurred serious philosophic and scientific inquiry."[28] Disability[29] as we understand it, therefore, is not an "operative category;" rather, it is an expansive concept that typically involved terms such as "defect" to distinguish persons with physical anomalies.[30] According to Dwight Christopher Gabbard, "disability . . . may be anachronistic, but it still can be usefully deployed in eighteenth-century studies to the extent that it addresses the anomalous body's relation to cultural environment."[31] Therefore, when scholars position Poynton into the discourse of disability, they examine her blindness in order to demonstrate the social and cultural functions of an eighteenth-century understanding of deformity.

Furthermore, Lennard J. Davis, a leader in the field of disability studies within the humanities, explains, "by narrativizing an impairment, one tends to sentimentalize it and link it to the bourgeois sensibility of individualism and the drama of an individual story."[32] This is why life writing and disability studies are complimentary theories, and also why Poynton's poetry, if we extend the genre of life writing to include literature in verse, lends itself so well to this type of analysis.

Interpellation, specific to disability studies,[33] is the process through which people with disabilities are constituted as "disabled" via cultural institutions and discourses of normalcy.[34] This process is problematic because it groups individuals under the umbrella term "abnormal" and inscribes them as substandard citizens. It encourages discrimination. Poynton suffers the effects of interpellation when she was and is passed over by audiences of both the eighteenth and the present century. She counteracts this process, however, via her poetry. Perhaps the reason her work is frequently overlooked is because critics have not read her work closely enough to discover the ways in which Poynton overcomes her obstacle of "deformity" and demonstrates her ability as a poet.

Before we situate Poynton in this context, it is important to demonstrate disability's connection with developing understandings of sex and gender during the eighteenth century. The movement of feminist disability studies revises what is already known about disability to "question our assumptions that disability is a flaw, lack, or excess" and argues that disability "is a cultural interpretation of human variation rather than an inherent inferiority."[35] Feminist disability studies not only "retrieves overlooked experiences and under theorized critical perspectives, it strives to rewrite oppressive social scripts."[36] In Poynton's case, the "oppressive social script" involved is the lack of recognition due to her blindness. For example, as Chris Mounsey shrewdly discusses in this volume's introduction, in her poem "Address to a Bachelor, On a Delicate Occasion. Inserted by Desire," Poynton recapitulates an uncomfortable experience occurring the night before.[37] Reluctant, confused, and blushing, Poynton is the butt of men's jokes because she cannot relieve herself on her own. Her experience is overlooked, and even mocked, because she is blind. Her reaction is to record the experience in verse and, presumably, send the poem to the very individual who caused her discomfort. The assumption is that her blindness is debilitating in regards to the act of writing, but it is her very blindness that prompts her to write, to represent in words her experience.

To represent Poynton as a blind eighteenth-century woman poet is accurate, but it categorizes her as an anomaly rather than a poet, and encourages the reader to center their understanding of Poynton around her blindness—which, for the purposes of this article and in the context of life writing and feminist disability studies is very important—instead of her poetry, which is more important. Although Poynton herself encouraged her anomalous identity as a poet so that she might gather more subscribers and audiences, this approach to her poetry no longer serves. Poynton probably organized a subscription list by following the example of Blacklock, whose 1756 edition of *Poems by Mr. Thomas Blacklock* also had a long list of subscribers. What is unique about Poynton's poetry is her method of gathering subscriptions by traveling through various counties and exhibiting it aloud.

Disability is an effect of power relations, which Poynton inverts by reciting her poetry to present audiences. There are several components at work in this exchange between the speaking, Poynton, and the listeners, her audience. First, by simply being blind, she neither acknowledges the fact that she is being gazed upon, nor does she gaze back. Her poetry reflects this; she often emphasizes that external charms and the accompanying acts of seeing and being seen are not as praiseworthy as virtue.[38] This allows her to recite poetry without distraction or concern over how her audience receives her during her performance. Additionally, Poynton refuses the hierarchy of the "defective" subject below the able subject by performing her poetry aloud, in front of an audience, as the center of attention. A significant amount of the poetry in her first volume exemplifies this structure, especially in the three odes that Poynton includes, all variations of the same theme.

Poynton's advertisement for her first collection, printed in *The Birmingham Gazette* on September 12, 1768, describes the upcoming volume as containing odes, elegies, songs, epistles, enigmas, and satires. She does not mention that they are primarily composed with little or no preparation, what she later calls extempore. Her subscribers presumably knew this; extempore poetry was a popular genre throughout the century[39] and many subscribers probably witnessed her poetry while she traveled throughout the counties of Staffordshire, Warwickshire, Leicestershire, and Cheshire. Poynton's announcement is the first example of her reading her own work, and thus reading her own life experience as an author. She writes that her first volume is an act of flattery—to herself—and that she wishes to publish her poems based on the assumption that they will be read by "the good-natur'd World, as well as the judicious critic."[40] Reflecting on her education, she writes that "since she is not sufficiently acquainted with Authors to dress her work with refin'd Quotations, her Thoughts wear no other Embellishment than Simple Nature, for to that fair one she is alone indebted."[41] Here, Poynton signals her method of composition: she relies on what she knows to write poetry rather than what she has learned about the genre. Her poems, therefore, are unique hybrids of common forms of verse that often reflect on the content she knows best—her own experiences. In the advertisement, Poynton includes what she calls a "Consolatory Ode on her Misfortune," which "was what first inspired her Genius."[42] The fact that Poynton writes her advertisement in the third person is indicative of the manner in which she reads her own writerly narrative. The use of third person accomplishes two things: first, it allows her to distance herself from her work in order to comment upon it without immediately revealing her motive, and second, it allows her to reflect upon the form and content of her poetry without appearing to do so and thus losing credibility.

Poynton's particular use of the word "Genius" most likely refers to her "natural ability or capacity" or her "quality of mind" that accommodates "the special endowments which fit a man for his particular work."[43] She demonstrates this genius by including a segment of her own poetry to allow audiences to read it and judge for themselves. What's missing from this rhetoric is the typical appeal to a women writer's readership to excuse her ignorance regarding the norms of

poetical composition. Instead, Poynton merely recounts her blindness and conse-
quential struggles. Her lack of vision is not an excuse for poor writing; rather, it is
a compelling argument meant to convince literary patrons to subscribe to her first
volume. Poynton's strategy is manipulative. After all, at this point in the publication process, she already has more than 1300 subscribers, which she notes at the
end of the announcement as if to affirm her poetry's worth.

> The brief ode, the first of the three, reads in full,
> With gen'rous pity, sure each breast must glow,
> For those who (like me) drink the cup of woe;
> Tho' great my loss, just heav'n the loss did send,
> And I to heav'n without reluctance bend:
> Since sighs and tears cannot my sight regain,
> Why should I then of adverse fate complain?
> Thus may I patient ever bear my woe,
> And still revere the hand that gave the blow.[44]

This, as we'll see, is similar to the following odes that she publishes in the volume
proper. The language is similar, and Poynton retains the invocation to the audience's pity in each poem. What's most interesting about this particular ode is that
the first two lines are reserved for the audience, as if to acknowledge their pity
and offset it with the poet's own. Her perspective changes after the first two lines,
however, to address her reflections on her own loss of sight. Poynton does this in
the following consolatory odes as well, but each time she does so, her language
changes and the meaning of the poem shifts accordingly.

The full-length ode published in *Poems on Several Occasions* establishes the
connections between what the genre of life writing reveals about a woman poet
and the reflections that result from the process of examining, or "envisioning," so
to speak, Poynton's own experience as a blind woman writer. Poynton's poem titled
"The following Consolatary [sic] ODE was the first Poetical Composition of the
AUTHOR'S" is the first in which we discover her blindness, and consequently, we
discover how Poynton reads and interprets her own narrative.

Her "Consolatary ODE," an appropriate example of the horizontal model
of life writing, begins by invoking the reader's pity: "The following Consolatary
ODE was the first Poetical Composition of the AUTHOR'S."[45] It seems strange,
at first, to suggest that Poynton considers herself as the reader—why would she
address herself in such a manner? The form of the poem lends insight into the
processes of self; she begins with a four-line stanza that orients the "reader," and

finishes the rest of the ode with twenty-five more lines, without stanza breaks, in heroic couplets. She writes, "Shoulds't thou, my Reader, lend a pitying sigh, / Ne'er ask for whom thy bosom heaves so high,"[46] which misleads the reader to believe that Poynton does not want their pity. However, if she is addressing herself as a reader, this first line is a reprimand against self-pity instead. The issue raised here is complicated: Poynton does not want the pity of the reader, whoever they may be, because pity is a difficult emotion for her to comprehend. Diderot, in his Essay on Blindness (composed about a decade after Poynton's first poems), would expound upon the same idea. He explains, "As of all the external signs which raise our pity and ideas of pain, the blind are affected only by complaint, I have, in general, no high thoughts of their sympathy and tenderness."[47] Poynton approaches her own capacity for affect in the same manner.

The first verse paragraph initiates the reader to the content of the poem—the form is immediately evident—and shifts from the second person "thou" to the first person possessive by the third line. The two pairs of lines, separated by the rhyme scheme, are disconnected. Poynton seems to encourage her reader not to pity her for her loss without explaining what her loss is or why she evokes feelings of pity in the first place. The stanza assumes that the reader already knows that the persona of the poem (the author, as established in the title), possesses some aspect of her being that evokes pity. Poynton's second couplet reads, "Though great my loss, just Heaven decreed it so, / Nor sighs, nor tears, can mitigate my woe."[48] More than anything else, she assures herself that her plight is "decreed," and pitying herself as disadvantaged is useless. When read closely, this is a remarkable instance of overcoming what even Poynton, as shown by these lines, considered a defect or deformity of her physicality. For not only is the author blind, she can barely use a writing instrument without being illegible. Nevertheless, she clearly does not believe her ability to compose verses is weakened by her blindness.

The very fact that Poynton cannot write with a pen but still overcomes the obstacle of the blank page despite her "lack," so to speak, echoes the common trope in feminist theory that describes the pen as a metaphorical phallus. Poynton has neither the pen nor the phallus, but neither matter; she writes anyway, even though she may not be able to examine the end result or correct errors in transcription, she is still in a position of power when dictating to her amanuensis what she wishes to say. The act is intensely reflective. Although a minor example, Poynton's ability to write without a pen—the mediator between her thoughts and the blank page—nonetheless contributes to the ways in which she overcomes both her blindness and her status as a woman writer with little formal education.

The middle of the ode narrates the event of Poynton's lack of vision, which she mentions numerous times in her poetry, noting its significance. Poynton never directly attributes the occasion of becoming a writer to her blindness, but its repeated mention suggests this is true. Following the first verse paragraph, which offers no insight as to why the poetic persona should or should not be pitied, Poynton reveals what causes her misery. She writes, "Full twice shining summers pass'd away, / The dread thirteenth, in darkness wrapp'd my day; / When on a rapid wing my dear sight fled, / And left me here, with drooping, mournful head."[49] Note that the poet does not mention her absence of vision and its effect on her writing. Instead she emphasizes that she is left "here," a word which resonates just before the caesura of the line. Where "here" is, she is not clear, but there is a sense of transformation at work in this phrase. Poynton is still "here," still blind. And yet, she is here as a writer, not merely a blind woman, and here in the poetry, representing herself in the best way she knows how.

The word "here" is temporal as well; it indicates the present process of self-reflection in Poynton's life writing. After all, self-reflection is her primary method of composition, as she cannot compose and edit her poetry visually via writing to any great extent. Poynton moves back and forth between tenses in the next six lines, indicating that the past physical "pain" of her blindness, which was "occasioned by a violent head-ach,"[50] mirrors her present emotional pain—an after effect of the pain of losing her sight from the unidentified illness she contracted at a young age, as well as the pain of no longer experiencing the joys that accompany sight. She writes, "How dull the hours! how slow they move away! / My ripening joys, by stern misfortune cross'd, / All blasted seem'd, and I to pleasure lost,"[51] indicating, at the onset of her blindness, that the passing of time becam· a drudgery for her, and she no longer locates pleasure in those things she once enjoyed. "For with my sight," Poynton continues, "each pleasing object flew; / Grant joys, kind Heav'n! more lasting and more true."[52] This sudden shift in emphasis from her blindness to her religious sentiments regarding her misfortune is an interesting turn, but not a surprising one.

The manner in which Poynton turns her narrative from one of loss to one of redemption is common in her poetry; she often begins to sermonize toward the end of her verses. This corresponds to the extempore tradition that was first begun by preachers and other ministers of the church. Poynton, who was an Anglican,[53] appropriates this tradition.[54] Jacqueline George, in her article, "Public Reading and Lyric Pleasure: Eighteenth Century Elocutionary Debates and Poetic Practice," argues that public reading that was often extempore, and involved sermons delivered by clergymen, gradually became more and more popular in the domestic sphere as women began to recite literature.[55] She explains that the movement of public reading created a "double consciousness" that "fashioned readers who, in private, would be fully prepared to engage in the imaginative arena of lyric poetry."[56] This is an instance of appropriation to be sure, but in Poynton's case she appropriates the form of extempore verse even further by orally delivering her work outside of the domestic sphere, in public and advertised settings, to promote the first volume of her poetry. Elocution, of course, involves a reader reciting another's text. Poynton reverses the model and becomes a poet who recites her text and reads and reflects upon its content simultaneously in order to make sense of her experience.

Poynton reads her narrative in this manner to demonstrate that her approach to blindness is to accept it and write regardless. The "Consolatary [sic] Ode" consoles Poynton as it relates the circumstances of her blindness and her subsequent life of writing, traveling across various counties, and composing poetry for willing audiences. By writing this poem almost twenty years after her loss of sight, Poynton demonstrates just how she uncovers new ways to see via writing. Thus, writing is enabling for her. That the subject of "the first Poetical Composition of the Author's" is the occasion of Poynton's blindness is telling, therefore, because it shows an outside reader just how Poynton reassures herself that there is reprieve for her blindness, albeit imagined at this point in her life. Her ability to imagine what she considers heaven is remarkable; the two most prominent images of paradise in the poem involve shining "bright mansions" and flowing "rivers of pleasure."[57] Briefly, she provides herself with an alternative to the darkness. This is a theme throughout a number of her poems, especially those whose subject is blindness directly. For instance, Poynton addresses a blind young man later in the volume with the lines, "Nor once repine, what tho' depriv'd of sight, / If we are blest but with internal light. / Those inward eyes that MILTON names, my friend, / Beam with eternal rays that have no end."[58] Again, Poynton substitutes earthly vision for "internal light," light that originates in her imagined divine realm. The light she describes is, according to Poynton, common to blind poets like Milton and Blacklock, which latter she praises in preceding poems as possessing matchless powers and equals him to Milton and Homer. Both poets' "inward eyes" are superior to external vision, Poynton claims, and rather than have sight she prefers to replace "external" vision with their "eternal rays" of light. Poynton emphasizes her subtle play on the words external and eternal in the following lines: "How empty then must be external sight, / When it's compar'd unto celestial light!"[59] Life's scenes are illusions, she explains, and just as in the odes, encourages the blind young man and herself to forgo sight in order to gain interminability in heaven. Poynton thus borrows language from Blacklock, who, as Joseph Spence explains in the preface to Blacklock's *Poems*, refers to light as something beyond mere brightness or daylight, but as something signifying heaven. He uses words like "immortal" and "glory," and Poynton mimics his approach to represent light metaphorically in order to combat her own physical and emotional darkness.[60]

To conclude the consolatory ode, Poynton seeks resolution, but articulates it in a strange manner. She writes, "For resignation best can sooth our woe, / However dire appears the fatal blow."[61] This line is problematic. That Poynton is resigned to her fate seems to contradict the rest of the poem, which acknowledges the poetic persona's misfortune but shifts midway to offer future solutions. This line on resignation, therefore, masks what Poynton is really demonstrating here— through writing her narrative via poetry, she discovers a method of consoling herself and momentarily escaping from her blindness. Poynton sees more about her situation than she lets on.

The second full-length consolatory ode, included in the same volume of poetry, is titled "Consolatory REFLECTIONS, that have Occasionally occurred on that most lamentable Incident, My LOSS of SIGHT: with some few Alterations and Additions, to what I had at first composed upon this melancholy subject."[62] This new poem on the same theme—Poynton's blindness—is a deeper reflection on the event than the first. Poynton once again invokes the poet's reader in the first line. In fact, she uses the same language, word for word, which suggests that the first two lines are purposely ambiguous as to who the reader of the poem is. Poynton's revision, however, further indicates that she is the primary reader of both the poem and of the event.

Poynton's extempore poems would not have been recited perfectly by her each time she included them on her tour, nor would they be transcribed accurately each time. The differences in the two poems are a matter of imperfect transcription, Poynton's misremembering, or her deliberate revision. If we are to believe that she read her life through the lens of her poetry, then the third possibility is the most relevant and deserves more exploration.

Thus, the first significant revision occurs in the third line, where Poynton replaces the "Though my great loss" of the original with "Tho' my hard fate." The new line makes Poynton's blindness appear inevitable, whereas the first suggests more of a medical circumstance that occasioned her loss of vision.[63] The rest of the first quatrain proceeds as before, until we reach the fifth line. In the original poem, Poynton finishes her quatrain and offers a break between the first four lines and the rest of the poem, perhaps to signal the levity of her topic. In the second poem, however, she forgoes the line break and continues, "Twelve shining summers I was bless'd with sight, / But then deny'd the chearful rays of light."[64] These lines are significantly more ambiguous than the original lines, which merely relate the commencement of Poynton's blindness at a young age. Instead, the lines lead the reader to interpret in two ways: that Poynton either was "deny'd" her sight by some omnipotent force, or she "deny'd" it herself. The syntactical structure of the sentence, along with the semicolon in place of a common or enjambment, suggests the latter.

The second volume of Poynton's poetry, published twenty-four years after her first volume, was titled *Poems by Mrs. Pickering* and included similar extempore poems and poems composed as though they were journal entries or narratives of Poynton's daily life.[65] The fact that this volume is published under the name Priscilla Pickering and not Priscilla Poynton seems problematic at first, but in the event, it reinforces Poynton's ability to read her life through the lens of her poetry. After she was married Poynton presumably stopped traveling to promote her poetry and, deprived of her audience, wrote much less. The poems she did write try to replicate her previous models, but are not as successful as the first volume. That she published under another name may be a strategy to position herself as an emergent blind author—thus portraying herself as an anomaly once again in order to gain a new reading public—but this interpretation seems disingenuous. Perhaps she published as Priscilla Pickering because, after her marriage, she considered her life much different from that of Priscilla Poynton's life, and could not reconcile the two. The poetry of this volume, therefore, is significantly weaker than that of the first, and the volume even includes poems by her editors, who possibly manipulated Poynton in her blindness and used her to promote their own work. There is no evidence to suggest that Poynton was aware of these poems' inclusion in her volume—she does not mention it anywhere in the text. In fact, there is almost nothing concrete to suggest that Poynton and Pickering is the same person except for a few minor instances: in the 1789 advertisement for the new volume and the occasional referral to "Prissy," a nickname of Poynton's that occurs in both volumes.

Like *Poems on Several Occasions*, Poynton published an advertisement in *The Birmingham Gazette* for *Poems by Mrs. Pickering*. It reads much like the one published previously; Poynton once again depicts herself as a novel, unique, and struggling poet. The 1789 advertisement explains that she "sustained many Losses in the Year 1770, through unavoidable contingencies,"[66] but this is the only hint that Mrs. Pickering and Priscilla Poynton are the same woman. In this volume, Poynton is less focused on portraying herself simply as a blind writer and chose instead to write about tangible events and circumstances in her life—in fact, this collection lends itself more easily to discussions of poetry and life writing because the poems included here are almost exclusively addressed to Poynton's acquaintances, and very few are labeled extempore. At this point in her life, after her marriage, Poynton probably secured a more reliable amanuensis to help her communicate via writing and poetry. She abandoned her recurring blindness theme and focused instead on specific events from her life, such as her marriage, her husband's death, and letters to relatives.

Poynton died in 1801. On June 15 her obituary in *The Birmingham Gazette* sparsely reads, "Died—Mrs. Pickering, of this town, who some time ago published a volume of poems by subscription. She had been blind about 50 years."[67] Nothing is known about the circumstances of her death, but we can assume, from the sparse reception of her poetry and the stressful monetary situation she readily admits, that she died in a state of discomfort.[68] Over two hundred years after her death, not much is known about Poynton except what she reveals herself—and to herself—via the life writing of her poetry. This is why, to combat the mentality that a woman writer who is not reviewed or does not appear in full-length criticism is not a worthy scholarly pursuit, using her poetry to discover her value as an eighteenth-century author is significant work. Poynton's poetry offers itself to analysis beyond anecdotal scholarship to advance a wider argument. Additionally, Poynton provides an example of why disability studies as a modern methodology might require more historical context to stand alone—it must address the gendered implications of the period in which it was written as well as the cultural understanding of disability, or "deformity," as it was presented in the eighteenth century.

Notes

1. For example, see Janet Todd, "Poynton, Priscilla [Pickering]," *A Dictionary of American and British Women Writers 1660–1800*, (Totowa, New Jersey: Rowman & Allanheld, 1985; Joseph Wittreich, *Feminist Milton*, (Ithaca: Cornell University Press, 1987); Fiona Pitt-Kethley, *The Literary Companion to Sex* (New York: Random House, 1992); Claudia N. Thomas, *Alexander Pope and His Eighteenth-Century Women Readers* (Carbondale: Southern Illinois University Press, 1994); Germaine Greer, *Slip-shod Sibyls: Recognition, Rejection and the Woman Poet* (New York: Viking, 1995); Simon Dickie, *Cruelty and Laughter: Forgotten Comic Literature and the Unsentimental Eighteenth Century* (Chicago: The University of Chicago Press, 2011.); Bill Overton, "Journeying in the Eighteenth-century: British Verse Epistle," *Studies in Travel Writing* 13, no. 1 (2009): 3-25; and Felicity A.

Nussbaum, *The Limits of the Human: Fictions of Anomaly, Race, and Gender in the Long Eighteenth Century* (Cambridge: Cambridge University Press, 2003).

2. Judith Fetterley, "Reading about Reading: 'A Jury of Her Peers,' 'The Murders in the Rue Morgue,' and 'The Yellow Wallpaper'" in *Gender and Reading*, ed. Elizabeth A. Flynn and Patrocinio P. Schweickart (Baltimore: Johns Hopkins University Press, 1986), 149.

3. Fetterley, "Reading about Reading," 150.

4. Priscilla Poynton, *Poems on Several Occasions by Miss Priscilla Pointon of Lichfield* (Birmingham: T. Warren, 1770), lxiii–lxiv.

5. A full literature review consists of eighteen sources, most of which discuss Poynton marginally.

6. Marlene Kadar, introduction to *Essays on Life Writing: From Genre to Critical Practice* (Toronto: University of Toronto Press, 1992), 4.

7. It should be noted here that contemporary scholarship on life writing focuses on secular life writing. Initial scholarship on life writing focused primarily on the spiritual.

8. Paula R. Backscheider and Catherine E. Ingrassia, introduction to Part II: "Poetry as Life Writing," *British Women Poets of the Long Eighteenth Century: An Anthology* (Baltimore: Johns Hopkins University Press, 2009), 291–300 and Felicity Nussbaum, *The Autobiographical Subject* (Baltimore: Johns Hopkins University Press, 1989).

9. "Essay Towards a History of Mankind," *The Annual Register, or a View of the History, Politics, and Literature, for the year 1771*, (London, 1779), 193.

10. Marlene Kadar, introduction to *Essays on Life Writing*, 4.

11. Marlene Kadar, introduction to *Essays on Life Writing*, 5.

12. Marlene Kadar, introduction to *Essays on Life Writing*, 10.

13. Backscheider and Ingrassia, "Poetry as Life Writing," 291.

14. Backscheider and Ingrassia, "Poetry as Life Writing," 292.

15. Susan Sniader Lanser, *Fictions of Authority: Women Writers and Narrative Voice* (Ithaca, NY: Cornell University Press. 1992), 7.

16. Lanser, *Fictions of Authority*, 15.

17. Lanser, *Fictions of Authority*, 15.

18. Lanser, *Fictions of Authority*, 19.

19. Explained in Edward Larrissy, *The Blind and Blindness in Literature of the Romantic Period* (Edinburg: Edinburg University Press, 2007), 15.

20. William R. Paulson, "Introduction: Unseeing the Eye," in *Enlightenment, Romanticism, and the Blind in France* (Princeton: Princeton University Press, 1987), 15.

21. Denis Diderot, *Lettre sur les auveugles, a l'usage de ceux qui voyent* (Londres, 1749), translated as *A Letter on Blindness for the use of those who have their sight*, (London: William Bingley, 1770).

22. Paulson, "Introduction: Unseeing the Eye," 15.

23. Paulson, "Introduction: The Unseeing Eye," 12.

24. Paulson, "Introduction: Unseeing the Eye," 12.

25. These revisions, of course, may be due to an imperfect transcriber or the extempore way in which she composed, but this is to go beyond the remit of the present essay.

26. Poynton, *Poems on Several Occasions*, 12.

27. See David M. Turner, *Disability in Eighteenth Century England: Imagining Physical Impairment* (London: Routledge, 2012).

28. Helen Deutsch and Felicity Nussbaum, introduction to *Defects: Engendering the Modern Body* (Ann Arbor: University of Michigan Press, 2000), 7.

29. Disability studies does not diagnose, it presupposes some aspect of the person as disabled, or unable to function typically in some respect, with varying degrees of severity. It is cultural, situated within social contexts, not medical or rehabilitative.

30. Lennard J. Davis, "Dr. Johnson, Amelia, and the Discourse of Disability in the Eighteenth Century," in *Defects: Engendering the Modern Body*, 57.

31. Dwight Christopher Gabbard, "Disability Studies and the British Long Eighteenth Century," *Literature Compass* 8:2 (2011), 85.

32. Lennard J. Davis, *Enforcing Normalcy: Disability, Deafness, and the Body*, (New York: Verso, 1995), 4.

33. Interpellation, a Marxist term, is typically used in conjunction with the concept of hailing, which connotes an awareness of subjects.

34. Rosemarie Garland-Thomson, "Feminist Disability Studies," *Signs: Journal of Women in Culture and Society* 30, no. 2 (2005): 1558.

35. Garland-Thomson, "Feminist Disability Studies," 1557.

36. Garland-Thomson, "Feminist Disability Studies," 1558.

37. Poynton, *Poems on Several Occasions*, 31.

38. See, for example, "The Following Lines by the Author, to Her Cousin Miss M. B. of Chester, On Entering Her Teens," in Poynton, *Poems on Several Occasions*, 36–7.

39. For more information on extempore poetry, see Anne Milne, *Lactilla Tends Her Fav'rite Cow: Eco-critical Readings of Animals and Women in Eighteenth-Century British Labouring-Class Women's Poetry* (Lewisburg: Bucknell University Press, 2008) and Backscheider and Ingrassia, *British Women Poets of the Long Eighteenth Century: An Anthology.*

40. "Priscilla Pointon," *Notes and Queries* 9 (1866): 355.

41. "Priscilla Pointon," *Notes and Queries* 9 (1866): 355.

42. "Priscilla Pointon," *Notes and Queries* 9 (1866): 355.

43. "genius, n.," *Oxford English Dictionary*, 2nd ed. (Oxford: Oxford University Press, 1989).

44. "Priscilla Pointon," *Notes and Queries* 9 (1866): 355.

45. Poynton. *Poems on Several Occasions*, 11.

46. Poynton, *Poems on Several Occasions*, 11.

47. Denis Diderot, *An Essay on Blindness, In a Letter to a Person of Distinction; Reciting the most interesting Particulars relative to Persons born Blind, and those who have lost their Sight. Being an Inquiry*

into the Nature of their Ideas, Knowledge of Sounds, Opinions Concerning Morality and Religion, &c., (London: J. Barker, 1780), 20–21.

48. Poynton, *Poems on Several Occasions*, 11.

49. Poynton, *Poems on Several Occasions*, 11.

50. Poynton, *Poems on Several Occasions*, 12. See author's note.

51. Poynton, *Poems on Several Occasions*, 12.

52. Poynton, *Poems on Several Occasions*, 12.

53. Poynton was married at St Michael's parish church, Shotwick in Cheshire, an Anglican church.

54. For instance, Poynton writes an elegy to the Reverend John Davenport, the vicar of St. Nicholas Church in Leicester, and Anglican parish Pointon, *Poems on Several Occasions*.

55. Jacqueline George, "Public Reading and Lyric Pleasure: Eighteenth Century Elocutionary Debates and Poetic Practice," *ELH* 76, no.2 (2009): 393.

56. George, "Public Reading and Lyric Pleasure," 372.

57. Poynton, *Poems on Several Occasions*, 12.

58. "The following lines, extempore, to a blind young Gentleman, who was so obliging to send the Author a Song of her own composing set to Music," in Poynton, *Poems on Several Occasions*, 84–85.

59. Poynton, *Poems on Several Occasions*, 85.

60. Thomas Blacklock, *Poems by Mr. Thomas Blacklock. To which is prefix'd, an account of the life, character, and writings, of the author, by the Reverend Mr. Spence, Late Professor of Poetry, at Oxford* (London: R. and J. Dodsley, 1756), xxxviii.

61. Poynton, *Poems on Several Occasions*, 12.

62. Poynton, *Poems on Several Occasions*, 99.

63. It is worthwhile to point out that Poynton removes the author's note explaining the reason for her blindness from the second ode.

64. Poynton, *Poems on Several Occasions*, 99.

65. Priscilla Pickering, *Poems by Mrs. Pickering. To which are added Poetical sketches by the author, and translator of Philotoxi Ardenæ* (Birmingham: E. Piercy, 1794).

66. John Alfred Langford, *A Century of Birmingham Life: Or, a Chronicle of Local Events, from 1741-1841* (Birmingham: E.C. Osborne, 1868), 384.

67. Langford, *A Century of Birmingham Life*, 384.

68. Weston may be exaggerating here, but he reports in the preface to the second volume that Poynton has expressed to him, "My Husband is dead . . . and I have not a Friend in the world." He goes on to say that her situation was desolate and her calamity irredeemable.

10

GOD GRANT US GRACE, THAT WE MAY TAKE DUE
PAINS, TO PRACTICE WHAT THIS EXERCISE CONTAINS;
TO WHICH, IF WE APPLY OUR BEST ENDEAVOUR, WE
SHALL BE HAPPY HERE, AND BLESS'D FOR EVER.

Thomas Gills: An Eighteenth-Century Blind Poet
and the Language of Charity

Chris Mounsey

AS THE SCOPE OF HISTORIES of disabilities widens it might be asked what special angle a study of the literary production of a disabled person might bring. To this question, I might give the usual answer that while histories of disabilities attempt to draw charts of the currents of history, the study of the work of disabled writers can give us detailed pictures of individual people caught up in the waves and eddies of the tides of historical change and continuity. But to this I would like to add the suggestion that histories and literary studies can heuristically come together methodologically when focused on narrow issues.

In the final chapter of his excellent *Down and Out on the Streets of London*,[1] Tim Hitchcock explores the technique he has used to create an history out of the lives of individual poor people using novels, poems, paintings, coroners' inquests, pamphlet literature, newspaper accounts, settlement examinations, workhouse reports and legal contracts, and the records of petty sessions and hospitals in order to "create an admittedly constructed, but convincing, vision of the past." The better to explain the strengths and limitations of his technique, Hitchcock extends his metaphor of vision to one of sight:

> The attempt here has been to use each of these sources to form one lens in an insect-like compound eye. The image drawn from poetry is myopic. The scene revealed in novels, full of cataracts. Account books, subject to astigmatism, and court records as distorted as the rest. But together, balanced one against the other, they bring a single image in to a sharper focus; made just a little clearer with the addition of each new source. The images brought together in this way are each distorted, and

the single view created by their combination contains all the flaws of each of its components.

Hitchcock's metaphor is both evocative and suggestive, and I find his methodology fitting for the project of variability outlined in the introduction. There is no attempt to trace origins or truths in the sources, but it expects a basic understanding of the situation of those people described derived from a commonly held feeling of embodiment.

In this essay I shall look at the poetry written by a blind man facing destitution, trying his best to make money the only way he can. Like Hitchcock, I shall be presenting evidence from a variety of disparate sources, using all the tricks and partial truths that the construction of a single narrative implies. Nevertheless, I believe I shall present as clearly as possible, a recognizable voice of a blind man faced with his dilemma. With the same assurance as Hitchcock, I think it is possible to conclude with some accuracy that the story of Thomas Gills of St. Edmundsbury demonstrates how much a disabled man wanted to be independent and established a complex relationship with the parish poor law for his income. I shall begin with a brief account of the history of the economic situation in which Gills found himself, before moving on to an account of the way in which he manipulated the publishing world and his readership to his own ends.

As such, this essay could be read as a "history from below,"[2] and more specifically as part of a subset of the history of poor people, since disabled people were often excluded from work and had to rely upon the poor laws or charities for their income. Added to the poor laws is the contextualization of the literary output of a disabled author over a number of years, which can give a broader picture of his self-presentation and attempts at self-sufficiency in the "economy of makeshifts"[3] than is possible using the snapshots of evidence that Hitchcock uses in his brief accounts of poor people. By bringing together the techniques of understanding texts in their contexts, with the context of the poor law, and reading both from the context of a disabled person with an identifiable disability, we can read the overlap of these three contexts with some precision.

An excellent historiography of the study of the poor in this period comes from Steven King and Alana Tomkins in their Introduction to *The Poor in England 1700–1850*,[4] where they argue that the "economy of makeshifts" was the chief way in which "poor households cobbled together a wide variety of sources and benefits ranging from ultra-legitimate wage labour to the fragile advantage gained when a landlord withheld foreclosure."[5] Working from the wide variety of methods of making an income or staving off the collection of a debt, King and Tompkins demonstrate that "'the economy of makeshifts' has become the organizing concept for a number of historians of English welfare . . . [rather than] parish poor relief."[6] Their argument rests on the indubitable fact (if there are facts in history) that households could not rely on state poor relief since "Essentially the Poor Law (and indeed other types of welfare) was resourced by a finite line of supply in the face of potentially infinite demand."[7] The essays in their collection witness the fact that "a coherent, predictable pattern of relatively reliable relief supplying comprehensive benefits to individuals has not been proved to exist for the whole of England."[8]

What will become important to the present essay is King and Tompkins's argument that "the old Poor Law was statutory only in as much as it compelled the propertied to contribute to the maintenance of the poor, it did not proscribe the format of distributions of a sufficiency of its benefits."[9] Thus, the essays tell us of poor people's desperate attempts to "cobble together" a subsistence as best they can, and from wherever they can, since there was no guarantee that they would receive money from the poor law fund.

A dissenting note to the work of these historians is the lawyer Lorie Charlesworth, who argues in *Welfare's Forgotten Past* that those who contend the "economy of makeshift" have forgotten the effects of the statutory nature of welfare.[10] "The forgotten of [Charlesworth's] title, is that many scholars are unaware of the extent of the legal foundation that ensured poor law was not simply a local custom, able to mutate over time in response to changing circumstances as other unofficially negotiated 'social rules.' Rather it constituted a slowly evolving fixed legal point of reference." For Charlesworth, welfare was not therefore a matter for local debate, but rather "a complex, nuanced and sophisticated system based upon rights." What seems to be wanting in this argument, however, is an explanation of the mechanism that rights were implemented on the hard edge of need. A poor person might have a right to relief but how were they to convince those whom the Old Poor Law compelled to benefaction of the reality of their indigence and that they were not simply idle, or a cheat. Whether or not this mechanism was "a complex, nuanced and sophisticated system based upon rights" it seems likely to have been achieved, as King and Tompkins argue, through "the face-to-face nature of parish government (at least in the rural south and midlands parishes), and supposing that they used local knowledge of people and resources, along with the powers of persuasion, to negotiate welfare deals."[11] And it is at the moment of the face to face where the problem lies since it meant that poor people had to argue again and again for their welfare, which might or might not be granted year by year.

Faced with the continual process of asking for money that might be met with denial, poor people typically turned to the "rhetoric of powerlessness" which has been the subject of some debate among historians since the 1990s. At first such pleading was read uncritically, but since Thomas Sokoll's *Essex Pauper Letters*,[12] their language—the genuine language of the poor—has been more carefully contextualized. Sokoll notes:

> The writing is tentative, hesitant, evasive; or, on the other extreme, coarse, rough, rude, clumsily offensive. . . . [But] The pauper letter always derives from the specific circumstances of an individual case.[13]

Here, I would gloss the idea of pleading an individual case as a strategic rather than a passive gesture, and King and Tompkins note that "historians [are] increasingly according agency to the parish poor."[14] As in the economy of makeshifts, the language of address by the poor to their benefactors comprised many forms.

In the story of Thomas Gills, who as a blind man we might believe to have been an uncontested case for poor law welfare, we find three distinct phases marked by his poetry: the production of a catechism for children which was aimed at the widest possible audience,[15] a moment of temporary remission when he briefly regained his sight and the use of his legs,[16] and a return to publishing his catechism.[17] The first phase suggests that Gills was trying to make as much money as possible from his writing, and while the second phase must have been sheer joy for him, it would have jeopardized his parish welfare, and thus was probably announced as temporary so he could return to his former source of income in the third phase. Thus, we find that his account of his recovery is presented using the "rhetoric of powerlessness" and was published along with an account of what it is like to be blind, "On the Misery of Blindness," lest his remission raised a question about the genuineness of his disability. The parish records of St. Mary in St. Edmundsbury, Suffolk record his death in January 1716 as "Thomas Gills, A Blind Man," which tells us that he was finally known by his disability. Nevertheless, the fact that he published his catechism and poems, suggests that he was never certain either that he deserved welfare, or that welfare would be forthcoming. What emerges from the evidence of the three phases is a constant heart-searching and struggle by Gills to try to make a living for himself so that he did not have to rely entirely upon an income stream that might fail him.

Thomas Gills of St. Edmunds Bury

Nothing is known about the life of Thomas Gills, who called himself "the Blind Man of St. *Edmunds Bury* in *Suffolk,*" except for his six extant publications. In these works, the only biographical information we have about Gills is contained in the "Address to the Charitable Buyer"[18] and in the account of his infirmities in the poems about his remission, relapse, and his life as a blind man. The ecclesiastical history of Bury St. Edmunds and of its poor houses are however both well documented and may account for the way Gills seems to have regarded himself as a blind man within the history of disabled people.

In 1914, when the Diocese of St. Edmundsbury and Ipswich was created, St. James's was made the cathedral, but the huge edifice was originally the great church of the Abbey of St. Edmundsbury and a seat of immense local power. It was the burial place of King Edmund who was killed by the Danes in 869 and gained a reputation for miracles performed at the shrine of the martyr king. In 945 the abbey was granted jurisdiction over the town free from secular interference, and later, in 1020, Canute granted the abbey freedom from episcopal control. At the same time, the abbey was rebuilt and became a Benedictine Establishment. Its overweening power seems to have been the reason for its twice being attacked and destroyed by the townspeople. The first attack, in 1327, was fifty years before the Great Rising, or Peasants' Revolt of 1381, when the town took a second opportunity to show their displeasure at the power of the church, where after they displayed the abbot's head on the town gate. There is also a legend that the Barons met in St. James's to discuss their Charter of Liberties that would become the Magna Carta. If the currents of history suggest that East Anglia was important in the growing sense of equality that marked the end of Medieval serfdom, maybe Thomas Gills's sense of himself as deserving of respect both as a blind man and as having a useful role in the economy, is not so surprising.

Whether Gills lived with his family or alone or in a Workhouse is not known, but the town was one of the earliest to set up a house under the Elizabethan Poor Laws.[19] The first workhouse in Bury St. Edmunds was in Whiting Street and dates before 1621 when a house in Churchgate Street was adapted for the purpose. After 1630 Moyse's Hall, a twelfth century edifice overlooking the town square was used as a workhouse, a house of correction, and the town gaol. By the early eighteenth-century the town had two workhouses, one in Eastgate Street for the parish of St. James, and one in Schoolhall Street for St. Mary's. By 1747, the town's workhouses catered for 250 poor people. All this suggests that Bury St. Edmunds was well furnished with the mechanisms of Poor Relief. If Gills lived in a workhouse (or even if he lived alone or with family where he would still have received poor rate money) he would not have been required to work: being blind he would have been classed as "Impotent." The fact that he did, and that he was successful, suggests that he at least did not think himself incapable of making a contribution to society.

Gills's enterprise is demonstrated by his choice of publishing his work in London rather than Bury St. Edmunds. Eighteenth-Century Collections Online (ECCO) suggests there were only about 150 publications in Bury throughout the century, with most dating from the 1790s, but this is typical of the weakness of basing that database on central libraries. Recent work in Winchester by Norbert Schurer discovered over 2,000 unrecorded publications in a similar provincial town based around a local newspaper publisher, and a similar pattern of publication can be predicted from the extant publications from Bury.

Thomas Baily and William Thompson worked between two printing houses in Stamford, Lincolnshire and Bury St. Edmunds. A single copy of a newspaper, the *Suffolk Mercury or Bury Post,* can be found on ECCO.[20] Dating from Monday, October 11, 1731, the header notes that it is "Vol. 22 No. 41." The format of three sides of international news gleaned from other newspapers and one side of local information such as advertisements, accidental deaths and drownings, the Bill of Mortality and the prices of grain and drugs, is usual for a local weekly newspaper. The identifying number "41" confirms this since Monday, October 11 was in the forty-first week of the year. This would further suggest that the newspaper began in 1709, twenty-two years before 1731, giving us the volume number at one per year. Although this dates the newspaper's foundation two years after Gills's first catechism (1707), it would be hard to argue that Baily and Thompson started their publishing house in Bury St. Edmunds with the publication of so huge an undertaking: a local newspaper more usually followed a series of smaller publication ventures.[21]

Only eleven other works of these publishers are available on ECCO and all are the sort of small undertaking typical of a local publishing house. There are four reprints of Ned Ward's comic writings,[22] three sermons by local ministers,[23] two political pamphlets on local issues (Navigation to the sea from the Norfolk towns of Lyn, Wisbeech, Spalding and Boston;[24] and Land Tax, published from Stamford[25]) and one collection of (three very short) novels.[26] ECCO dates the earliest publication by Baily and Thompson, Ned Ward's *A Satyr against Wine,* to 1712. Since the first edition, from Bragg in London, is dated 1705,[27] Baily and

Thompson's may be earlier than the recorded date. Only further work in local libraries could turn up a fuller list of publications.

The advertisements in Baily and Thompson's existing books show a much wider range of books and pamphlets both published by themselves and by others.[28] One title they advertise in one of two versions of Ned Ward's *Honesty in Distress: but Reliev'd by No Party* (1721?)[29] is particularly interesting. *The Weekly Exercise: Or, Plain and Easie Instructions for Youth*[30] may be a version of Gills's catechism. Baily and Thompson's title appears to be derived from what is probably the most enduring of the lines of Gills's work, the last quatrain:

> God grant us Grace, that we may take due Pains,
> To practice what this *Exercise* contains;
> To which, if we apply our best Endeavour,
> We shall be happy here, and bless'd for ever.[31]

Likewise, Gills's preface "to the Charitable Buyer" explains the easy nature of the verse:

> My Stile is low, so should it be,
> To suit a Child's Capacity:[32]

The long explanatory subtitle of *The Weekly Exercise* follows the subject matter of Gills's catechism: "Shewing First, The many Obligations Men are under to serve God. And, Secondly, How they may do it in the best Manner: Particularly, How they of the Church of England ought to behave themselves, whose Service and Prayers are herein fully Explain'd, and prov'd to be warrantable and Orthodox, by Quotations and Cases from Scripture, and the Examples of the Apostles themselves, and Rendered easie and intelligible to the meanest Capacities."[33] Furthermore, *The Weekly Exercise* is advertised to be sold at "Price Two-Pence, or 12s. a Hundred to those that are Charitably disposed to give them away" the same pricing structure of J. Downing's "Second Edition Enlarged" of Gills' catechism, printed in London in 1716.

Baily and Thompson sold another moral piece, by the seventeenth-century poet Henry Peacham,[34] *The Worth of a Penny*,[35] which was probably reprinted from a 1703 edition that was originally published in London by Samuel Keble. The piece is of the same type as Gills's catechism and aimed at improving the morals of ordinary people, so we might ask why Gills did not choose the local publisher for the works that are associated with his name.

I would argue that the answer lies in Baily and Thompson's list: everything they published was either previously published elsewhere by dead authors or by the wealthy, such as the satirical poem, *Lincolnshire* (1720) that was "Printed for the Author;"[36] or ministers of religion,[37] or people with a political axe to grind who wanted the widest audience for their ideas and had someone to foot the bill for printing. In this they were typical of local publishers who were only interested in selling popular items, or pieces that cost them nothing but the time of setting the type. But there is no evidence they paid anything to writers. For Thomas Gills to make money out of his writing he did not fit with the economic model underpinning local publishers: he had to turn to London where publishers were becoming used to paying for copy.

In this essay there is no need for me to rehearse the argument of Brean Hammond's *Hackney for Bread*,[38] which charts the rise of the professional writer in London between 1670 and 1740. What I wish to add to Hammond's magisterial work is that an insignificant blind and lame poet should be added to the list of imaginative professional writers who attempted to make money from his writing.

Instructions for Children

The first edition of Gills's catechism *Instructions for Children in Verse* (1707) is noted to have been published in London but no publisher is named. From the start Gills is forthright in his economic intention for the piece when he tells his reader that

> my Condition is as low,
> Poor, Blind and Lame, and being so.
> I can no better Way descry
> Than this to get a penny by.
> Then pray dislike not what I do,
> To help my self and others too:
> And if you Buy this Book of me,
> You do Two Acts of Charity:
> To Children good Advice you give,
> And grant me wherewithal to Live. [39]

We have explored the second act of charity in some detail, although it might now be argued that granting Gills the "wherewithal to Live" is a disguise for the hard economic facts of his enterprise. The first act of charity, giving children good advice, would have been equally fraught with difficulty, but once again Gills was remarkably successful.

Gills writes following the headings "Duty to God, and first of Prayer," "Of Respect to the Name of God," "Of Keeping the Lord's Day," "Duty to Parents," "Duty to Relations and others," "Of Stealing," "Of Lying," "Duty to Old People," "Duty to Poor People," and ends with the quatrain quoted in the title of this essay. His explanations are certainly fitted to a child, and the jingling verse would suggest a child learning by rote the importance of prayer, the way to follow five of the Ten Commandments and to perform three social duties. Gills begins:

> Q. From whence, dear Child, does all that's Good proceed
> A. All Good from God Almighty comes indeed:
> We can no Gift, nor Grace, nor Blessing have,
> But what we from his Goodness must receive.
> Q. And how should we God's Blessings seek to gain?
> A. By Prayer we must those Gifts of God obtain.[40]

I have located six other catechisms written for children that were published in the first ten years of the eighteenth century but none is so easy to follow and all have a subtext that highlights the version of Christianity held by the author. What is so powerful about Gills's simple language for children is that it does not fixate on a particular issue which defines a sect or group of Christians, but gives a simple lesson fitted to the mind of a child.

The Presbyterian Catechism of the Reverend Assembly of (Westminster) Divines,[41] claimed it was "all fitted both for Brevity and Clearness to this their Form of Sound Words of the benefit of Christians in General, and of Youth and Children, in Understanding in particular."[42] It was not. The first question and answer was:

> Q. What is the chief end of Man?
> A. Mans chief end is to glorifie GOD *a*, and to enjoy Him for ever *b*.

Each footnote mark indicated a passage in the Bible which supposedly glossed the statement. Thus, footnote *a* to 1 Corinthians 10:31 explained to a child the process of glorifying God: "Whether therefore ye eat, or drink, or whatsoever ye do, do all to the glory of God." Likewise footnote *b* explained enjoying God: "Whom have I in heaven but thee? and there is none upon earth that I desire beside thee. My flesh and my heart faileth: but God is the strength of my heart, and my portion for ever."[43] If the first footnote suggests that we eat, drink and be merry to glorify God, then all well and good, but the second footnote seems wildly at odds with the answer to the question.

Likewise, Josiah Woodward's Anglican Catechism,[44] which claimed it "explain[ed] the Substance of the Christian Religion Suited to the Understanding of Children and the Meanest Capacities,"[45] is carefully glossed, though it does not print out the verses in the bible to which his questions and answers refer. His first questions are quite different from the presbyterians but would be equally baffling to a child.

> Q. What is Man?
> A. A Reasonable Creature, consisting of Soul and Body.
> Q. What is a Creature?
> A. A Being Created of God.
> Q. What is it to be Created?
> A. To be produced out of nothing?[46]

The misprinted question mark at the end of the third answer is perhaps a foretaste of what is to come, as children are questioned on Man's Corruption, Redemption, the Covenant of Grace, Baptism, the Lord's Supper, of a Christian Life, of Christian Hope and lastly of Everlasting Punishment, where "Eternity" is explained as "A Duration without end."[47] With its explanations of "Some Terms," and prayers, the catechism also comes in at three times the length of Gills's.

I have chosen to excerpt the Westminster Divines' and Woodward's catechisms not as extreme examples but examples of the six extreme positions on Christianity that the other catechisms display. All of the others privilege an aspect of Christianity that the author believes to be the most important. For Richard Kidder,[48] who ended his life as Anglican Bishop of Bath and Wells, the most important thing was not to exclude those who tended to Nonconformist beliefs from the Anglican communion, while at the same time avoiding Roman Catholic doctrine. Thus, his catechism follows a carefully worded route through the elements of Anglican-based church worship that represents a believer's life: baptism, the creed, the commandments, and the Lord's Prayer. He is careful for the child to define only two sacraments, Baptism and Holy Communion,[49] as the requirements for the deliverance from sin and the hope of heaven.

Thomas Cooke,[50] another Anglican who wrote his for Merchant Taylor's School, also follows the pattern of church worship: baptism, the creed, the commandments and the Lord's Prayer, and the two sacraments. However, the catechism is more thorough and his answers longer, concentrating on the difference between the earthly body represented by the father's name and the spiritual body represented by the Christian name. At 60 pages this catechism would represent a great task of rote learning albeit that the questions might act as prompts.

The pattern is followed in a similar way by Peter Hewit,[51] a third Anglican, although the balance of his catechism is dramatically different. Chancellor of St. Fin Barre's Cathedral in Cork, Hewit was in charge of theological education of a small congregation scattered throughout a large diocese that was largely Roman Catholic. He follows through the exegesis of baptism, the creed, the commandments and the Lord's Prayer as a preparation for confirmation of young adults, and without an exploration of sacraments. His position is explained at the beginning with an exposition of the nature of catechism itself, and the whole is concluded by an exhortation to families to pray together morning and evening, with examples of long prayers to be said by the father and by the children. His congregation will more usually pray at home than in church.

Writing his catechism from the nonconformist (Particular Baptist) standpoint, Benjamin Keach,[52] is openly controversial and calls out replies such as those we have already seen. The Child's Instructor was written in 1664 and became instantly famous when its author was pilloried for its schismatical and seditious attack on child baptism.

Gills's catechism is not directed to a distinct market, or a particular age group. The argument of the first part of this essay would suggest that he was writing for commercial rather than doctrinal reasons. To make money to support himself as a blind man, his work does not exclude any potential buyer. Thus, his first reminder to his readers is that he is not ordained, so his work cannot cause controversy:

> 'Twas from another hand I took
> The Subject of this little Book;
> For I myself am no Divine,
> The Verse and Rhime is only mine.[53]

And nor does it. Throughout, Gills's charming rhymes exhorts children to the proper deportment during prayers, rather than what to pray:

> Q. What manner do you think you ought to pray in?
> A. I ought to Kneel while I my Prayers am saying;
> On both my Knees, (for one will not suffice)
> And towards Heaven lift up my Hands and Eyes;
> I must Kneel upright too, not lean or loll
> Against a Stool, or Chair, or Bed, or Wall;

> Nor must I Laugh, or Look another Way,
> Nor with my Toys, or with my Fingers play,
> Nor stop to speak to others while I pray.[54]

Here we read that even in admonition, Gills's touch is light, as he is also in remembering that children will copy the bad examples of their elders. On the subject of taking the Lord's Name in vain he writes:

> Q. And yet some People counted Good no doubt,
> You hear for every trifling Cause cry out,
> And often say, O Jesus! Or O God.
> A. Yes, I hear, and think 'tis very odd
> That such as they should be so much to blame,
> And learn us little ones to do the same;
> For what ill Words we hear old Folks repeat,
> We Children are too apt to imitate.
> And thus God's Name is with Contempt abus'd,
> Which in a Holy Manner shou'd be us'd.[55]

Like a truly professional writer for children, Gills makes sure throughout the catechism that his words are not just for the children but for their parents as well. Thus, when he admonishes a child to go to Sunday School, he reminds the parents of their duty also:

> My Parents, or my Friends, must careful be
> To make me do my Duty punctually;
> And what may make me good they often ought
> To teach, or send me where I may be taught:
> For if these Things they take no Care to do,
> And I prove Wicked, they are Guilty too;
> Because my Parents know, or should know, what
> Is most for my own Good if I do not.[56]

To be sure, Gills uses the trick of the all-seeing God to ensure good behavior of the perfect child:

> And what my Parents bid me I must do,
> Not only in their sight, but Absence too;
> Or else by cheating them I give Offence
> To God, who sees my Disobedience.[57]

But it must be argued that he has a keen understanding of human nature, and how the child is father to the man:

> Now if I do not practice this whilst Young,
> Can I who had my own Will all along
> Deny it when my Passions grow more strong?[58]

Perhaps the strongest section of the verse is when Gills puts a beautifully constructed list of those things that make children most obnoxious to their parents into the mouth of the child:

> Why then if I love Idleness and Play,
> And will not Learn to Work, nor Read, nor Pray,
> Or if I Stamp, or Cry, or take it Ill,
> And Fret because I cannot have my Will;
> Or if I be addicted to tell Lies,
> Speak Naughty Words, or call ill Names likewise;
> If I be Dainty, and refuse to Eat
> Without my Sawce, or choicest Bits of Meat;
> Or if though Pride I Envy and Repine
> At others better cloath'd, and dress'd more fine,
> Or those Despise whose Cloaths are worse than mine;
> If I be Peevish, Quarrelsome, or Loud,
> Inquisitive, Affected, Vain, or Proud;
> If any one of these ill Inclinations,
> And such like Humours, Faults, and Naughty Passions,
> My careful Parents never should neglect me,
> But contradict my Humour, and correct me,
> For whilst these Humours I in others see,
> I find how odious they would look in me,
> And how mischievous their Effects would be.[59]

This is not to say that Gills does not bring treatment of those with his own disability into the list of good behaviors that he heaps upon the child, and in a most Old Testament cycle of revenge:

> Q. And don't you think 'tis likewise very bad
> To mock at Folks Deform'd, or Fools, or Mad?
> A. Tis ill to scoff at Peoples Misery,
> And if I do so God may angry be,

And with the like Affliction punish me;
I ought to have Compassion on their Woe,
And give God Thanks because I am not so.[60]

But it is no surprise that Gills's humor gives specific praise to that reply in the voice of the questioner, which brings us back to the topic of this essay:

Q. You say well Child, now tell me One Thing More
Concerning your Behaviour to the Poor?
A. The Poor I must relieve if I be able,
With Money, or with something from the Table;
For what I give the Poor I lend the Lord;
But if I can no other Alms afford,
I'll pray for them, and pity their Distress,
And always speak to them with Tenderness;
For whosoever does the Poor contemn,
His Maker does reproach in scorning them.[61]

Gills is here reminding the buyer of his pamphlet of their duty to pay their poor rate at the same time that they conclude their reading of the pamphlet they have bought from him to subsidize his poor rate payment. Furthermore, by putting the idea of giving to the poor into the minds of the children who are to be catechized by his words, he will put the idea back into the minds of their parents as the children remind their parents of the lesson.

That Gills's was a successful strategy is demonstrated in three ways. First, *Instructions for children* was reprinted in 1709 exactly as it appeared in 1707, as though it had not been reset, which suggests that it might have in continual production over three years. Publishers did not keep plates made up as they had limited sets of fonts. Second, a companion volume which gives similar advice to older children, *Advice to Youth: or Instructions for Young Men and Maids* was published at the same time as the second edition, also in London, and also in the form of a dialogue. Third, Joseph Downing, who published the Woodward catechism we explored above, republished Gills's *Instructions* twice, in 1712 and 1716, with different titles. The later edition is the version which sold at "2d each or 12s per hundred." This was no small achievement. Downing has 812 titles to his name on the ECCO database, and was a major publisher for the Society for the Reformation of Manners, the Society for the Propagation of the Gospel, the Society for the Propagation of Christian Knowledge and the Charity School movement. Gills did not live to reap the benefit of the final success of his little book as he died in

January 1716.[62] As I noted above he was buried at St. Mary's church and entered as "A Blind Man" in the burial record.

From this we see Thomas Gills as a self-publicist of his poverty, but at the same time as an entrepreneur who went to some lengths to finance himself. In the economy of makeshifts within which he most probably lived, Gills comes across as remarkably driven by a desire for independence.

The Recovery and Blindness Poems

Gills's publications of 1710 demonstrate the precarious nature of living on charity, and the fact of there being two complementary poems becomes the more telling when we read his poem "Upon the Recovery of his Sight and the Second loss thereof" counterbalanced by the second in the same pamphlet, "On the Misery of Blindness." "Upon the Recovery" hints that Gills suffered from cortical strokes from which it is typical to have a series of partial recoveries of sight and the use of limbs followed by relapse. The second reminds his readers what it means to be blind, if only for intermittent periods. It confirms that he really knows what blindness is and that he is not feigning to cheat the Poor Law system—or them.

Gills is repetitively careful to make sure that his readers understand his self-identification as a blind man. Thus, "Upon the Recovery" begins with lines reminding his readers that he had been blind before recounting the miracle of his return to sight:

> Long had I languish'd in continual Night,
> Long mourn'd the grievous loss of strength and sight,
> Long had I sought to have the cause remov'd,
> In vain Advices, Means and Medicines prov'd.
> When lo, the Almighty looking with Compassion
> Upon my Darkness, Grief and Desolation,
> Was pleas'd of his meer bounty to restore
> Part of that Sight and Strength I had before.[63]

When we get to the second page of the pamphlet, and presumably after the reader has bought the poem, Gills gives details of the return of his sight:

> gradually and slowly came my Sight,
> At first confusedly I saw Day-light,
> And knew when it was Gloomy, and when Bright.
> Then Humane Bodies when approaching near,

> Strange moving Forms like Shadows did appear.
> Next distinguished Colours near the Eye,
> And various Objects I discern'd when nigh,
> Which afterwards at distance I discry.[64]

In the event, Gills's recovery was so enabling that he managed to walk alone to other towns, something that must have been difficult for his friends, let alone the Overseers of the Poor to accept.

> Then cou'd I walk th' adjacent Fields alone,
> And sometimes ramble to a Neighbouring Town.
> Oh ! what delight I took to tread the Fields,
> And view the Beauties Spring and Summer yields.[65]

Thus, Gills tells his readers that although he could move about unaided, between himself and the "Beauties . . . A subtile Vail of Dimness interpos'd:" he can see but only partially. Furthermore, at the bottom of the second page, he reminds his readers of

> the Fleeting state of Worldly Joys,
> Which each Mischance or Malady destroys.[66]

Whence, he relapses once again into being crippled and "stone blind":

> My Head and Eye were seized with grievous pain
> The Cause, Defluctions and an Inflammation,
> Th' Effect, of Sight a Second Deprivation.[67]

From which after some time and treatment, sight returns once more:

> Thou now hast given me a breathing space,
> And made my Sickness, Pains and Sorrows cease;
> Thou hast restor'd me some small light
> Enough with care to guide my steps aright.[68]

Faced with this cycle of illnesses, Gills resigns himself to the decline in his health, but like the child whom he catechized, he promises God:

> Thy Holy Will be always done on me;
> I'll strive to be content whate'er it be.[69]

Thus he declares of himself:

> He is not wholly vanquish'd in the Field,
> Who tho' he falls o'erpowered, yet ne'er will yield.[70]

Nevertheless, even though he declares himself a wounded soldier on the battlefield of life, his final call to his reader reminds them to value their senses.

> You who enjoy Health, hearing, Speech and Sight,
> Oh! Prize and use those benefits aright;
> Inestimable is their worth, and no Man
> Ought to esteem them less for being Common;[71]

Gills's tone in this poem must be understood in the same way as the rhetoric of powerlessness[72] adopted by paupers in their begging letters to overseers, and therefore ought to be read with some caution. Gills is positioning himself as the fit beneficiary of charity, and specifically as a writer whose poems are worthy to be bought for charity even if they are not a great species of writing. With this in mind, if we read the balance between the joy of his returned sight with the redoubled sadness of his "second loss" alongside the admonition to his readers to value their sight, it becomes more clear that the poem is less a fountain of sorrow than a strategy for inducing charity, and thus it concludes with the lines:

> READER, if in these following Lines you find
> Nought worth your Time or Money, please to know
> The Author is Unlearned, Lame and Blind;
> And'tis no wonder if his Verse be so.
> Yet wholly lost you Money will not be,
> Because bestowed on one in Poverty.[73]

Continuing the rhetoric of powerlessness, Gills completes his 1710 pamphlet with "On the Misery of Blindness." Poems evoking what it is like living as a blind person would become a typical vehicle for deriving charity employed by blind writers during the eighteenth century (the example from Priscilla Pointon in this volume is another). The model for such verses is Milton's *On his Blindness*,[74] but where Milton fondly asks "Doth God exact day-labour, light denied?" and answers himself, "They also serve who only stand and wait," Gills's independence underlying the rhetoric of powerlessness cannot allow himself to regard himself as "waiting" and his discomfort with his situation has to be given voice. Thus, he describes his day-to-day existence as "tiresome idleness," and while eve this has to be qualified, he ends the poem with a conventional Christian acceptance of his earthly life.

> His only comfort is, (and sure 'tis better,
> Than all the World's delights can give, and greater,)
> That if he does his Cross with patience bear,
> Make Heaven his only hope, his aim, his care,
> And uses pious Thoughts, and frequent Prayer, . . .
> Then will his Miseries end and Joys begin.
> From his dark Cage his Spirit takes its flight,
> To boundless Regions of Eternal Light,
> Where in Immensive Joy and Pleasure he
> Shall Everlasting Glorious Objects see.[75]

It is just possible that being blind on earth will ensure his place in heaven.

The publication gives no assignment of where it was printed, so it may be the work of Baily and Thompson. The ECCO copy suggests it was a quick job carried off on cheap paper scraps. It may have brought him little or no monetary reward, but it was possibly his most important publication as it established his condition in the face of charges that he might have feigned his blindness. In turn then, we might look upon his catechism as an attempt to be economically self-sufficient in order that he did not have to face repeated and impertinent questioning about the state of his health.

Conclusion

Whatever was Gills's fate, the value of work like his was recognized at least in Bury St. Edmunds. In 1786, Edmund Gillingwater, keeper of the Work-Houses in Harleston in Suffolk noted with sadness: "the almost universal neglect of moral instruction of the poor is the source of those numerous and enormous vices, which are now become both the disgrace and terror of mankind."[76] His suggestion for the cure of such vices might have been Gills's catechism:

> Let us but look into our work-houses, for instance, on the Lord's Day, and see how it is observed.—How seldom shall we find there, that the poor are constantly and regularly brought to Divine service. How seldom are they catechized and otherwise instructed in the principles

of Christianity. How seldom are they informed of their dependence on their Creator, and their indispensable duty towards him.[77]

Notes

1. Tim Hitchcock, *Down and Out on the Streets of London* (London: Humbledon, 2005). The author graciously granted me access to this text using the original word documents, which do not, of course, bear the same paginations as the published version, so I will not give any.

2. A term which may be dated from as early as A.L. Morton, *A People's History of Britain*, (London: Gollancz, 1938).

3. See Olwen Hufton, *The Poor of Eighteenth Century France 1750–1789* (Oxford: Clarendon, 1974).

4. Steven King and Alana Tomkins, eds. *The Poor in England 1700–1850*, (Manchester: Manchester University Press, 2003).

5. King and Tompkins, *The Poor in England*, 8.

6. King and Tompkins, *The Poor in England*, 1.

7. King and Tompkins, *The Poor in England*, 9.

8. King and Tompkins, *The Poor in England*, 10.

9. King and Tompkins, *The Poor in England*, 11.

10. Lorie Charlesworth, *Welfare's forgotten past: a socio-legal history of the poor law*, (Abingdon: Routledge, 2010) [Kindle edition used which has no text-to-voice page numbers].

11. King and Tompkins, *The Poor in England*, 7.

12. Thomas Sokoll, *Essex Pauper Letters 1731–1837*, (Oxford: Clarendon Press, 2001)

13. Sokoll, *Essex Pauper Letters*, 7.

14. King and Tompkins, *The Poor in England*, 7.

15. Thomas Gills, *Instructions for Children, in Verse* (London, 1707), Eighteenth Century Collections Online, Gale (CW3324642157); Thomas Gills, *Advice to Youth: or Instructions for Young Men and Maids* (London, 1708/9?), Eighteenth Century Collections Online, Gale (CW3312252458); Thomas Gills, *Instructions for Children*, in Verse (London, 1709), Eighteenth Century Collections Online, Gale (CW3312804968).

16. Thomas Gills, *Upon the Recovery of his Sight and the Second Loss Thereof* (London? 1710?), Eighteenth Century Collections Online, Gale (CW3311512092).

17. Thomas Gills, *Useful and Delightful Instructions by way of Dialogue between the Master & his Scholar, Containing the Duty of Children* (London: J. Downing, 1712), Eighteenth Century Collections Online, Gale (CW3311512077); Thomas Gills, *Useful and Delightful Instructions by way of Dialogue between the Master & his Scholar, Containing the Duty of Children, The Second Edition Enlarg'd* (London: J. Downing, 1716), Eighteenth Century Collections Online, Gale (CW3310481438). These are both largely identical to *Instructions for Children*. The enlargement of the second edition consists only of better printing of the same text over seven more pages and two new short speeches to be said before public examination.

18. Gills, *Instructions for Children*, 2. It is to the 1707 edition to which I make all references to Gills catechism throughout this essay.

19. Strangely the *Oxford English Dictionary*, 2nd ed. (Oxford: Oxford University Press, 1989) dates the word "workhouse" only to 1652 with reference to the Poor Laws, although many town histories record such places from the early seventeenth century.

20. *Suffolk mercury: or, Bury post* (Bury St. Edmunds: Baily and Thompson, Monday 11 October 1731), Eighteenth Century Collections Online, Gale (CB3326829097). There are no copies recorded in the Burney Collection.

21. This was also the publication pattern for Thomas Gent, who published the blind poet, John Maxwell's poems in York.

22. Edward Ward, *Honesty in distress: but reliev'd by no party. A tragedy, as it is acted on the stage of the world. Act I. Scene the palace. Honesty alone. Honesty and a courtier. Honesty and a lady. Honesty and a footman. Honesty alone. Act II. Scene Westminster-Hall, with the court sitting. Honesty among the lawyers. The lawyers speeches concerning honesty. Honesty and . . . Act III. Scene . . . Honesty begging along the city . . . draper. A precise apothecary and his man. Honesty and an ale-house keeper. Honesty and a grocer. Honesty and a hosier. Honesty and the merchants. Honesty starved to death. To which is added, a satyr against the corrupt use of money* (Bury St. Edmunds, Suffolk: Baily and Thompson, 1721?), Eighteenth Century Collections Online, Gale (CB3331342863).

Edward Ward, *The rise and fall of madam Coming-Sir: or, An Unfortunate slip from the tavern-bar, Into the Surgeon's Powdering-Tub* (Stamford, Lincolnshire and St. Edmond's Bury: Thompson and Bailey, 1720?), Eighteenth Century Collections Online, Gale (CW3309954349).

Edward Ward, *A satyr against wine. With a poem, in praise of small beer. Written by a gentleman in a fever, occasion'd by hard drinking.* The second edition (St. Edmunds Bury, Suffolk and Stamford, Lincolnshire: Thompson and Baily, 1712?), Eighteenth Century Collections Online, Gale (CW33330865852).

23. Francis Harvey, *The dangers and mischiefs of instability in matters of religion consider'd. A sermon preach'd at the Arch-Deacon's visitation, at Sudbury, on Thursday, April 20, 1721. A.M. rector of lawshall in Suffolk; and chaplain to the Right Honourable the Earl of Bristol. Printed at the request of the clergy* (Bury St. Edmunds, Suffolk: Baily and Thompson, 1721), Eighteenth Century Collections Online, Gale (CW3326679938).

Thomas Birch, *The unreasonableness of revenue, and the great duty of Christian-charity; consider'd. In two sermons: Preach'd at Botesdale-chapel in Suffolk, August 21 and 28. 1720. A.B. lecturer of the said chapel* (Bury St. Edmunds, Suffolk: Baily and Thompson, 1720?), Eighteenth Century Collections Online, Gale, (CB3326543246).

Francis Peck, *Ad magistratum: a sermon preached before the mayor and aldermen of Stamford In the County of Lincoln, in the Parish-Church of the Blessed Virgin; at the Inauguration of a new Mayor, Oct. 6. 1720. A. B. Curate of King's-Cliffe, in the County of Northampton. Published to prevent Misrepresentations* (Stamford, Lincolnshire and Bury St. Edmunds, Suffolk: Thompson and Baily, 1720?), Eighteenth Century Collections Online, Gale, (CW3322788913).

24. Charles Kinderley, *The present state of the navigation of the towns of Lyn, Wisbeech, Spalding, and Boston. The rivers that pass through those places, and the countries that border thereupon, truly, faithfully, and impartially represented* (Bury St. Edmunds, Suffolk: Baily and Thompson, 1721), Eighteenth Century Collections Online. Gale, (CW3306552396).

25. *Proposals for taking off the land-tax: likewise ways and means for easing the nation of all the other taxes; to the great advancement of trade, and Benefit of the Nation in General. Being a project for raising above three millions per annum. Humbly submitted to the consideration of the Honourable House of Commons* (Stamford: Baily and Thompson, 1713), Eighteenth Century Collections Online, Gale, (CW3306540868).

26. *Three delightful novels, displaying the stratagems of love and gallantry. Novel I. The lucky misfortune. . . . Novel II. The noble recompence. . . . Novel III. The loves of Edgar, King of England.* (Bury St. Edmunds, Suffolk: Baily and Thompson, 1720?), Eighteenth Century Collections Online, Gale, (CW3313826242).

27. Edward Ward, *A satyr against wine. With a poem in praise of small beer. Written by a gentleman in a fever, occasion'd by hard drinking.* (London: Bragg, 1705), Eighteenth Century Collections Online. Gale, (CW3310733701).

28. There are nineteen titles.

29. The publication date of 1721 (which is given for both, although the advertisements differ in each) is probably inaccurate. Of the other works advertised all are by Ward and all were originally published in the first ten years of the eighteenth century. The only other work which might give us a clearer date of publication is Francis Peck, *An Exercise upon the Creation.* The first edition of this was published in 1716, on his graduation to BA from St. John's College, Cambridge and ordination (ODNB). The British Library Catalogue gives the date of 1717, but the copy is lost. The advertisement offers "The Second Edition Corrected."

30. No copies have been found.

31. Gills, *Instructions for children*, 15. Emphasis added.

32. Gills, *Instructions for children*, 2.

33. Ward, *Honesty in Distress*, unpag.

34. Henry Peacham, (1578-1644?) Peacham is best known as the author of *The Compleat Gentleman* (London: 1634).

35. Henry Peacham, *The worth of a penny: or, a caution to keep money. With the causes of the scarcity, and misery of the want thereof, consider'd under the following Heads, viz. the . . . Causes why Men are without Money, and are Three . . . I. Excess in Diet, Drinking, and Apparel. II. Gaming, and Recreations. III. Idleness and Improvidence, either in themselves, or their Servants. IV. The Character of a dejected Spirit for want of Money. V. The Misery of the Want of Money. VI. It compelleth to offend against Body and Soul. VII. The Vertue of Frugality, and the Definition of it. VIII. The Derivative of the Word Penny, and the Value of is. IX. The many good Uses that a Penny may be put to. X. Cautions to save Money in Diet, Apparel, and Recreations. XI. The English, of all Nations in Europe, the most prosuse in their Expences. XII. Of good Husbandy in Apparel. XIII. Many excellent Examples of Moderation in it. XIV. Of Recreation, and the Benefits that are received by it. XV. Four excellent Cautions to be observ'd in Play, &c.* (St. Edmund's Bury: Baily and Thompson, 1725?), Eighteenth Century Collections Online, Gale, (CW3305452375).

36. Gentleman in Lincolnshire, *Lincolnshire. A poem* (Bury St. Edmunds, Suffolk, 1720), Eighteenth Century Collections Online, Gale, (CW3309769436).

37. Francis Peck bought the living of Goadby Marwood in Leicestershire for £400 in 1723, which suggests he was independently wealthy. He was the son of a merchant in Stamford, and educated at Charterhouse before Cambridge.

38. Brean S. Hammond, *Professional imaginative writing in England, 1670-1740: 'hackney for bread'* (Oxford: Clarendon Press, 1987).

39. Gills, *Instructions for children*, 2.

40. Gills, *Instructions for children*, 3.

41. The Westminster Assembly was set up by the Long Parliament to restructure the Church of England along Presbyterian lines and met between 1643 and 1649.

42. Westminster Assembly, *The shorter catechism, composed by the Reverend Assembly of Divines. With the proofs thereof, out of the scriptures, in words at length. Which are either some of the former quoted places, or others gathered from their other Writings: All fitted both for Brevity and Clearness to this their Form of sound Words. For the Benefit of Christians in General, and of Youth and Children, in Understanding in particular, that they may with more ease acquaint themselves with the Truth, according to the Scriptures, and with the Scriptures themselves* (Edinburgh: John Reid, 1702), Eighteenth Century Collections Online, Gale, (CW3321606620), unpag.

43. Westminster Assembly, *The Shorter Catechism*, 1702, unpag.

44. Josiah Woodward, *A short catechism, explaining the substance of the Christian religion suited to the understanding of children, and the meanest capacities* (London: J. Downing, 1709), Eighteenth Century Collections Online, Gale, (CW3323333701).

45. Josiah Woodward, *A Short Catechism*, title page.

46. Josiah Woodward, *A Short Catechism*, 7.

47. Josiah Woodward, *A Short Catechism*, 32.

48. Richard Kidder, *An help to the smallest children's more easie understanding the church-catechism. By way of question and answer. Drawn up for the use of a certain parish in London by the rector thereof* (London: H. Hills, 1709), Eighteenth Century Collections Online, Gale, (CB3329893928).

49. Roman Catholics number seven sacraments.

50. Thomas Cooke, *A brief but plain explication of the church-catechism. Designed for the use of the scholars in Merchant-Taylors-School, and of the Children Educated in Christ's-Hospital, those particularly which are brought up in the Grammar-School thereunto belonging* (London: J. Wale, 1706), Eighteenth Century Collections Online. Gale, (CW3323387679).

51. Peter Hewit, *A brief and plain explication of the catechism of the Church of England; In sundry short and familiar questions and answers, composed for the use and benefit of families: that hereby parents of children, &c. may be directed how to instruct those that are committed to their charge and trust, in the right understanding of the true grounds and principles of the Christian faith and practice. To which is annexed, an exhortation to family devotion* (London: Awnsham and John Churchill, 1704), Eighteenth Century Collections Online, Gale, (CB3326642102).

52. Benjamin Keach, *The child's delight: or instructions for children and youth. Wherein all the chief principles of the Christian religions are clearly (though briefly) opened. Necessary to Establish young People in God's Truth, in opposition to Error in these perilous Times. Together With many other things,*

both Pleasant and Useful, for the Christian Education of Youth; with Letters to Parents. Adorned with several Copper Cuts, teaching to Spell, Read, and cast Accompts. With a short Dictionary interpreting hard Words and Names. Likewise, a Form for a Bond, Bill, or Receipt; And a Table showing the Interest of any Sums, &c. Fitted for the use of Schools, and useful for all Families, The Third Edition (London: William and Joseph Marshall, 1704?), Eighteenth Century Collections Online, Gale, (CW3321382880).

53. Gills, *Instructions for Children*, 2.

54. Gills, *Instructions for Children*, 7–8.

55. Gills, *Instructions for Children*, 9.

56. Gills, *Instructions for Children*, 10.

57. Gills, *Instructions for Children*, 11.

58. Gills, *Instructions for Children*, 11.

59. Gills, *Instructions for Children*, 12.

60. Gills, *Instructions for Children*, 15.

61. Gills, *Instructions for Children*, 16.

62. Since the New Style calendar, which began the year on January 1, did not come into general usage until 1751, it is not certain whether Gills died in what we would now call January 1717, from which we might deduce that he did benefit from the second publication by Downing.

63. Gills, *Upon the Recovery*, 1–2.

64. Gills, *Upon the Recovery*, 2.

65. Gills, *Upon the Recovery*, 2.

66. Gills, *Upon the Recovery*, 2.

67. Gills, *Upon the Recovery*, 3.

68. Gills, *Upon the Recovery*, 4.

69. Gills, *Upon the Recovery*, 4.

70. Gills, *Upon the Recovery*, 4.

71. Gills, *Upon the Recovery*, 4.

72. See King and Tompkins, *The Poor in England*, p.7.

73. Gills, *Upon the Recovery*, 1.

74. John Milton, *Poems &c upon severall occasions in English and Latin*, (London: Thomas Dring, 1673), 59.

75. Gills, *Upon the Recovery*, 7.

76. Edmund Gillingwater, *An essay on parish work-houses: containing observations on the present state of English work-houses; with some regulations proposed for their improvement. By Edmund Gillingwater, Overseer of the Poor, at Harleston, Norfolk* (Bury St. Edmund's: J. Rackham, 1786), Eighteenth Century Collections Online, Gale, (CW3304658747).

77. Gillingwater, *Essay on Work-Houses*, 2–3.

Allen, Hannah. "A Narrative of God's Gracious Dealings With that Choice Christian Mrs. Hannah Allen, (Afterwards Married to Mr. Hatt,) Reciting the great Advantages the Devil made of her deep Melancholy, and the Triumphant Victories, Rich and Sovereign Graces, God gave her over all his Strategems and Devices." In *Voices of Madness: Four Pamphlets, 1683–1796*, edited by Allan Ingram. Thrupp: Sutton Publishing, 1997.

Anderson, Julie, and A. Carden-Coyne. "Enabling the Past: New Perspectives in the History of Disability." *European review of history/ Revue européenne d'histoire* 14, no. 4 (2007): 447–57.

———. *War, disability and rehabilitation in Britain: "soul of a nation."* Manchester: Manchester University Press, 2011.

Andrews, Jonathan and Andrew Scull. *Customers and Patrons of the Mad Trade: The Management of Lunacy in Eighteenth-Century London.* Berkeley: University of California Press, 2003.

——— and Andrew Scull. *Undertaker of the Mind: John Monro and Mad-Doctoring in Eighteenth-Century England.* Berkeley: University of California Press, 2001.

Anon. *Aesop Unveil'd: or, the Beauties of Deformity.* London, 1731.

———. "Essay Towards a History of Mankind." In *The Annual Register, or a View of the History, Politics, and Literature, for the year 1771*, 490–93. The Third Edition. London, 1779.

———. "Priscilla Pointon." *Notes and Queries* 9 (1866): 355.

———. "A Case Humbly Offered to the Consideration of Parliament." In *Gentleman's Magazine* 33 (1762): 25–6.

———. *Proposals for Redressing Some Grievances Which Greatly Affect the Whole Nation.* London: J.Johnson, 1740.

———. *Proposals for taking off the land-tax: likewise ways and means for easing the nation of all the other taxes; to the great advancement of trade, and Benefit of the Nation in General. Being a project for raising above three millions per annum. Humbly submitted to the consideration of the Honourable House of Commons.* Stamford: Baily and Thompson, 1713. Eighteenth Century Collections Online, Gale. CW3306540868.

———. *The Ugly Club Manuscript, 1743–1754.* Housed at Liverpool Central Library, Liverpool, United Kingdom.

———. *Three delightful novels, displaying the stratagems of love and gallantry. Novel I. The lucky misfortune.... Novel II. The noble recompence.... Novel III. The loves of Edgar, King of England.* Bury St. Edmunds, Suffolk: Baily and Thompson, 1720?. Eighteenth Century Collections Online, Gale. CW3313826242.

Anstey, Peter R. "The Experimental History of the Understanding from Locke to Sterne." *Eighteenth-Century Thought*. 4 (2009): 143–69.

———. "Literary Responses to Robert Boyle's Natural Philosophy." In *Science, Literature and Rhetoric in Early Modern England*, edited by Juliet Cummins and David Burchell. Aldershot: Ashgate, 2007.

Armstrong, Nancy. *Desire and Domestic Fiction: A Political History of the Novel*. Oxford: Oxford University Press, 1987.

Ayers, Michael. *Locke: Epistemology and Ontology*. London: Routledge, 1993.

Backscheider, Paula R. *Eighteenth-Century Women Poets and Their Poetry: Inventing Agency, Inventing Genre*. Baltimore: Johns Hopkins University Press, 2005.

——— and Catherine E. Ingrassia, eds. *British Women Poets of the Long Eighteenth Century: An Anthology*. Baltimore: Johns Hopkins University Press, 2009.

Bacon, Francis. "Of Deformity." In *The Major Works*. Oxford: Oxford University Press, 2008. 426.

———. *Essays moral, economical, and political*. London: T. Bensley, 1798.

Banerjee, Chinmoy. "Tristram Shandy and the Association of Ideas." *Texas Studies in Literature and Language* 15, no. 4 (1974): 693–706.

Bannerman, Anne. *Poems*. Edinburgh: Mundell, 1800.

Barker-Benfield, G. J. *The Culture of Sensibility: Sex and Society in Eighteenth-Century Britain*. Chicago: University of Chicago Press, 1996.

Barrell, John. "'The Dangerous Goddess': Masculinity, Prestige, and the Aesthetic in Early Eighteenth-Century Britain," *Cultural Critique* 12 (1989): 101–31.

Battie, William. *A Treatise on Madness*. London: J. Whiston and B. White, 1758.

Baynton, Douglas C. *Through Deaf Eyes, A Photographic History of a Deaf Community*. Washington DC: Gallaudet University Press, 2007.

Belcher, William. "Address to Humanity: Containing, a Letter to Dr. Thomas Monro: A Receipt to Make a Lunatic, and Seize his Estate; and a Sketch of a True Smiling Hyena." In *Voices of Madness: Four Pamphlets, 1683–1796*, edited by Allan Ingram. (Thrupp: Sutton Publishing, 1997).

Birch, Thomas. *The unreasonableness of revenue, and the great duty of Christian-charity; consider'd. In two sermons: Preach'd at Botesdale-chapel in Suffolk, August 21 and 28. 1720. A.B. lecturer of the said chapel*. Bury St. Edmunds, Suffolk: Baily and Thompson, 1720?. Eighteenth Century Collections Online, Gale. CB3326543246.

Blacklock, Thomas. *Poems by Mr. Thomas Blacklock. To which is prefix'd, an account of the life, character, and writings, of the author, by the Reverend Mr. Spence, Late Professor of Poetry, at Oxford*. London: R. and J. Dodsley, 1756.

Borsay, Anne. *Disability and social policy in Britain since 1750: a history of exclusion*. Basingstoke: Palgrave Macmillan, 2005.

———. "History, Power and Identity." In *Disability Studies Today*, edited by Colin Barnes, Michael Oliver, and Len Barton, 98–118. Cambridge: Polity, 2002.

Boyle, Robert. *The Sceptical Chymist*. London, 1661.

Braddock, David L., and Susan L. Parish. "An Institutional History of Disability." In *Handbook of Disability Studies*, edited by Gary L. Albrecht, Katherine D. Seelman, and Michael Bury, 11–68. Thousand Oaks: Sage, 2001.

Bredberg, Elizabeth. "Writing Disability History: Problems, perspectives and sources." *Disability & Society* 14, no.2 (1999): 189–201.

Breed, Bryan. *From scorn to dignity: a brief history of disability.* London: New European, 2008.

Briggs, Peter M. "Locke's Essay and the Tentativeness of Tristram Shandy." *Studies in Philology* 82, no. 4 (1985): 493–520.

Bruckshaw, Samuel. "One More Proof of the Iniquitous Abuse of Private Madhouses." In *Voices of Madness: Four Pamphlets, 1683–1796,* edited by Allan Ingram. Thrupp: Sutton Publishing, 1997.

———. "The Case, Petition and Address of Samuel Bruckshaw, who Suffered a Most Severe Imprisonment for Very Nearly the Whole Year." In *Voices of Madness: Four Pamphlets, 1683–1796,* edited by Allan Ingram. Thrupp: Sutton Publishing, 1997.

Burch, Susan. "Disability History: Suggested Readings—An Annotated Bibliography." *The Public Historian* 27, no. 2 (Spring 2005): 63–74.

Burke, Edmund. *A Philosophical Enquiry into the Origin of our Ideas of the Sublime and Beautiful.* Oxford: Oxford University Press, 2009.

———. *A philosophical enquiry into the origin of our ideas of the sublime and beautiful.* London: R. and J. Dodsley, 1757.

Burney, Frances. *Camilla: Or, A Picture of Youth.* Oxford: Oxford World's Classics, 2009.

Byrd, Max. "The Madhouse, the Whorehouse, and the Convent." *Partisan Review* 44, no.2 (1977): 268–78.

Caruth, Cathy, ed. *Trauma: Explorations in Memory.* Baltimore: Johns Hopkins University Press, 1995.

———. *Empirical Truths and Critical Fictions: Locke, Wordsworth, Kant, Freud.* Baltimore: Johns Hopkins University Press, 1991.

———. *Unclaimed Experience: Trauma, Narrative, and History.* Baltimore: Johns Hopkins University Press, 1996.

Castiglione, Baldassarre. *The Book of the Courtier.* Translated by Charles S. Singleton. Garden City: Doubleday, 1959.

Cavell, Stanley. *Must We Mean What We Say?* New York: Charles Scribner & Sons, 1969.

Cavendish, Margaret. *Ground of natural philosophy divided into thirteen parts: with an appendix containing five parts / written by the . . . Dvchess of Newcastle.* London: A. Maxwell, 1668.

———. *Observations upon Experimental Philosophy.* Edited by Eileen O'Neill. Cambridge: Cambridge University Press, 2001.

———. *Philosophical and physical opinions written by . . . the Lady Marchioness of Newcastle.* London: William Wilson, 1663.

———. *Philosophical letters, or, Modest reflections upon some opinions in natural philosophy maintained by several famous and learned authors of this age, expressed by way of letters / by the thrice noble, illustrious, and excellent princess the Lady Marchioness of Newcastle.* London, 1664.

Chalmers, David. *The Conscious Mind: In Search of a Fundamental Theory.* New York: Oxford University Press, 1996.

Charlesworth, Lorie. *Welfare's forgotten past: a socio-legal history of the poor law.* Abingdon: Routledge, 2010.

Cobbett, William. *The Parliamentary History of England, from the Earliest Period to the year 1803*, Volume 15, 1753–1765. London: T. C. Tansard, 1813.

Cooke, Thomas. *A brief but plain explication of the church-catechism. Designed for the use of the scholars in Merchant-Taylors-School, and of the Children Educated in Christ's-Hospital, those particularly which are brought up in the Grammar-School thereunto belonging*. London: J. Wale, 1706. Eighteenth Century Collections Online. Gale. CW3323387679.

Cooper, Anthony Ashley, Third Earl of Shaftesbury. *Askêmata, Standard Edition: Complete Works, Correspondence, and Posthumous Writings*. Volume 2.6. Stuttgart: Frommann-Holzboog Verlag, 2011.

———. *Characteristics of Men, Manners, Opinions, Times*. Edited by Lawrence E. Klein. Cambridge: Cambridge University Press, 1999.

Croxall, Samuel. *The Fables of Aesop, With a Life of the Author*. London, 1793.

Cruden, Alexander. "The London-Citizen exceedingly injured or a British inquisition display'd, in an account of the unparallel'd case of a citizen of London, bookseller to the late Queen, who was in a most unjust and arbitrary Manner sent on the 23d of March last, 1738, by one Robert Wightman, a mere Stranger, to a private madhouse Containing, I. An Account of the said Citizen's barbarous Treatment in Wright's Private Madhouse on Bethnal-Green for nine Weeks and six Days, and of his rational and patient Behaviour, whilst Chained, Handcuffed, Strait-Wastecoated and Imprisoned in the said Madhouse: Where he probably would have been continued, or died under his Confinement, if he had not most Providentially made his Escape: In which he was taken up by the Constable and Watchmen, being suspected to be a Felon, but was unchain'd and set at liberty by Sir John Barnard the then Lord Mayor. II. As also an Account of the illegal Steps, false Calumnies, wicked Contrivances, bold and desperate Designs of the said Wightman, in order to escape Justice for his Crimes, with some Account of his engaging Dr. Monro and others as his Accomplices. The Whole humbly addressed to the Legislature, as plainly shewing the absolute Necessity of regulating Private Madhouses in a more effectual manner than at present." In *Voices of Madness: Four Pamphlets, 1683–1796*, edited by Allan Ingram. Thrupp: Sutton Publishing, 1997.

Curtis, Lewis Perry, ed. *Letters of Laurence Sterne*. Oxford: Oxford University Press, 1965.

Darwin, Erasmus. *Zoonomia; or, The laws of organic life*. London: J. Johnson, 1794–1796.

Davie, Donald. *The Eighteenth-Century Hymn in England*. Cambridge: Cambridge University Press, 1993.

Davis, Lennard J. *Bending over Backwards: Essays on Disability and the Body*. New York: New York University Press, 2002.

———. *Enforcing Normalcy: Disability, Deafness, and the Body*. New York: Verso Press, 1995.

Davoine, Françoise and Jean-Max Gaudillière. *History Beyond Trauma*. Translated by Susan Fairfield. New York: Other Press, 2004.

De'Porte, Michael. *Nightmares and Hobbyhorses: Swift, Sterne, and Augustan Ideas of Madness*. San Marino: Huntington Library Press, 1974.

Defoe, Daniel, *The secret history of the October Club: from its original to this time. By a member*. London, 1711.

———. *A Review of the State of the English Nation*. London: J. Roberts, 1706.

———. *Augusta triumphans or, The way to make London the most flourishing city in the universe: first, by establishing an university . . . concluding with an effectual method to prevent street robberies, and a letter to Coll. Robinson on account of the orphan's tax*. London: J. Roberts, 1728.

Deleuze, Gilles. *Foucault*, Ed. De Minuit, 1968.

Derrida, Jacques. "Cogito and the History of Madness." In *Writing and Difference*, translated by Alan Bass, 36–77. (London: Routledge and Keegan Paul, 1978).

———. *Of Grammatology*. Translated by Gayatri Chakravorty Spivak. Baltimore and London, Johns Hopkins University Press, 1987.

Deutsch, Helen and Felicity Nussbaum, eds. *Defects: Engendering the Modern Body*. Ann Arbor: University of Michigan Press, 2000.

———. *Loving Dr. Johnson*. Chicago: Chicago University Press, 2005.

———. *Resemblance and Disgrace*. Cambridge: Harvard University Press, 1996.

Dewhurst, Kenneth. *Dr. Thomas Sydenham, 1624–1689: His Life and Original Writings*. Berkeley: University of California Press, 1966.

———. *John Locke Physician and Philosopher: A Medical Biography*. London: Wellcome Historical Medical Library, 1963.

———. *John Locke, 1632–1704, Physician and Philosopher: A Medical Biography with an Edition of the Medical Notes in His Journals*. London: Wellcome Historical Medical Library, 1963.

Dickie, Simon. "Hilarity and Pitilessness in Mid-Eighteenth Century: English Jestbook Humor," *Eighteenth-Century Studies* 37, no. 1 (2003): 1–22.

———. *Cruelty and Laughter: Forgotten Comic Literature and the Unsentimental Eighteenth Century*. Chicago: The University of Chicago Press, 2011.

Diderot, Denis. *An Essay on Blindness, In a Letter to a Person of Distinction; Reciting the most interesting Particulars relative to Persons born Blind, and those who have lost their Sight. Being an Inquiry into the Nature of their Ideas, Knowledge of Sounds, Opinions Concerning Morality and Religion, &c.* London: J. Barker, 1780.

Eagleton, Terry. *The Ideology of the Aesthetic*. Oxford: Blackwell, 1990.

Edgeworth, Maria. *Belinda*. Oxford: Oxford's World Classics, 2009.

Erikson, Kai. "Notes on Trauma and Community." In *Trauma: Explorations in Memory*, edited by Cathy Caruth, 183–200. Baltimore: Johns Hopkins University Press, 1995.

Evelyn, Mary. Letter to Ralph Bohun. In *Paper Bodies: A Margaret Cavendish Reader*, edited by Sylvia Bowerbank and Sara Mendelson, 91–92. Peterborough: Broadview Press, 2000.

Fetterley, Judith. "Reading about Reading: 'A Jury of Her Peers,' 'The Murders in the Rue Morgue,' and 'The Yellow Wallpaper.'" In *Gender and Reading*, edited by Elizabeth A. Flynn and Patrocino P. Scweickart, 147–164. Baltimore: Johns Hopkins University Press, 1986.

Fielding, Henry. *Joseph Andrews* and *Shamela*. Oxford: Oxford University Press, 1999.

Fluchère, Henri. *Laurence Sterne: From Tristram to Yorick*. Oxford: Oxford University Press, 1965.

Fonda, Jane and Jon Voigt. *Coming Home*. Movie. Directed by Hal Ashby. 1987. Los Angeles, CA: United Artists.

Foucault, Michel. *Histoire de la Folie à l'Age classique*. Plon, 1961. Reprint, Ed.Gallimard, 1972.

———. *Madness and Civilization*. Translated by Richard Howard. New York: Vintage Books, 1988.

———. *Naissance de la Clinique*. PUF, 1963.

———. *Surveiller et punir*. Ed. Gallimard, 1975.

———. *The Order of Things: An Archaeology of the Human Sciences*. Translated by Alan Sheridan. New York: Harper and Rowe, 1973.

Foyster Elizabeth "At the limits of liberty: married women and confinement in eighteenth-century England." *Continuity and Change* 17 (2002): 39–62.

Frank, Robert G. "Thomas Willis and His Circle: Brain and Medicine in Seventeenth-Century Medicine." In *The Languages of Psyche: Mind and Body in Enlightenment Thought: Clark Library Lectures, 1985–1986*, edited by George S. Rousseau, 107–146. Berkeley: University of California Press, 1990

Froide, Amy. *Never Married: Single Women in Early Modern England.* Oxford: Oxford University Press, 2007.

Fudge, Erica. *Brutal Reasoning: Animals, Rationality, and Humanity in Early Modern England.* Ithaca: Cornell University Press, 2006.

Gabbard, D. Christopher. "From Idiot Beast to Idiot Sublime: Mental Disability in John Cleland's *Fanny Hill*." *PMLA* 123, no. 2 (2008): 375–89.

———. "Disability Studies and the British Long Eighteenth Century." *Literature Compass* 8 no.2 (2011): 80–94.

Garland-Thomson, Rosemarie. "Feminist Disability Studies." *Signs: Journal of Women in Culture and Society* 30, no.2 (2005): 1557–87.

Gaukroger, Stephen. "The Role of Natural Philosophy in the Development of Locke's Empiricism." *British Journal for the History of Philosophy* 17, no.1 (2009): 55–83.

Gentleman in Lincolnshire. *Lincolnshire. A poem.* Bury St. Edmunds, Suffolk, 1720. Eighteenth Century Collections Online, Gale. CW3309769436.

George, Jacqueline. "Public Reading and Lyric Pleasure: Eighteenth Century Elocutionary Debates and Poetic Practice." *ELH* 76, no.2 (2009): 371–97.

Gillingwater, Edmund. *An essay on parish work-houses: containing observations on the present state of English work-houses; with some regulations proposed for their improvement. By Edmund Gillingwater, Overseer of the Poor, at Harleston, Norfolk.* Bury St. Edmund's: J. Rackham, 1786. Eighteenth Century Collections Online, Gale. CW3304658747.

Gills, Thomas. *Advice to youth: or, instructions for Young men and maids. By Thomas Gills, the Blind Man of St. Edmunds-Bury, Suffolk.* London, 1709. Eighteenth Century Collections Online, Gale. CW3312252458.

———. *Instructions for children, in verse. By Thomas Gills, the Blind Man of St. Edmund's-Bury in Suffolk.* London, 1709. Eighteenth Century Collections Online, Gale. CW3312804968.

———. *Instructions for children, in verse. By Thomas Gills, the Blind Man of St. Edmunds Bury in Suffolk.* London, 1707. Eighteenth Century Collections Online, Gale. CW3324642157.

———. *Thomas Gills of St. Edmund's Bury in Suffolk, upon the recovery of his sight, and the second loss thereof.* Bury St Edmunds?, London?, 1710. Eighteenth Century Collections Online, Gale. CW3311512092.

———. *Useful and delightful instructions by way of dialogue between the master & his scholar, containing the duty of children. Composed in verse, after a very Plain, Easie, Delightful and Natural Manner: And humbly recommended to the Use of Children of both Sexes, train'd up in the Charity-Schools.* London: J. Downing, 1712. Eighteenth Century Collections Online, Gale. CW3311512077.

———. *Useful and delightful instructions, by way of dialogue between the master & his scholar. Containing the duty of children. Composed in verse, after a very Plain, Easie, Delightful and Natural Manner: And humbly recommended to the Use of Children of both Sexes, train'd up in the Charity-Schools.*

The second edition enlarg'd. London: J. Downing, 1716. Eighteenth Century Collections Online, Gale. CW3310481438.

Gonda, Caroline, "Sarah Scott and 'The Sweet Excess of Paternal Love.'" *Studies in English Literature, 1500–1900* 32, no.3 (1992): 511–35.

Goodey, C. F. *A history of intelligence and "intellectual disability": the shaping of psychology in early modern Europe.* Farnham: Ashgate, 2011.

Greer, Germaine. *Slip-shod Sibyls: Recognition, Rejection and the Woman Poet.* New York: Viking, 1995.

Hammond, Brean S. *Professional imaginative writing in England, 1670–1740: 'hackney for bread.'* Oxford: Clarendon Press, 1987.

Harper, Andrew. *A Treatise on the real cause and cure of insanity; in which the nature and distinctions of this disease are fully explained, and the treatment established on new principles.* London: Stalker and Walter, 1789.

Harrison, Susanna. *Songs in the Night, by a young woman under deep affliction.* London: R. Hawes, 1780.

Harvey, Francis. *The dangers and mischiefs of instability in matters of religion consider'd. A sermon preach'd at the Arch-Deacon's visitation, at Sudbury, on Thursday, April 20, 1721. A.M. rector of lawshall in Suffolk; and chaplain to the Right Honourable the Earl of Bristol. Printed at the request of the clergy.* Bury St. Edmunds, Suffolk: Baily and Thompson, 1721, Eighteenth Century Collections Online, Gale. CW3326679938.

Hay, William. *Deformity: An Essay.* London: George Faulkner, 1754.

———. *An Essay on Civil Government.* London: R. Gosling,1728.

———. *Martial's Epigrams Selected, Translated and Imitated.* London: R. & J. Dodsley, 1775.

———. *Mount Caburn: A Poem.* London: J.Stagg, 1730.

———. *Religio Philosophi: or, the principles of morality and Christianity illustrated from a view of the universe, and man's situation in it.* London: R.& J. Dodsley, 1753.

———. *Remarks on the Laws relating to the Poor, with Proposals for their better Relief and Employment.* London: J. Stagg, 1731.

Haywood, Eliza. *The Distressed Orphan, or Love in a Mad-house.* New York: Published for the William Andrews Clark Memorial Library and the UCLA Center for Seventeenth- and Eighteenth-Century Studies by AMS, 1993.

Hazlitt, William. *The Complete Works of William Hazlitt in Twenty-One Volumes, vol. 6, Lectures on the Comic Writers and Lectures on the Age of Elizabeth.* Edited by P.P. Howe. London: J.M. Dent and Sons, Ltd., 1931.

Hewit, Peter. *A brief and plain explication of the catechism of the Church of England, In sundry short and familiar questions and answers, composed for the use and benefit of families: that hereby parents of children, &c. may be directed how to instruct those that are committed to their charge and trust, in the right understanding of the true grounds and principles of the Christian faith and practice. To which is annexed, an exhortation to family devotion.* London: Awnsham and John Churchill, 1704. Eighteenth Century Collections Online, Gale. CB3326642102.

Hitchcock, Tim. *Down and Out on the Streets of London.* London: Humbledon, 2005.

Hirschmann, Nancy J. "Freedom and (Dis)Ability in Early Modern Political Thought." In *Recovering Disability in Early Modern England*, ed. Allison P. Hobgood and David Houston Wood, 167–86. Columbus: Ohio State University Press, 2013.

Hobgood, Allison P. "Caesar Hath the Falling Sickness: The Legibility of Early Modern Disability in Shakespearean Drama." *Disability Studies Quarterly* 29, no. 4 (2009). Accessed May 1, 2013. http://www.dsq-sds.org/article/view/993/1184.

———. and David Houston Wood. Introduction to *Disability Studies Quarterly* 29, no. 4 (2009). Accessed May 1, 2013. http://www.dsq-sds.org/issue/view/42.

Hufton, Olwen. *The Poor of Eighteenth Century France 1750–1789.* Oxford: Clarendon, 1974.

Hunter, Richard Alfred and Ida Macalpine. *Three Hundred Years of Psychiatry, 1535–1860: A History Presented in Selected English Texts.* Oxford: Oxford University Press, 1963.

Hutchison, Iain. *A history of disability in nineteenth-century Scotland.* Lewiston: Edwin Mellen Press, 2007.

Iser, Wolfgang. *Laurence Sterne: Tristram Shandy.* Cambridge: Cambridge University Press, 1988.

Jackson, Peter. *A Pictorial History of deaf Britain.* Winsford: Deafprint, 2001.

James-Cavan, Kathleen. Introduction to *Deformity: An Essay* by William Hay, 9–19. Victoria, University of British Columbia Press, 2004.

Johnson, Samuel. *A Dictionary of the English Language. . . .* Vol 2. 2nd Edition (corrected). London, 1760.

———. *A Dictionary of the English Language. . . .* Vol 2. 3rd Edition. London, 1765.

Jones, Robert W. "Obedient Faces: The Virtue of Deformity in Sarah Scott's Fiction." In *Defects: Engendering the Modern Body*, edited by Helen Deutsch and Felicity Nussbaum, 280–302. Ann Arbor: University of Michigan Press, 2000.

Jordan, Robert. *The Eye of the World.* New York: T. Doherty Associates, 1990.

Kadar, Marlene, ed. *Introduction to Essays on Life Writing: From Genre to Critical Practice.* Toronto: University of Toronto Press, 1992.

Keach, Benjamin. *The child's delight: or instructions for children and youth. Wherein all the chief principles of the Christian religions are clearly (though briefly) opened. Necessary to Establish young People in God's Truth, in opposition to Error in these perilous Times. Together With many other things, both Pleasant and Useful, for the Christian Education of Youth; with Letters to Parents. Adorned with several Copper Cuts, teaching to Spell, Read, and cast Accompts. With a short Dictionary interpreting hard Words and Names. Likewise, a Form for a Bond, Bill, or Receipt; And a Table showing the Interest of any Sums, &c. Fitted for the use of Schools, and useful for all Families.* The Third Edition. London: William and Joseph Marshall, 1704?. Eighteenth Century Collections Online, Gale. CW3321382880.

Keymer, Thomas, ed. *Laurence Sterne's Tristram Shandy: A Casebook.* Oxford: Oxford University Press, 2006.

———. *Sterne, the Moderns, and the Novel.* Oxford: Oxford University Press, 2002.

Kidder, Richard. *An help to the smallest children's more easie understanding the church-catechism. By way of question and answer. Drawn up for the use of a certain parish in London by the rector thereof.* London: H. Hills, 1709. Eighteenth Century Collections Online, Gale. CB3329893928.

Kim, James. "'good cursed, bouncing losses': Masculinity, Sentimental Irony, and Exuberance in Tristram Shandy." *The Eighteenth Century* 48, no. 1 (2007): 3–24.

Kinderley, Charles. *The present state of the navigation of the towns of Lyn, Wisbeech, Spalding, and Boston. The rivers that pass through those places, and the countries that border thereupon, truly, faithfully, and impartially represented.* Bury St. Edmunds, Suffolk: Baily and Thompson, 1721. Eighteenth Century Collections Online, Gale. CW3306552396.

King, Ross. "Tristram Shandy and the Wound of Language." *Studies in Philology* 92, no. 3 (1995): 291–310.

King, Steven, and Alana Tomkins, eds. *The Poor in England 1700–1850: An Economy of Makeshifts.* Manchester: Manchester University Press, 2003.

Klein, Lawrence E. *Shaftesbury and the Culture of Politeness: Moral Discourse and Cultural Politics in Early Eighteenth-Century England.* Cambridge: Cambridge University Press, 1994.

Kramnick, Jonathan. *Actions and Objects from Hobbes to Richardson.* (Stanford: Stanford University Press, 2010).

Kristeva, Julia and Jeanine Herman "Liberty, Equality, Fraternity, and . . . Vulnerability" *WSQ: Women's Studies Quarterly* 38, nos.1&2 (2010): 251–68.

Kromm, Jane E. "The Feminization of Madness in Visual Representation." *Feminist Studies* 20 (1994): 507–35.

Krystal, Henry. "Trauma and Aging: A Thirty-Year Follow-Up." In *Trauma: Explorations in Memory,* edited by Cathy Caruth, 76–99. Baltimore: Johns Hopkins University Press, 1995.

Lamb, Jonathan. "Sterne, Sebald, and Siege Architecture." *Eighteenth-Century Fiction* 19, nos. 1&2 (2006): 21–41.

Langford, John Alfred. *A Century of Birmingham Life: Or, a Chronicle of Local Events, from 1741–1841.* Birmingham: E.C. Osborne, 1868.

Lanser, Susan Sniader. *Fictions of Authority: Women Writers and Narrative Voice.* Ithaca: Cornell University Press. 1992.

Larrissy, Edward. *The Blind and Blindness in Literature of the Romantic Period.* Edinburgh: Edinburgh University Press, 2007.

Laub, Dori. "Truth and Testimony: The Process and the Struggle." In *Trauma: Explorations in Memory,* edited by Cathy Caruth, 61–75. Baltimore: Johns Hopkins University Press, 1995.

Lazarus, Emma. "The New Colossus." Accessed September 3 2013. http://www.libertystatepark.com/emma.htm.

Levi-Strauss, Claude. *Anthropologie structural deux.* Plon, 1973.

———. *Anthropologie Structurale.* 1958. Reprint Plon, 1974.

———. *L'impossible prison. Recherches sur le système pénitentiare au XIXe siècle.* Edited by Michelle Perrot. Le Seuil, 1980.

———. *La Pensée sauvage.* Plon, 1962.

Lewis, Jane Elizabeth. *The English Fable: Aesop and Literary Culture, 1651–1740.* Cambridge: Cambridge University Press, 1996.

Linthicum, Liz. "Integrative Practice: Oral History, Dress and Disability Studies." *Journal of Design History* 19, no. 4 (2006): 309–18.

Linton, Simi. *Claiming Disability: Knowledge and Identity.* New York: New York University Press, 1998.

Locke, John. *Of the Conduct of the Understanding.* Cambridge: J. Archdeacon, 1781.

———. *An Essay concerning Human Understanding, 4th edition.* Edited by. P.H. Nidditch. Oxford: Oxford University Press, 1975.

Longmore, Paul K. and Laurie Umansky. *The New Disability History: American Perspectives.* New York: New York University Press, 2001.

Lonsdale, Roger, ed. *Eighteenth Century Women Poets: An Oxford Anthology.* Oxford: Oxford University Press, 1989.

Lund, Roger D. "Laughing at Cripples: Ridicule, Deformity, and the Argument from Design." *Eighteenth-Century Studies* 39, no.1 (2005): 91–114.

Markley, Robert. "Sentimentality as Performance: Shaftesbury, Sterne, and the Theatrics of Virtue." In *The New Eighteenth Century: Theory, Politics, English Literature,* edited by Felicity Nussbaum and Laura Brown, 210–30. New York: Methuen, 1987.

Matthew, H. C. G. and Brian Harrison, eds. *Oxford Dictionary of National Biography.* Oxford: Oxford University Press, 2004.

McKeon, Michael. "Historicizing Patriarchy: The Emergence of Gender Difference in England, 1660–1760." *Eighteenth-Century Studies* 28, no. 3 (1995): 295–322.

Meade, Teresa and David Serlin, eds. "Disability and History." *Radical History Review* 94, Special Issue, (Winter 2006).

Meynell, G.G. "Locke as the Author of Anatomia and De Arte Medica." *The Locke Newsletter* 25 (1994): 65–73.

Michael, Emily, and Fred S. Michael, "Corporeal Ideas in Seventeenth-Century Psychology." *Journal of the History of Ideas* 50, no.1 (1989): 31–48.

Millon, Theodore, with contributions from Seth D. Grossman and Sarah E. Meagher. *Masters of the Mind: Exploring the Story of Mental Illness from Ancient Times to the New Millennium.* Malden: Wiley Blackwell, 2004.

Milne, Anne. *Lactilla Tends Her Fav'rite Cow: Ecocritical Readings of Animals and Women in Eighteenth-Century British Labouring-Class Women's Poetry.* Lewisburg: Bucknell University Press, 2008.

Milton, John. "Sonnet XX, On His Blindness." In *The Complete Works of John Milton,* edited by Laura Lunger Knoppers. Oxford: Oxford University Press, 2008.

Mitchell, David T. and Sharon L. Snyder, eds. *The Body and Physical Difference: Discourses of Disability.* Ann Arbor: University of Michigan Press, 1997.

———. and Sharon L. Snyder. *Narrative Prosthesis: Disability and the Dependencies of Discourse.* Ann Arbor: University of Michigan Press, 2000.

Monro, John. *Remarks on Dr Battie's treatise on madness.* London: John Clarke, 1758.

Morton, A.L. *A People's History of Britain.* London: Gollancz, 1938.

Mottolese, William C. "Tristram Cyborg and Toby Toolmaker: Body, Tools, and Hobbyhorse in Tristram Shandy." *Studies in the English Language* 47, no. 3 (2007): 679–701.

Mounsey, Chris. ed. *Developments in the Histories of Sexualities: In Search of the Nor. 'al.* Lewisburg: Bucknell University Press, 2013.

———. *Being the Body of Christ: Towards a Twenty First Century Homosexual Theology for the Anglican Church.* Sheffield: Equinox, 2012.

Mulvey, Laura. "Visual Pleasure and Narrative Cinema." *Screen* 16, no.3 (1975): 6–18.

Munch, Edvard. "The Modern Eye." Art Exhibition. Tate Modern. Bankside, London. August 12, 2012.

Neilsen, Kim E. *A Disability History of the United States.* Boston: Beacon Press, 2012.

Nelson, Holly Faith, and Sharon Alker. "Conway: Dis/ability, Medicine, and Metaphysics." In *The New Science and Women's Literary Discourse: Prefiguring Frankenstein*, edited by Judy A. Hayden, 65–83. New York: Palgrave Macmillan, 2011.

———. "Writing 'Science Fiction' in the Shadow of War: Bodily Transgressions in Cavendish's *Blazing World*." In *Travel Narratives, the New Science, and Literary Discourse, 1569–1750*, edited by Judy Hayden, 103–21. Aldershot: Ashgate, 2012.

Nestor, Deborah. Introduction to *The Distressed Orphan, or Love in a Madhouse*, by Eliza Haywood, iii–xxii. New York: Published for the William Andrews Clark Memorial Library and the UCLA Center for Seventeenth- and Eighteenth-Century Studies by AMS, 1993.

New, Melvyn. "Sterne and the Narrative of Determinateness." *Eighteenth-Century Fiction* 4, no. 4 (1992): 315–29.

Nussbaum, Felicity A. *The Autobiographical Subject*. Baltimore: Johns Hopkins University Press, 1989.

———. "Feminotopias: The Pleasures of 'Deformity' in Mid-Eighteenth-Century England." In *The Body and Physical Difference: Discourses of Disability*, edited by David Mitchell and Sharon L. Snyder, 161–73. Ann Arbor: University of Michigan Press, 1997.

———. *The Limits of the Human: Fictions of Anomaly, Race and Gender in the Long Eighteenth Century*. Cambridge: Cambridge University Press, 2003.

Nussbaum, Martha C. *Frontiers of Justice: Disability, Nationality, Species Membership*. Cambridge: Harvard University Press, 2006.

———. *The Therapy of Desire: Theory and Practice in Hellenistic Ethics*. Princeton: Princeton University Press, 2009.

O'Connor, Timothy. *Person and Causes: The Metaphysics of Free Will*. Oxford: Oxford University Press, 2000.

Osborne, Dorothy. *Letters to Sir William Temple*. Harmondsworth: Penguin, 1987.

Overton, Bill. "Journeying in the Eighteenth-century: British Verse Epistle." *Studies in Travel Writing* 13, no.1 (2009): 3–25.

Oxford English Dictionary. 2nd ed. 20 vols. Oxford: Oxford University Press, 1989.

Pargeter, William. *Observations on maniacal disorders*. Reading: Smart and Cowslade, 1792.

Park, Katharine, and Lorraine Daston, eds. *Early Modern Science*, Cambridge: Cambridge University Press, 2006.

Parker, Fred. *Scepticism and Literature: An Essay on Pope, Hume, Sterne, and Johnson*. Oxford: Oxford University Press, 2003.

Parry-Jones, William. *The Trade in Lunacy: a study of private madhouses in England in the eighteenth and nineteenth centuries*. London: Routledge and Keegan Paul, 1971.

Paulson, Ronald. *The Beautiful, Novel, and Strange: Aesthetics and Heterodoxy*. Baltimore: Johns Hopkins University Press, 1996.

Paulson, William R. *Enlightenment, Romanticism, and the Blind in France*. Princeton: Princeton University Press, 1987.

Peacham Henry. *The worth of a penny: or, a caution to keep money. With the causes of the scarcity, and misery of the want thereof, consider'd under the following Heads, viz. the . . . Causes why Men are without Money, and are Three . . . I. Excess in Diet, Drinking, and Apparel. II. Gaming, and Recreations. III. Idleness and Improvidence, either in themselves, or their Servants. IV. The Character of a dejected Spirit for want of Money. V. The Misery of the Want of Money. VI. It compelleth to offend against Body and Soul. VII. The Vertue of Frugality, and the Definition of it. VIII. The Derivative of the Word Penny, and the Value of is. IX. The many good Uses that a Penny may be put to. X. Cautions to save Money in Diet, Apparel, and Recreations. XI. The English, of all Nations in Europe, the most prosuse in their Expences. XII. Of good Husbandy in Apparel. XIII. Many excellent Examples of Moderation in it. XIV. Of Recreation, and the Benefits that are received by it. XV. Four excellent Cautions to be observ'd in Play, &c.* . St Edmund's Bury: Baily and Thompson, 1725?. Eighteenth Century Collections Online, Gale. CW3305452375.

———. *The Compleat Gentleman*. London, 1634.

Peck, Francis. *An Exercise upon the Creation*. Cambridge, 1716.

———. *Ad magistratum: a sermon preached before the mayor and aldermen of Stamford In the County of Lincoln, in the Parish-Church of the Blessed Virgin; at the Inauguration of a new Mayor, Oct. 6. 1720. A. B. Curate of King's-Cliffe, in the County of Northampton. Published to prevent Misrepresentations.* Stamford, Lincolnshire and Bury St Edmunds, Suffolk: Thompson and Baily, 1720?. Eighteenth Century Collections Online, Gale. CW3322788913.

Perry, Ruth. *Novel Relations: The Transformation of Kinship in English Literature and Culture, 1748–1818*. Cambridge: Cambridge University Press, 2004.

Pickering, Priscilla. *Poems by Mrs. Pickering. To which are added Poetical sketches by the author, and translator of Philotoxi Ardenæ*. Birmingham: E. Piercy, 1794.

Pitt-Kethley, Fiona. *The Literary Companion to Sex*. New York: Random House, 1992.

Porter, Roy. *Mind-Forg'd Manacles: A History of Madness in England from the Restoration to the Regency*. London: Athlone Press, 1987.

Poynton, Priscilla. *Poems on Several Occasions by Miss Priscilla Pointon of Lichfield*. Birmingham: T. Warren, 1770.

Reid, Thomas, and John Haldane. "An essay by Thomas Reid on the conception of power." *Philosophical Quarterly* 51 (2001):1–12.

———. *Essays on the Active Powers of Man*. Edinburgh: John Bell, 1788.

———. *Essays on the Intellectual Powers of Man*. Edinburgh: John Bell, 1785.

Richardson, Jonathan. "Imagining Military Conflict in the Seven Year's War." *Studies in the English Language* 48, no. 3 (2008): 585–611.

Richardson, Samuel, *Pamela: Or, Virtue Rewarded*. London: C. Rivington, 1740.

Rogers, John. *The Matter of Revolution: Science, Poetry and Politics in the Age of Milton*. Ithaca: Cornell University Press, 1996.

Romanell, Patrick. *John Locke and Medicine: A New Key to Locke*. Buffalo: Prometheus Books, 1984.

Rorty, Richard. *Philosophy and the Mirror of Nature*. Princeton: Princeton University Press, 2009.

Rowe, Elizabeth Singer. *Devout Exercises of the Heart in Meditation and Soliloquy, Prayer and Praise. By the late Pious and Ingenious Mrs. Rowe. Review'd and Published at her Request, by I. Watts, D.D.* London: R. Hett, 1738.

Sarasohn, Lisa T. *The Natural Philosophy of Margaret Cavendish: Reason and Fancy during the Scientific Revolution*. Cambridge: Cambridge University Press, 2001.

Scarry, Elaine. *The Body in Pain*. Oxford: Oxford University Press, 1985.

Schneewind, J. B. *The Invention of Autonomy: A History of Modern Moral Philosophy*. Cambridge: Cambridge University Press, 1998.

Schweik, Susan. *The Ugly Laws: Disability in Public.* New York: New York University Press, 2009.

——. "Disability Politics and American Literary History: Some Suggestions." *American Literary History* 20, no. 1–2 (2008): 217–37.

Scott, Sarah. *A Description of Millennium Hall.* Toronto: Broadview Press, 1995.

——. *Agreeable Ugliness: or, the Triumph of the Graces. Exemplified in real life and fortunes of a young lady of some distinction.* London: R. and J. Dodsley, 1754.

Scull, Andrew, Charlotte MacKenzie, and Nicholas Hervey. *Masters of Bedlam: The Transforming of the Mad-Doctoring Trade.* Princeton: Princeton University Press, 1996.

——. *Museums of Madness: The Social Organization of Insanity in Nineteenth-Century England.* New York: St. Martin's Press, 1979.

Siebers, Tobin. *Disability Theory.* Ann Arbor: University of Michigan Press, 2008.

Smith, Bonnie G., and Beth Hutchison, eds. *Gendering Disability.* New Brunswick: Rutgers University Press, 2004.

Snyder, Sharon L. and David T. Mitchell. "Re-engaging the Body: Disability Studies and the Resistance to Embodiment." *Public Culture* 13, no. 3 (2001): 367–89.

Sokoll, Thomas. *Essex Pauper Letters 1731–1837.* Oxford: Clarendon, 2001.

Soud, Stephen. "'Weavers, Gardeners, and Gladiators': Labyrinths in Tristram Shandy." *Eighteenth-Century Studies* 28, no. 4 (1995): 397–411.

Spence, Joseph. *Crito: or, A Dialogue on Beauty.* London: R. Dodsley, 1752.

Staves, Susan. *Married Women's Separate Property in England, 1660–1833.* Cambridge: Harvard University Press, 1990.

Steele, Richard. "On Personal Defects; Proposals for an Ugly Club." In *Selections from the Tatler, Spectator, and Guardian,* edited by Austin Dobson, 172. Oxford: Clarendon Press, 1885.

Sterne, Laurence. *The Life and Opinions of Tristram Shandy, Gentleman.* Edited by Melvyn New. London: Penguin Books, 2003.

Stiker, Henri-Jacques. *A History of Disability.* Translated by William Sayers. Ann Arbor: University of Michigan Press, 1999.

Suffolk mercury: or, Bury post. Bury St. Edmunds: Baily and Thompson, Monday 11 October 1731. Eighteenth Century Collections Online, Gale. CB3326829097.

Sydenham, Thomas. *Methodus curandi febres.* London: 1666.

——. *The Whole Works of that Excellent Practical Physician, Dr. Thomas Sydenham.* London, 1734.

Tadié, Alexis. *Sterne's Whimsical Theatres of Language: Orality, Gesture, Literacy.* Aldershot: Ashgate, 2003.

Taylor, Stephen and Clyve Jone. *Tory and Whig.* Woodbridge: Boydell Press, 1998.

Terry, Jennifer, and Jacqueline Urla, eds. *Deviant Bodies: Critical Perspectives in Science and Popular Culture.* Bloomington: Indiana University Press, 1995.

Thomas, Claudia N. *Alexander Pope and His Eighteenth-Century Women Readers.* Carbondale: Southern Illinois University Press, 1994.

Todd, Janet. *A Dictionary of American and British Women Writers 1660–1800.* Totowa: Rowman & Allanheld, 1985.

Turner, David M. *Disability in eighteenth-century England: Imagining Physical Impairment.* London: Routledge, 2012.

Two Ordinances of the Lords and Commons Assembled in Parliament. London, 1647.

Van der Kolk, Bessel A. and Onno Van der Hart. "The Intrusive Past: The Flexibility of Memory and The Engraving of Trauma." In *Trauma: Explorations in Memory*, edited by Cathy Caruth, 158–82. Baltimore: Johns Hopkins University Press, 2005.

Van Peer, Willie. "Mutilated Signs: Notes toward a Literary Paleography." *Poetics Today* 18, no. 1 (1997): 33–57.

Simo Vehmas, "What Can Philosophy Tell Us about Disability?" In *Routledge Handbook of Disability Studies*, eds. Nick Watson, Alan Roulstone, and Carol Thomas, 298–309. New York: Routledge, 2012.

Voitle, Robert. *The Third Earl of Shaftesbury, 1671–1713.* Baton Rouge: Louisiana State University Press, 1984.

Wainwright, Geoffrey and Karen Westerfield Tucker eds. *The Oxford History of Christian Worship.* Oxford: Oxford University Press, 2005.

Walmsley, Jonathan. "Sydenham and the Development of Locke's Natural Philosophy." *British Journal for the History of Philosophy* 16, no.1 (2008): 65–83.

Ward, Edward. *A satyr against wine. With a poem, in praise of small beer. Written by a gentleman in a fever, occasion'd by hard drinking.* London: Bragg, 1705. Eighteenth Century Collections Online, Gale. CW3310733701.

———. *A satyr against wine. With a poem, in praise of small beer. Written by a gentleman in a fever, occasion'd by hard drinking.* The second edition. St Edmunds Bury, Suffolk and Stamford, Lincolnshire: Thompson and Baily, 1712?. Eighteenth Century Collections Online, Gale. CW33330865852.

———. *Honesty in distress: but reliev'd by no party. A tragedy, as it is acted on the stage of the world. Act I. Scene the palace. Honesty alone. Honesty and a courtier. Honesty and a lady. Honesty and a footman. Honesty alone. Act II. Scene Westminster-Hall, with the court sitting. Honesty among the lawyers. The lawyers speeches concerning honesty. Honesty and . . . Act III. Scene . . . Honesty begging along the city . . . draper. A precise apothecary and his man. Honesty and an ale-house keeper. Honesty and a grocer. Honesty and a hosier. Honesty and the merchants. Honesty starved to death. To which is added, a satyr against the corrupt use of money.* Bury St. Edmunds, Suffolk: Bailey and Thompson, 1721?. Eighteenth Century Collections Online, Gale. CB3331342863.

———. *The rise and fall of madam Coming-Sir: or, An Unfortunate slip from the tavern-bar, Into the Surgeon's Powdering-Tub.* Stamford, Lincolnshire and St Edmond's Bury: Thompson and Bailey, 1720?. Eighteenth Century Collections Online, Gale. CW3309954349.

Watt, Carol. *The Cultural Work of Empire: The Seven Years' War and the Imagining of the Shandean State.* Toronto: University of Toronto Press, 2007.

Westminster Assembly. *The shorter catechism, composed by the Reverend Assembly of Divines. With the proofs thereof, out of the scriptures, in words at length. Which are either some of the former quoted places, or others gathered from their other Writings: All fitted both for Brevity and Clearness to this their Form of sound Words. For the Benefit of Christians in General, and of Youth and Children, in Understanding in particular, that they may with more ease acquaint themselves with the Truth, according to the Scriptures, and with the Scriptures themselves.* Edinburgh: John Reid, 1702. Eighteenth Century Collections Online, Gale. CW3321606620.

Wheeler, Roxann. *The Complexion of Race: Categories of Difference in Eighteenth-Century British Culture.* Philadelphia: University of Pennsylvania Press, 2000.

Willis, Thomas, Kenneth Dewhurst, John Locke, and Richard Lower. *Thomas Willis's Oxford Lectures.* Oxford: Sandford Publications, 1980.

———. "Of Stupidity or Folly." In *The London Practice of Physick: Or the whole Practical Part of Physick Contained in the Works of Dr. Willis.* 489–90. London, 1685.

———. *Two Discourses Concerning the Soul of Brutes: Which Is That of the Vital and Sensitive of Man.* Translated by Samuel Pordage. Gainesville: Scholars' Facsimiles & Reprints, 1971.

Wittreich, Joseph. *Feminist Milton.* Ithaca: Cornell University Press, 1987.

Wolfe, Charles T. "Empiricist Heresies in Early Modern Thought." In *The Body As Object and Instrument of Knowledge: Embodied Empiricism in Early Modern Science,* edited by Charles T. Wolfe and Ofer Gal, 333–344. Dordrecht: Springer, 2010.

Wolfe, David E. "Sydenham and Locke on the Limits of Anatomy." *Bulletin of the History of Medicine* 35, no. 3, (1961): 193–220.

Woodward, Josiah. *A short catechism, explaining the substance of the Christian religion suited to the understanding of children, and the meanest capacities.* London: J. Downing, 1709. Eighteenth Century Collections Online, Gale. CW3323333701.

Wright, David. *Down's: the history of a disability.* Oxford: Oxford University Press, 2011.

Wright, John P. "Association, Madness, and the Measures of Probability in Locke and Hume." In *Psychology and Literature in the Eighteenth Century,* edited by Michael De'Port and Christopher Fox, 103–27. New York: AMS Press, 1987.

Yaffe, Gideon. *Manifest Activity: Thomas Reid's Theory of Action.* Oxford: Oxford University Press, 2004.

Zimmer, Carl. *Soul Made Flesh: The Discovery of the Brain and How It Changed the World.* New York: Free Press, 2004.

Emile Bojesen is a senior lecturer in Education at the University of Winchester. His current research is into the theory and practical means underpinning a democratically responsive state education which would include the promotion and facilitation of self-education. Aesthetic and physical education are areas of particular interest within this context.

Jess Keiser is a postdoctoral research fellow at Rice University's Humanities Research Center. He has published articles on it—narratives and eighteenth-century neuroscience. He is currently completing a book entitled *Nervous Fictions*, which will explore how eighteenth-century writings on the brain influenced experiments in literary form.

Jason S. Farr recently defended his dissertation, "Queer Deformities: Disability and Sexuality in Eighteenth-Century Women's Fiction," at the University of California, San Diego, where he has specialized in British literature and culture of the long eighteenth century, deaf and disability studies, and gender and sexuality studies. He has a forthcoming publication on Frances Burney's Camilla in *The Eighteenth Century: Theory and Interpretation*, and is currently working on a project that explores the emergence of deaf education in England and Western Europe, 1640–1783.

Dana Gliserman Kopans is an assistant professor of literary and cultural studies at Empire State College in Saratoga Springs, NY. She works in eighteenth-century British literature and culture, and her interests are in gender and in the intersections of legal, medical, and cultural history. Other work concerns her personal obsessions of tea and chocolate.

Sharon Alker, an associate professor of English at Whitman College, has published a plethora of articles in the long eighteenth century, including works on James Hogg, Robert Burns, Maria Edgeworth, Daniel Defoe, John Arbuthnot, and John Galt. She has co-edited several essay collections on Scottish writers. Most recently, she is working, with Holly Faith Nelson, on a book on the literary representation of the siege in the Restoration and early eighteenth century.

Paul Kelleher is an assistant professor of English at Emory University. He has published several articles in the fields of eighteenth-century studies and queer theory, and recently has completed his first book, *Making Love: Sentimentalism and the Literary History of Sexuality*. His current book project explores the intersections of sympathy and disability across several genres, including eighteenth-century moral philosophy and twenty-first-century film.

Jamie Kinsley is a Ph.D. candidate at Auburn University. Her dissertation, "Speaking Silences: Poetry in Prose Fiction," examines how women writers such at Mary Wroth, Jane Barker, and Charlotte Lennox integrated their own poetry in their prose fictions to create a discourse for female experience. In addition to disability studies, her interests lie in women's writing, genre theory and interdisciplinary studies.

Jess Domanico is an instructor of English at Point University in West Point, Georgia. Her interests are broad, and include the rhetoric of disability, issues of accessibility in the classroom, and late eighteenth-century women poets like Priscilla Poynton. Her current research involves the physical and emotional benefits of equine facilitated therapeutics, a field dedicated to modern-day enabling.

Anna K. Sagal is a graduate student of English Literature at Tufts University. Her research interests include disability studies, feminist theory and women's studies, science and literature studies, and Restoration theatre. She is currently working on her dissertation, entitled "Women Writers and Fictions of Experiment: 1666–1790."

Holly Faith Nelson, professor and chair of English at Trinity Western University, has published widely on British literature of the seventeenth and long eighteenth centuries. Her publications include, *Through a Glass Darkly: Suffering, the Sacred, and the Sublime in Literature and Theory*, *Robert Burns and Transatlantic Culture*,

French Women Authors: The Significance of the Spiritual, 1400–2000, and *Topographies of the Imagination: New Approaches to Daniel Defoe.*

Chris Mounsey worked for several years in theatre before an accident and four months immobility, in which reading was the only possible occupation, led to an academic career. Degrees in philosophy, comparative literature and English from the University of Warwick followed, and a doctorate on Blake founded an interest in the literature of the eighteenth century. Dr. Mounsey, who now teaches at the University of Winchester, is author of *Christopher Smart: Clown of God* and editor of *Presenting Gender, Queer People* and *Developments in the Histories of Sexualities* (for Bucknell University Press). He is also author of *Understanding the Poetry of William Blake through a Dialectic of Contraries,* (Lewiston, 2011), and *Being the Body of Christ,* (Sheffield, 2012).